THE DEVIL'S HORSEMEN

THE DEVIL'S HORSEMEN

A THOUSAND YEARS OF CONQUEST BY EURASIAN STEPPE HORSE ARCHERS

JEM DUDUCU

AMBERLEY

For Bertan and Inji, the Devil's horsemen in my life.

First published 2025

Amberley Publishing
The Hill, Stroud
Gloucestershire, GL5 4EP

www.amberley-books.com

ISBN 978 1 3981 2291 8 (hardback)
ISBN 978 1 3981 2292 5 (ebook)

British Library Cataloguing in Publication Data.
A catalogue record for this book is available
from the British Library.

1 2 3 4 5 6 7 8 9 10

Typesetting by SJmagic DESIGN SERVICES, India.
Printed in the UK.

Appointed GPSR EU Representative: Easy
Access System Europe Oü, 16879218
Address: Mustamäe tee 50, 10621, Tallinn, Estonia
Contact Details: gpsr.requests@easproject.com,
+358 40 500 3575

CONTENTS

Introduction 7

1 Life on the Steppe 14

2 The Origins of the Hunnic Empire 26

3 Attila the Hun 39

4 The Avars and the Magyars 61

5 The Turks 82

6 The Ottomans 107

7 Temujin 148

8 The Mongols after Genghis Khan 180

9 Emir Timur 231

10 Babur and the Mughal Empire 259

Conclusion 276

Bibliography 279

Index 281

INTRODUCTION

Determining an exact date for the start of the Eurasian Steppe nomad story is notoriously difficult. The steppe is vast, and we are looking at a culture that didn't leave behind much evidence. Even early sedentary populations can be difficult to detect if their sites were isolated from modern population centres (for example, Petra). This is why archaeologists love to uncover ancient cities preserved in deserts; the level of information they provide is essential to an understanding of that society and adds enormously to even the best guesswork. But the steppe nomads were constantly on the move, travelling from location to location via horseback and staying for only short periods of time in any one place. They lived in tents, kept no written records and made only what they used, so how is it possible to know where they went and how they lived?

Then there is the very real question of funding for the archaeological work that might reveal more about these nomadic people. It is far easier to obtain grants to study the civilisations we know, like the Romans or even the Mongols, than to obtain them for more obscure world cultures. The well-known names attract attention, and further archaeological work is seen as a practical way to enhance the revenues of the universities, museums and related organisations that stand to benefit from new discoveries. But when it comes to the Bronze Age Eurasian Steppe nomads, archaeologists are looking for a needle in a haystack; they are seeking a society without a name and discoveries that will not cause ripples of excitement in the popular press. It is a thankless task.

There is some fragmentary evidence from 5,000 years ago of these people breaking into three distinct groups: some moved to the western steppe, more moved to central Asia, and a third group migrated to the eastern steppe. Some settled just to the north of the Black Sea and began farming wheat and barley, and did not go down the path of the more itinerate lifestyle. There is fragmentary evidence of clashes with the Persian empire, and on into China there is some evidence of large groups of raiders arriving from the direction of the steppes. That there are records of these raids shows that they had a serious impact. A couple of bandits wouldn't be worth mentioning in a chronicle, but there is no detail beyond a few bald references.

The first mention of any kind of confederation or empire associated with these people occurred in the first millennium BC, when the Scythians enter the records. The name is not unfamiliar, and their culture is known for its distinctive style of metalwork, which shows that the Scythian culture had evolved sufficiently to support artisans. It was a level of sophistication that wouldn't be matched for many centuries by other groups explored in this book.

Archaeological finds from these societies stretch across the Eurasian Steppe – possibly an indication of the extent of their power, and at the very least proof that they were heavily involved in the early days of the Silk Road. The Romans knew of them as fearsome cavalry and hired them as mercenaries to support the legions. But while these people may have been fearsome warriors honing their skills in battle, they were not conquering neighbouring empires. China may have been raided, but these people didn't conquer it.

All we can say with any certainty is that by the first millennium BC, the basic frameworks of communication, organisation, culture and language were already in existence for these people and will be seen again and again in the future waves of expansion discussed within these pages. This timeline means the steppe nomads possess one of the longest-lasting cultures in world history.

Attila the Hun and Genghis Khan are names that echo down the centuries, and almost everyone knows of the Turks; many even know of the Magyars and Emir Timur. But each of these is put in a separate category. This seems to make sense. After all, Attila the Hun died in Europe a thousand years before Timur died in central Asia. At first glance there is nothing to connect these two men. And yet there is.

In the modern Republic of Türkiye, schoolchildren are taught about the 'Turkish' empires of the past. The idea has a nationalist agenda, asserting as it does that this modern country of very ethnically mixed peoples is somehow the same as the great Mongol Khans. Putting aside the jingoistic exaggeration, there is a core of truth to the idea.

There are many books about the above individuals and their empires, but very few (at least in English) have set down the whole narrative, the true story that what Attila started in the 5th century AD, Tamerlane and his descendants would finish at the time of the Renaissance, thus concluding a thousand years of conflict. But there is another, less well-reported story of culture, tolerance and trade. Why? Because the culture, religion, traditions, technology and ethnicities of these people were essentially the same. We tend to see the nations of medieval Europe as similar because they, too, had a unifying religion, culture and way to wage war, but by no means did they display any kind of brotherly love. This is the analogy to consider when thinking about the nomadic cultures of the Eurasian Steppe, because the nomads lasted longer and had a greater impact on the world than any medieval alliance.

Hollywood loves to immortalise great stories from history, and while it has churned out endless movies and TV shows about the Romans and the Tudors, the nomads of the Eastern Steppe have been largely ignored. Even when their story manages to make it to the silver screen, it is always problematic. In *Attila the Hun* (1954), Anthony Quinn played the lead with a big droopy moustache. It was neither well reviewed nor a hit. Or there's the 2001 TV miniseries about Attila, this time starring the very Scottish (even when he plays a Spartan) Gerard Butler. Tamerlane gets classier treatment in *Tamburlaine the Great* Parts I and II by Christopher Marlowe from the 16th century, and he is also a key character in *Turandot*, the 1920s opera by Puccini, but so far Hollywood hasn't even bothered with him. Kublai Khan got a Netflix show, although he's seen through the lens of a European, hence the show's name: *Marco Polo*. Perhaps the most hard done by is Genghis Khan, who had a European-made film starring Omar Sharif in 1965, but even worse was the ethnically and historically insensitive *The Conqueror* in 1956, when it was John Wayne's turn to wear the droopy moustache. Wayne was completely miscast, which he admitted as soon as he saw the film. Even worse, it was filmed on one of the US nuclear test sites, leading to dozens of cast and crew developing and dying of cancer (I go into this in more detail in my book *Forgotten History*). So, while these people and leaders have arguably had a greater impact on world history than any other ruler or empire, they are largely non-existent in popular culture.

That said, there is one piece of pop culture that could serve as a summary of this entire book and that is the play *The Mongol Khan*, written in 1998 by the poet B. Lkhagvasuren. With a title like that it would be safe to assume it's about Genghis Khan or one of his successors, but no. The play is set a thousand years earlier and is about a leader of the Hunnu empire (referred to as the Xiongnu by contemporary Chinese records). Hunnu is another name for the people we in the West call the Huns. Here we have the story of the culture that is directly linked to Attila and the hordes that fought the Roman Empire, but the name of the play immediately brings to mind the medieval empire of the Mongols, who would at times fight European knights. The point of the stage spectacular is to dazzle, to bring to life (via exaggeration and mind-blowing set pieces) a complex and vibrant but forgotten civilisation. It is not factual history, but a set of myths made real. In western literary terms it's more *Lord of the Rings* than *Henry V*.

From the time of its first production in the 1990s the play has had a difficult relationship with the Chinese authorities and the Chinese Communist Party in particular. The authorities want unity, and unity in China means looking to Han Chinese history, not that of other ethnicities, and the Hunnu (Xiongnu) were outright enemies of the Han. To the western eye it all might be lumped together as Chinese, whereas in reality *The Mongol Khan*'s very un-Han-like origins and the story it tells have been a point of real concern. When it was revived in China in the 2020s it faced open hostility from the authorities and was shut down. So, a theatrical piece about a long-dead civilisation was seen as provocative if not dangerous to China in the 21st century. There was a happy ending to the production when it toured Europe and garnered good reviews. It was, as *The Times* newspaper pointed out, the first play written by a Mongolian to be performed in Britain.

Today, the ancestors of the people of the Eurasian Steppe still appear in surprising ways. In September 2023, there was news of a new Defence Minister in Ukraine, a man called Rustem Umerov, who was identified as a Crimean Tatar. This showed the ethnic variety in the Kyiv government, but also sent signals to Moscow that Ukraine was not backing down on the recapture of the Crimean Peninsula. Soon after, during Pope Francis' visit to Mongolia, eyebrows were raised when he praised Genghis Khan's tolerance of many faiths. While accurate, his comment omitted any mention of the huge scale of massacres carried out by Genghis Khan and the other great khans of the Mongol Empire.

The story of these nomadic people is in many ways the story of Asia (including India and China), the Middle East and Europe for a millennium, which is something no other culture can say. Only once in history were Poland and Japan under threat by the same enemy at the same time, and that enemy was the Mongol Empire. Their history is our history, and the story of these people is the closest we have to an encapsualtion of world history. But because they were the invaders, the so-called 'other', their impact was quickly forgotten once they left save for the terrifying legends about violence and barbarity. The purpose of this book is to reappraise these groups as people for what they were, and not as a great horde of demons disgorged from hell to prey on sinners as a punishment from God. But this is not a revisionist work. Many massacres occurred under the blades and bows of these tribes, and they will not be ignored. But like everything in life, it was all a little more complicated than the story you think you know.

I have wanted to write this story for more than 25 years. My dissertation at university was 'The Mongol Expansion of the 13th century and its Impact on the Crusading Movement'. Twenty years later, my first published book was *Deus Vult: A Concise History of the Crusades*, and both the Turks and the Mongols play an integral part in it. I have also written

The Sultans: The Rise and Fall of the Ottoman Rulers and their World, in which the Turks and Tamerlane are key to the narrative. If you have read either of these you will be familiar with some of the stories in this book, but this time I am looking at them from a different perspective. So now, more than ten years after writing *Deus Vult*, here I am again telling a story I have always wanted to share.

I

LIFE ON THE STEPPE

The Eurasian Steppe is a gigantic part of the world's land mass. Starting on the Chinese coast of the Pacific, it stretches across all of Asia and into Europe, ending at the Danube River in modern-day Hungary and Bulgaria after 5,000 miles. This important grassland biome is punctuated by mountain ranges and deserts, but if a person were to travel from the Pacific to Hungary there is a clear route all the way there, free of impassible cliff faces and canyons. It is so broad that a traveller can simply go around any such obstacles on the gradually undulating, grass-covered hills.

During the German invasion of the Soviet Union in the Second World War, Panzer divisions would drive across part of this largely flat, featureless landscape, and some diary entries describe the feeling of being at sea, with an ocean of grass in every direction and no landmarks or sign of habitation. Some found this endless bland steppe a little unnerving, but this ease of access and the plentiful supply of animal feed meant that the steppe acted as a natural path for migration as far back as the Palaeolithic Era. Part of the steppe crosses Siberia, a place that still had the last few mammoths at the time when the Egyptians were building the pyramids. The Palaeolithic Era predates agriculture, and while other cultures from Egypt, Babylon and the Indus Valley were starting agriculture in the Neolithic Era, tribes of the steppe never did. They found that there were other ways to harness the land, which led to a nomadic lifestyle in which tents, horses and yaks were the order of the day.

Time for a brief history on the domestication and weaponization of the horse. Horses appear to have been domesticated around 4,000 BC. At first, they were too small and lacked the strength to carry a grown man, particularly one with all the added weight of a warrior with weapons and armour. And so the chariot was invented. In every possible way inferior to cavalry, they were devised because, while a man could not sit for long on a horse, two were able to pull a wheeled platform from which archers could be more mobile than if they were on foot. The Battle of Kadesh in 1274 BC, between the Egyptians and the Hittites, is important for several reasons, most notably because it's the first ever battle where we have a decent description of what happened, but also because it is thought to have seen the largest number of chariots in a battle (5,000–6,000). 1274 BC is 500 years before the founding of Rome and 700 years before the Battle of Thermopylae. By the time we come into the classical era of the ancient world, chariots had given way to cavalry. The last holdout for this now obsolete invention was the Britons, who in the 1st century AD used them against the Roman legions... and lost.

Even if they did have cavalry, many of these cultures were yet to develop the key piece of equipment to make cavalry forces reliable: the stirrup. The first example of a stirrup can be found in the Assyrian Empire that covered much of modern-day Iraq and Iran and which is on the Eurasian Steppe. These horsemen were virtually born in the saddle, and the stirrup allowed them not only to stay on more easily but to free their hands from the reins so that they could wield a weapon or use a bow. Using a horse as a weapon platform made them, at the time, the best cavalry in the world. This one innovation made the old war chariot completely obsolete as a mounted archer was better in every measurable way. It should therefore surprise no one that the stirrup was rapidly adopted by all horse cultures across the central and eastern Eurasian Steppe – centuries before Europe knew of its existence.

Horses were vital to the culture for travel, food (both meat and milk), as beasts of burden and as weapons of war. A family's status would be measured by the number of horses they owned. While horses were highly regarded to the point where epic oral poems were written about them, they were not treated the same as horses in Europe. Eurasian horses were very rarely named. When Alexander the Great's horse Bucephalus died in modern-day Pakistan, he was so upset he named a city in its honour. No such gesture was ever made by any of the nomadic

Assyrian mounted archer – but no stirrup yet in evidence. (Courtesy British Museum, Carol Raddato, under Creative Commons 2.0)

warlords in this book. All the grooming and fussing and brushing of coats that happens in the West did not happen on the steppe, where horses were allowed to roam free and graze. A horse's spirit was thought to reside in its mane, so a thick, long, flowing mane was seen as the sign of a healthy animal. To differentiate the thousands of horses, families would refer to them by their colour and markings.

The horses themselves were relatively small compared to many European breeds; they also had longer hair, useful in the bitterly cold winters, and as such would be slightly slower over distance than their European counterparts. This is important as many chronicles talk about these various groups 'sweeping across the steppe' or 'riding like the wind' in battle. The steppe horses were not magical, although they would eventually get that reputation; it would take up to six months for a rider to travel from eastern Mongolia to the Danube if they were so inclined. Part of the success of these nomadic warriors was more likely down to two things: first, taking the initiative, so choosing the time and place to attack; and second, mobility. The fact that all their forces were mounted meant they were overall faster and more mobile than any force with infantry contingents and achingly slow baggage trains. The nomads rode with everything they needed and foraged off the land; they had no need for supply logistics.

Home life was substantially different to that of the sedentary populations of the world. The family home was a tent, that sturdy felt tent known as a yurt (the Mongolian term, which seems to have stuck in the English language, but they had other names in other cultures). They could be broken down and packed away within hours, meaning the family could make their way across the steppe as they followed their grazing herds. Livestock consisted mainly of horses and yaks, with some kinds of cattle and sometimes sheep and goats. The steppe was so vast, with an infinite amount of grass to feed the livestock, that it was far simpler to follow the herd than to start farms, erect fences and build barns to store hay.

Due to the itinerate nature of the people, there was no agriculture, and so there were no peasants. There are many records (particularly under the Mongols) of the wholesale massacre of peasants in their fields. This is separate to other violence and can be blamed on the fact that nomadic horsemen didn't understand the point of these poorly dressed people, scrabbling around in the dirt, jabbering in their alien tongues, who were not artisans and had no riches to trade. What was their purpose? How low could a human sink? And as history has shown on many occasions, if there is no understanding, there is no empathy – and that can lead to mass murder.

The main drawback to living in this biome is the lack of forests and thus wood. They existed but wood was far too precious to burn, so most fuel for the household fires was dried animal dung, still used in some remote communities today. Wood was for tools, weapons and frames for the tents, which were a marvel of design and ergonomics. Easy to put up over a wooden frame, their circular shape meant they rarely blew over (if a tent were to collapse in the middle of a winter blizzard it would likely spell certain death for the occupants). A central hole in the roof allowed the smoke to escape.

Tribes consisted of extended families; their sizes varied wildly, but it was the tradition throughout this era that everyone must belong to a group as a lone individual stood no chance on their own. Therefore, one of the most terrible punishments was exile. Family ties were strong but these alliances and loyalties led to a lack of trust between disparate groups. Violence and theft of livestock could happen at any time. Blood feuds could last generations. Marriage with women from other tribes was encouraged, and weddings provided opportunities to meet with other tribes, to socialise, share news, discuss plans and arrange further marriages to unify the two groups – or cause offence leading to conflict.

Men could have multiple wives. Sometimes these were through marriage alliances, other times they were the captured women of other tribes. These women could become slaves or marry, or sometimes both. Multiple wives, like a large number of horses, was a sign of status. Being able to feed a large family and having plenty of children was not only a sign of virility but also of wealth. It was usual for the first wife to be senior, with later wives taking orders from her. Depending on the tribe and the era these systems would change and flex, but as we shall see much later, they would be replicated on a much larger scale in several imperial courts.

A common misconception about some of the later groups such as the Turks and Mongols was that they were either Muslim (that would come later with integration with local communities) or they had no religion. This is not true, shamanistic practices were common, with elaborate ceremonies to commune with ancestors and offerings at holy sites such as the shores of the Caspian Sea. Soothsayers, myths and fireside retellings of old tales were commonplace. Giving thanks to a stream when you were thirsty didn't require a whole religious belief system, but many of these groups converted to new religions with no resistance or simply tolerated the many (often feuding) religions in their empires. When Attila the Hun met Pope Leo (more on that later) he showed the Pope respect not because he had any interest in becoming Christian, but because he recognised the trappings of a mystic and understood the deference the Romans showed him. Spirits and the nether world lurked on the edges of everything, in some ways no different to the Scandinavians who would be Christianised but remain wary of elves or trolls living in the darkest regions of the forests.

As with virtually all traditional societies, the structure was patriarchal, but it was surprisingly egalitarian. An aristocratic warrior class existed but it was based on meritocracy. The best warriors became known as the best warriors because they were; they were more likely to do better on the hunts and would, therefore, have more resources to provide for a larger family. This is the opposite of the aristocratic structures in Europe at the time, where a family name carried a certain level of authority, regardless of the abilities of the current generation.

Women had important roles. The tribal leader's mother was often seen as a fountain of wisdom, and some assumed the role of tribal shaman. There are a few examples of women becoming warriors, too. It was by no means a fair and equal society, but it did offer more scope for advancement than the ossified structures of imperial China or feudal Europe. This was even true for slaves, who were generally the losers in some kind of tribal war. Slavery was not endemic; slaves had to be fed and there was always pressure on the amounts of food available. But slaves were allowed to marry into their owner's families. So the whole society was surprisingly fluid, allowing the next generation to recover quickly after major setbacks in the previous one.

Today the idea of a 'Turkish' or 'Persian' rug is a sign of handmade quality. Rug manufacturing appears around the world in virtually all societies. Within their tents the home was made complete with colourful woollen rugs rather than a dirt floor. The women produced these from the animal hair available. Yak down is just as soft and durable as wool, perfect for rugs and blankets. Leather was also produced but most other textiles (and some of the finer examples of rugs including silk) were traded in the cities. Tashkent and Samarkand were large cities throughout this era and acted as staging posts on the Silk Road where the tribes traded fine bows, slaves and the highest quality birds of prey for metal swords and arrow heads.

Which brings us to the Silk Road. That name was never used by the people at the time; the term was popularised in 1877 by the German traveller and writer Ferdinand von Richthofen (uncle of the famous WWI fighter pilot). There was never actually just one road and a better translation of what Richthofen had written would be the 'Silk Route', meaning a network of pathways and areas that travellers crossed (largely over the Eurasian Steppe) to bring goods from China to the Middle East and vice versa. It began in the 2nd century BC and continued into the time of Tamerlane, but it was with the rise of European merchant shipping and the discovery of America, combined with China starting to close itself off from the world, that led to its eventual end by the early 1500s. The most famous trade route in the world crisscrossed the very lands of the people this book is about. It should therefore come as no surprise that the fate of each one is intertwined with these trade routes, so the Silk Road will be making a regular appearance.

Sometimes these Asiatic nomads were the hired muscle to keep shipments from Damascus safe; other times they plundered and murdered any caravans they could find. At other points they would be overlords of the whole steppe and so in control of all trade, ensuring they positively benefitted from the obligatory tax revenues. These routes brought the benefits of wealth and diplomacy, and dangers such as disease along with them. If there was internecine war amongst the steppe nomads, trade suffered.

Languages varied but they came from two common roots. The first and most widespread was a Turkic base which evolved into the modern languages of Azerbaijan, Uzbekistan, the Crimean Tatars and, of course, Türkiye. The second was the Mongolian Uighur languages, still extant in the modern country of Mongolia, areas of Inner Mongolia and Xinjiang in China, where they spread and evolved. These two roots are distinct but within them are similarities. Think of the difference between French and Italian, both Romance languages, with similar grammar and vocabulary, that have slowly drifted apart over the centuries. Magyar in Hungary is the language that has diverged the most and is now more closely connected to the Slavic and Finnish languages than to the originators of the language 1,200 years ago.

The refinements of an urban population were non-existent. Life was tough on the steppe. They were always on the move, always worrying about their livestock, fighting the elements or wolves or other tribes. Was there any time or inclination to invent the piano? While culture existed, it was rudimentary. Mongolian throat singing is highly evocative and unique, but it requires no musical instruments; similarly, these were not literate societies. The idea that 'history is written by the victors', is one that annoys me, and this entire book is a rebuttal of that. We have no accounts from Attila the Hun, only the European chronicles describing a very alien culture. Attila won, but the history was recorded by his vanquished foes. The same for the Magyars, early Turkish groups and Genghis Khan, and while we have records from the court of Emir Timur, he attacked so many different places we have more history written by the losers than the winning side.

Just to finish my rebuttal to the hot take above, the same is true for the Vikings, and once we are into the era of printing there are so many accounts from so many different sides that the idea that only the winners control the narrative is a nonsense. Indeed, there are many countries where national identity is intrinsically tied to some past defeat or injustice that the winning country has completely forgotten. There will be some examples of this later.

With the peoples of the steppe, however, we must treat some recorded history with caution. If a nation's army has just been defeated and the king was forced to retreat, the chronicles are not going to be complimentary about the foreign victors. Devil's Horseman, Scourge of God, Gog and Magog are just some of the fearsome labels applied to these people, and that's just in the West. Dehumanising the enemy is a common ploy and still goes on (in the 21st century the Ukrainians call the Russian invaders 'orcs', the malevolent humanoid monsters from *Lord of the Rings*). The steppe people were not a manifestation of evil but fellow humans who faced their own threats and were forced to move to new lands; they were simply trying to survive. Their methods could be horrifyingly bloody, but they were pragmatic solutions made by a pragmatic people who had to make the tough decisions or die on the steppe.

It was exceedingly rare for drought to destroy all the grassland, but disease and the general subsistence level of their existence meant that no food was wasted. For example, testicles are still considered a delicacy, and the meat from the cheeks and the eyeballs are thought to be the very choicest parts offered to guests as a gesture of great honour. In the 21st century such gestures provide some comic interludes as the locals know westerners don't enjoy eating eyeballs. A vivid pink mixture of animal blood and milk is considered to be a healthy and nutritious meal (technically it is, but you've got to keep it down), and another favoured drink is kumis – fermented yak's milk – both of which are still part of the staple diet of many nomadic peoples.

If the preceding information about food raises doubts about its nutritional efficacy, the nomads would agree with you because the key to their culture, military success and survival was hunting. Falconry has been around for at least 4,000 years and is prevalent in all Eurasian cultures. But whereas it evolved over time as a sport for the aristocracy (it's considered by some to be the oldest sport in the world), for the Asiatic nomads it was a necessity. Eagles, hawks and falcons are able to capture small mammals such as hares, muskrats and foxes, a valuable source of protein for the wandering tribes.

The key hunt occurred when the men would gather together but then spread out over a huge area to form a circle. Then they would ride towards each other, steadily decreasing the area where the animals within the circle could hide. The method required excellent coordination. Tribal leaders would learn who was reliable, who listened, who was too headstrong, and use that information when it came to war. Sometimes wolves or other apex predators were caught in the hunt, in which case seeing the marksmanship of a man with his bow in a life-or-death situation was also vital preparation for battle.

The bow was the main weapon of each of the groups. The standard bow across the world was the short bow. It was lethal at a hundred paces, but its penetrating power rapidly dwindled after that. The mightiest bow in all of history was the English/Welsh longbow. Able to kill at half a mile, at closer range (and with specific arrows) it could penetrate plate steel armour. It took so long to train to draw the bowstring of the 6ft bow that archaeological evidence suggests it caused the archer's vertebrae to fuse. Another problem with this bow was that it was not easily portable. Many of the battles that included longbowmen involved them setting up spiked barricades to break any cavalry charges coming at them, and the longbowmen certainly could not be drawn while mounted.

Enter the composite bow. This was the perfect weapon for these Asiatic tribes. Unlike the long or short bows, they were not made from a single piece of wood but were made instead from horn, wood and sinew bound together. Whereas the other types of bow, when drawn in profile look like the letter 'U', the composite bow had extra curves giving it more of a 'W' profile. These extra curves, together with the composite nature of the weapon, gave it far greater range and penetrating power than a short bow. It wasn't quite as powerful as a long bow, but what little power it sacrificed was made up for by the fact that it could be drawn quickly whilst riding on the back of a horse. The composite bow gave birth to the horse archers who would terrorise the known world for a millennium.

2

THE ORIGINS OF
THE HUNNIC EMPIRE

Originating from central Asia and the Caucasus region, the Huns are the first of our five groups in the five eras of steppe nomads. That's the best guess from the West. The Chinese had another name for them, and from that we get an understanding of the expanse of their conquests before Rome even knew of their existence. Known in China as the Xiongnu, they originated to the north of that country under a leader called Modu Chanyu, who founded the Xiongnu Empire in 209 BC. The problem here is that the names Hun and Xiongnu aren't even close and a sign that they are a localised version of something else. What these people called themselves is lost to time. Since these tribes did not have writing and preserved their stories through oral history, we know virtually nothing about Modu Chanyu apart from a few scant references in the Chinese chronicles. They were interested in him because he founded the empire the Chinese Han dynasty fought off and on for 250 years.

It is important to point out that the term 'empire' is quite different for nomadic societies when compared to something like the Roman Empire. If the year was 200 AD in Roman Gaul, evidence of it being part of a larger empire would be everywhere. The official language, architecture and currency would be obvious. Digging deeper, the way to wage war and the local laws, customs and religion would also have been Romanised. We call these 'empires' because there was a central authority unifying disparate groups into one civilisation.

Nomad empires were completely different. Historians make maps to show areas of influence, so in this case, the Xiongnu Empire is coloured in the same way the Roman would be. Except it was not one homogeneous area. The Xiongnu warbands would travel from town to town demanding tribute and it would be paid, but the local population retained and spoke their own language, had their own architecture and religion. Currency in the area would come from some far-flung and stable state, but the nomads had no interest in or ability to create a currency and treasury, or any kind of centralised administration. So, ironically, Han coins would be available around the Xiongnu Empire, even though the Xiongnu were the top of the pile in terms of military might, and no other groups dared to challenge their access to the assets of their 'empire'.

It was the Han–Xiongnu War and the mobile warbands of the Xiongnu that led to the construction of the early parts of what would be called when completed (after the Mongols were expelled in the 1300s) the Great Wall of China. These nomads were mobile, well-trained and lethal archers, but horse archers cannot break down walls. The Xiongnu started the war (the Han had no use for the endless grasslands) by raiding these sedentary populations. The advantage that all steppe peoples had was that they could always choose the time and the place of their attacks; the kingdoms they attacked had the same city in the same place every time.

Fighting occurred across much of northern China and the Han did inflict losses on the Xiongnu. This led to the nomads setting up camps to the north of the Gobi Desert. The Gobi is a cold desert and acts as a natural neutral zone between the Eurasian Steppe to the north and China to the south. There were occasions throughout history when both parties did try and surprise the other by travelling through it, but with no water and thousands of troops and horses needing it, the Gobi served as a natural obstacle, giving neither side an advantage.

A typical example of the kind of conflict that would occur is the Battle of Tian Shan, a place located in the Tian Shan Mountain range in the northwestern region of Xinjiang. In 99 BC, the Han general Li Guangli led approximately thirty thousand cavalrymen in an attack on the Xiongnu forces in Tian Shan. The Han had learned their lesson and had no infantry, so in theory the Han had the advantage as they had more soldiers and no baggage (literally). But the Xiongnu were on familiar territory and were born in the saddle rather than men who had trained to be cavalry. The Han attack was initially successful, with the Xiongnu suffering heavy losses. However, as the Han army withdrew, it was surrounded by enemy forces and cut off from escape. This shows the manoeuvrability not just of individual units, but the fluid cohesion of the entire force. The Han Chinese had come prepared to fight a familiar enemy and still they were outflanked. Many of the Han cavalry died of thirst or starvation. Eventually, Li escaped but by then almost 60 per cent of his force had lost their lives.

The reason the conflict dragged on for so long was that while the nomads could raid China any time they liked, they could never conquer the walled cities, and while China did sometimes win on the field of battle, the Xiongnu forces were simply better. Whereas Han China was one of the most densely populated nations in the world at the time, the Eurasian Steppe was very sparsely populated. The battle of Tian Shan was a decisive victory for the Xiongnu, but it came at a cost. Although the initial attack had been a success for General Li, the result was

The Tian Shan range, the 'Mountains of God/Heaven', on the border of China, Kazakhstan and Kyrgyzstan with Khan Tengri (7,010 m) at the centre. (Courtesy Chen Zhao under Creative Commons 02)

thousands of dead Xiongnu warriors. Such losses forced the Xiongnu to sue periodically for peace on favourable terms.

However, at other times the internal weakness was on the Chinese side. In 9 AD there was a palace coup, and a civil war broke out between the Han emperors and the new Xin emperor. The Xiongnu ignored it and just retook the western areas they had at times controlled before, including Xinjiang. By 23 AD the Xin had been vanquished and the Han had been reenergised and now had the time, the ability and the resources to push out the Xiongnu once and for all. This culminated in 73 AD in what has become known as Battle of Yiwulu, but battle is the wrong word. This was a campaign, a series of minor skirmishes, with two important results: First, the Xiongnu lost every one of the skirmishes and second, they were forced to retreat from

Xinjing. Raiding would continue but any serious threats of invasion from the Xiongnu were forestalled.

It was about this time that the Roman Empire began trading in earnest with the merchants of the Silk Road. Roman glassware from the 1st century AD has been found in China, and silk from the East was highly prized in Roman society. The fact that these items were found so far from their place of origin proves that no matter what was going on in western China, the overall picture across the steppe was one of stability. Merchants could travel along these routes, across thousands of miles, (relatively) safely. The Xiongnu Empire must have existed in some form to allow this trade to happen in the quantities that have been implied by both archaeology and historical records.

Because there are no internal records, we can only assume that with failure came infighting. All we can say with any certainty is that one of the largest empires in the ancient world evaporated without a trace. Underlying the fragmentary nature of the tribes is their genetics, a hotly contested topic. Roman writers from late antiquity (some were eyewitness accounts) describe people who we would nowadays call Mongolian. But there is a justifiable argument that this depiction is embedded in a totally negative viewpoint, describing them as barely human, so such features could have been exaggerated or added. In terms of the evidence, the nomads interbred with all types of peoples, including central Asians, Slavs and Han Chinese, so it's likely that there was a mix. As mentioned earlier, slaves were allowed to marry and reproduce within the tribes, which would invariably bring in more ethnic diversity. Indeed, the idea that 'Turk' is an ethnicity is a political, not a biological concept and has no basis in genetics.

Whispers of what was going on are found in a few records. The 2nd century AD geographer Claudius Ptolemy mentioned the Chuni tribe (a name Latinised from the original Greek) when listing tribes of the western Eurasian Steppe. He notes that they live 'between the Bastarnae and the Roxolani' or in modern terms, the area of Ukraine and southwestern Russia. This could well be location to which the Huns had migrated. The 5th-century historian Zosimus describes a tribe called the Urugundi who invaded the Roman Empire from the area of the Danube in 250 AD. The problem with this is he was writing more than a century after confirmed events and gives no further details. Is this another name for one of the Germanic tribes who we know attacked in the 3rd century? Was this a record of the first ever raid by the Huns? It's worth mentioning this if only to show how little we have about the Huns in the historical records.

There is another possibility to explain why some of these tribes headed west: the rise of the Rouran Khaganate. Essentially taking up the reins dropped by the Xiongnu, this was a new confederation of tribes north of China in what would be today Mongolia and parts of eastern Russia. While this empire is obscure, its tactics are not. The best way to think of it is as a proto-Mongolian Empire. Horse archers? Yes. A central ruler warlord? Absolutely. Savage acts of violence against civilian populations? Unfortunately, yes. It began forming in the 330s AD at exactly the same time that some of these peoples started heading west. From the perspective of the urban civilisations of Europe and Asia, peoples like the Huns or the Mongols appeared to have come from nowhere. It seems that each one of the five groups started expanding into new territories because of political instability on the steppe. Some of these forces were migrating away from war, with the Huns quite possibly being the first example of this. Timur and groups such as the Mongols were able to consolidate unity amongst warring factions and then harness that aggression to look outwards. In short, if the political situation in any culture is stable, nothing happens; it takes instability to create the conditions for radical change. A contemporary example (rather milder) would be working from home, a taboo in the early 21st century for office workers. But Covid arrived and we all *had* to work from home, so that even when the pandemic passed, conditions for hybrid working had been established. A concept impossible for companies to consider just a short time before, it now became commonplace.

There is scant information on the Rouran Khaganate. China lists some leaders (khagans) from the end of the 4th century into the 5th. But the group is important and will appear again. Its aggressive raiding and later collapse led to the migration of three key groups on top of the possible drive westwards of the Huns. As well as the Turks and the Crimean Tatars, the Avars are one of the groups that will be part of the Magyars' story.

The western part of the Eurasian Steppe is the Pontic–Caspian Steppe. This stretches from the Caucasus along the northern coast of the Black Sea and includes what today is southern Ukraine and the Crimea and continues downwards, just edging into Bulgaria and Moldova. This area is especially important in the study of linguistics. The Kurgan theory is the most widely accepted analysis to identify this area as the origin of the Indo-European languages dating back about 6,000 years. The reason for this is the area's access to the Eurasian Steppe and the Black Sea, which means it serves as a kind of crossroads for access to Europe, the Near East and Asia.

The Greeks called this Scythia, so it was known to the Romans, and by the 370s AD, a new group of nomads, thought to be the remnants of the Xiongnu, had moved into the area. They were called Huns by the Romans, and it seems they were attacking some of the other peoples looking for refuge in the Roman Empire while fleeing still others. The 4th century AD in Roman history was one of wave after wave of peoples being displaced from their lands further east. Some of the names became legendary, like the Vandals and the Goths, and some have been assumed to be western European, like the Franks (they were not), while others, like the Alans or the Greuthungi, have been forgotten.

In 376 AD, the Huns attacked the Germanic hinterland of the Roman Empire with forces so large as to have overwhelmed any local resistance. The Greuthungic King Ermanaric committed suicide rather than be captured by this new threat, which had appeared apparently out of the ether. To see suicide as the best option vividly shows how morale melted away and how rapid the advance was. Regardless, these attacks do not appear to have been a serious attempt at conquest, more a case of a reconnaissance in force or a raid on a large scale.

To put this campaign into context, two years later the Greuthungi would be part of a rebel confederation of Germanic tribes that would be in open conflict with the Eastern Roman Emperor Valens. The Germanic tribes would go on to win the Battle of Adrianople, killing Valens in the battle. So the forces that beat a Roman army were helpless against the Huns. And if the Greuthungi couldn't stop them, what chance did the Roman Emperors have?

What was driving this mass migration of peoples? There is no historical record. It seems likely that the frequent blood feuds and wars on the steppe had led to a more dominant force attacking some of the weaker ones, meaning that some groups felt the need to vacate the area. By the 4th century AD, it would have been known across the steppe that there was a stable empire to the west that could be considered either a safe refuge or potentially easy pickings, as the raids on Han China had proved. This is all conjecture (conjecture that I think is the most reasonable explanation), and while likely, there is no evidence in either historical records or archaeological findings. The problem for the Romans was that while the empire probably could have supported all these new people, had the empire been in its prime, it was far from that in the 4th century AD when Rome was in the grip of regular bouts of civil war. Its finances had dwindled to a tiny amount of what they had been a century earlier. By now of course the empire had been split in two, with the Western Roman Empire having the prestige of Rome as its capital, and the Eastern Roman Empire having Constantinople (arguably the largest city in the world at the time) as its capital. Sometimes the two emperors worked together, but at other times there was open hostility. The idea of Roman civilisation wasn't dead yet, but it was crumbling, and into this mess marched hundreds of thousands of new people.

Late Western Roman history is a long list of migrant tribes. The best way to think of these groups, from the perspective of the Roman Emperors, is that they were not Roman and therefore essentially disposable. Sometimes they were useful allies; at other times they would bite the hand that fed them and attack Roman lands. In 381, the Sciri and Carpi, together with at least some Huns, launched an unsuccessful attack on Pannonia (now western Hungary). Eunapius, the first eunuch to become a Roman consul, wrote of these events as a contemporary historian and reported that the Eastern Roman Emperor Theodosius I made peace with the Goths a year later in 382. He gave them land and cattle in order to form 'an unconquerable bulwark against the inroads of the Huns'. This is the first definitive display of concern about the rising threat of the Huns in Roman history. After this, the Huns are recorded to have launched a raid into Scythia Minor (modern-day Moldova and Bulgaria) in 384 or 385. A year later, the Greuthungi are back in the picture, fleeing the Huns into Thrace. This was the last serious migration into Roman territory until after the end of Hun rule, so this would indicate that the Huns were securely in control of eastern tribes beyond Rome's influence.

What had started as talk of these people called Huns becoming conquerors turned into a grim reality a generation later, when in 395 the Huns took on both the Roman Empire and the Persian-based Sasanian Empire. There were numerous clashes with Persia before the Hun cavalry penetrated deep into Sasanian lands, getting close to Ctesiphon (near Baghdad). But Hun forces were eventually defeated, and they were forced to retreat into the hinterlands to lick their wounds. They had been repelled, but it was a warning to new empires about the damage the horsemen from the steppe could do.

Uldin was the first name of a Hun known to the West. He seems to have clashed with Gothic tribes (now under theoretical Roman protection) along the eastern end of the Danube. Records are fragmented but Uldin may have pushed further west into Roman lands. It is unclear and chaotic, which is a fair summary of the attacks the Huns carried out on the Romans. From the perspective of Uldin, he had been testing the enemy to see what resistance could be expected and the answer was little. From the perspective of the Germanic tribes along the Danube, they had just been dealt a hammer blow from an alien force. The Huns were still on the periphery of the Roman world, but they wouldn't remain there for much longer.

At about this time there are references in Roman records to Huns not just being the enemy, but mercenaries too. By this time in Roman history the idea of legions full of citizen soldiers fighting in the armour we have all seen in the movies was long gone. The Romans might have been much poorer than they used to be, but they were still much richer than the Huns. If you can't beat them, try buying them.

In 400 AD, a Gothic leader named Gainas, who had once been installed as a *magister militum*, had been the loser in a rebellion against Roman authority. What he did next must be seen as an act of desperation if not stupidity. Having been unable to overpower the ever-weakening Roman rule, he marched his forces into Uldin's lands. Exactly what his plan was is unknown, but to march an army into the territory of the supreme military power in the area was an act of insanity. What happened next was the completely predictable defeat of Gainas by Uldin, who ordered his execution. Uldin then sent Gainas' head to Constantinople. This 'gift' likely meant Uldin was interested in cooperating with the Romans while he expanded his control over Germanic tribes and their territory. As described in the chronicles of Eunapius, the territory was regarded as little more than a buffer zone and of minimal concern to the powers in either Constantinople or Rome.

Why did the Vandals and Alans move into Gaul when they had been previously on the other side of the Rhine? This could well have been down to Uldin carrying out aggressive raids in the area in 406. Again, while contemporary records are incredibly thin, some historians seem to be mystified as to the reasons why these groups kept heading into the Roman Empire, but from the perspective of historians looking at the peoples of the Eurasian Steppe the answer is obvious: they weren't doing it by choice but were fleeing a conflict zone. As we have observed before, they may have been looking for peaceful sanctuary or someplace to conquer. Either way, the storm from the East was too strong to resist.

Somewhere in the maelstrom of raiding and violence Flavius Aetius became a political hostage as a teenager, first to Alaric I of the Visigoths, then to Uldin's court. For most of his late teens, this Roman citizen was living amongst the barbarians. He was able to see their customs, their courts and the way they waged war. It's very tempting to discuss the motivations of historical figures, but unless they thought to record them, everything is conjecture. So, all that can be said is that for 3 or 4 years this impressionable adolescent had the opportunity to see how the premier military power in eastern Europe organised itself. As we shall see, Flavius would later become one the last great Roman generals.

In 408 AD, Uldin was back. This time he crossed the Danube and pillaged Thrace. It was the perfect time to do so as the new Eastern Roman Emperor was Theodosius II, and he was just seven years old. As an indication of the state of the Roman Empire as a whole, it was around this time that the Roman army was ordered to leave Britain, never to return. This meant that Britain left the empire within a generation and was then defenceless against Germanic raiders.

The attack on Thrace was a serious attempt at invasion, or at least disruption, and while numbers are unknown, they must have been in the tens of thousands as the Eastern Romans knew they stood no chance of raising a force large enough to expel them. They tried to buy Uldin off, but on this occasion the amount he asked for was too high. So, Theodosius' advisors came up with a cunning plan to spend smaller amounts bribing Uldin's generals. This resulted in desertions and Uldin's force melted away like ice in the desert. Uldin himself escaped back across the Danube with what few forces he had left. After 408, he is not mentioned again in the annals. Whether he was deposed, assassinated or died of natural causes is unknown. Meanwhile, the Romans could breathe a sigh of relief; they had avoided a serious threat from the Huns ... for now.

Before we come to their infamous leader, two more years are important when considering the threat caused by the Huns. The year 412 was important because Olympiodorus of Thebes was sent as an emissary to 'the first of the kings' of the Huns, Charaton, Uldin's successor. Sadly, the records of this meeting are largely lost, but it does show that the Romans were willing once again to make a deal with the devil, presumably because they knew they couldn't stop Charaton if he directed all his forces against them. In that same year, the Huns raided Thrace again, a reminder of what they could do and how difficult it was to stop them.

In the year 422, the Huns were led by Ruga, their third leader in fourteen years. We have no idea what the fates of Uldin or Charaton were, but with their reputations for martial prowess it's unlikely that they died peacefully in their beds (Attila's demise may be the exception that proves the rule). It is also worth remembering that as the first serious incursions happened in the 370s and we are now in the 420s, the Huns had been a threat to the Roman Empire for fifty years. By now these nomads were far less alien, their tactics were known and some had even acted as mercenaries for Roman armies. But if they were more familiar, they were no less terrifying. In 422, a major Hun raid into Thrace was launched from the Danube. Even though Ruga reached the walls of Constantinople, he stood no chance of laying siege to the city, again highlighting that while horse archers are lethal on the field of battle, they are useless against stone walls. Ruga could do no more, and Emperor Theodosius II (now twenty-one) needed the Huns gone from the suburbs of his capital. Consequently, this raid ended in the first official peace treaty between the Huns and Rome. The Huns had to return to their lands, but the Romans had to pay an annual tribute of 350 pounds of gold. The Romans had managed to buy some time, but how much?

3

ATTILA THE HUN

Now we come to the first famous person in this book, a man so notorious he transcends history. Someone's politics are occasionally described as 'more right wing than Attila the Hun'. I have always found this an odd phrase as clearly this nomadic warlord had no concept of politics in any modern sense, but the point is that he is instantly seen as someone uncompromising and brutally pragmatic, someone to be feared.

Attila is, however, a fitting example of the problem with many of the people in the early chapters of this book. Since all our contemporary information comes from Latin and Greek sources, the vanquished enemies were never going to describe him in a neutral, non-nuanced way. The other problem with these records is that they are fragmentary. There are entire books dedicated to the man, but it quickly becomes obvious that the known facts fit into a handful of pages. Everything else is conjecture, plausible theory and a little archaeology.

To bring this point home, there is even serious debate about what the derivation of his name signifies. By this time the Hunnic Empire in the West was a polyglot, multi-ethnic society. The Huns were the overlords, but subjugated Germanic tribes also lived under their rule. As such, one theory is that the name Attila has a Germanic derivation meaning 'little father'; others argue that as his origins are from the steppe it's a Turkic composition that means 'oceanic or universal ruler'. As this is also the exact meaning of the title Genghis Khan, I side with the Turkic argument. But to not even know the origins of the name of such a famous figure in history shows that we are on the very fringes of written history. The only contemporary account of Attila is from Priscus of Panium, who was sent as an emissary to the court of the Huns. However, no extant copy of this incredibly important record exists. Instead, it has been preserved in later records by Procopius of Caesarea and Jordanis, who wrote a major work on the history of the Goths that included a section on the Huns, but these writers lived a century after the events.

When we last spoke of Ruga he had managed to ensure concessions from the Eastern Roman Empire and to secure an annual tribute of 350 pounds of gold. That was in 422. In 424, there is some evidence of the Huns fighting with Roman forces in North Africa. The gold had bought good will and shows that the Huns, while warlike, were neither an unstoppable force nor deaf to negotiations. The more we know about them, the less they appear to be a late antiquity collection of Terminators and more a tribe in marshal ascendancy. When most people think of the Huns or the Mongols, they think of hordes of horsemen appearing from the swirling mist, descending like a pack of wolves on various settlements before disappearing into the night just as suddenly as they had arrived. But the folk memory and the reality are utterly different. Indeed, Ruga even informed Theodosius II in 434 that he was planning to attack some tribes in Roman territory that he considered to be under his authority. Had he just been a ravenous warmonger he would have done it and to hell with the consequences. Ruga died in 435 before the campaign could be carried out.

Ruga's death left a power vacuum, and the Hunnic Empire was split between Ruga's two nephews, Bleda, who took the eastern half, and Attila, who took the western half. Again, there is debate about whether they had equal authority or if one was the senior partner. Those who believe the latter all agree that Bleda was the senior partner. Personally, I think the information is just too scant to make any assumptions, but in deference to that argument I will put Bleda's name first.

The two brothers started strong and were able to get the Romans to agree to the Treaty of Margus, with the annual tribute doubled. The treaty also opened Roman markets to trade with the Huns (a counterintuitive phrase) and agreed a ransom of eight solidi for all Romans taken captive. The treaty was a great success for Bleda and Attila and a little at odds with their image as bloodthirsty savages. So far, there had been more diplomacy and trade than fighting. The meeting was, however, typically Hunnish. As was the custom, Bleda and Attila took the meeting while mounted, surely an intimidating site for the Roman diplomats on foot.

With their western borders at peace, Bleda and Attila turned east and attacked the Sassanid Empire (Iran, Iraq and the Caucasus). They were thrown back in Armenia by the Sassanids, who also had well-trained cavalry forces. In 437, the Huns were back in Europe and the brothers sent contingents of their forces to fight with Flavius Aetius (who returns to the story now as a grown man) against the Burgundian kingdom on the Rhine led by King Gundahar. Gundahar had beaten Aetius a year earlier, but recognising he needed backup, Aetius looked to the Huns. It worked. Not only were the Burgundians defeated, but Gundahar was killed in battle. This has been immortalised in various Germanic myths, and Gundahar is seen as the origin of the Siegfried/Brunhild story, immortalised in Wagner's opera the *Ring of the Nibelung*. This is one example of a completely accidental Hunnic impact on European culture.

After this, Hun troops fought with Aetius to put down a revolt. The next year they were fighting with the Romans (but not Aetius) against the Visigoths in Toulouse. This campaign failed to capture the city, but to the east they were more successful. There is a passing mention in the records of their conquest of peoples in Scythia, meaning their empire was stretching ever further east, where it was largely unopposed. This meant that Bleda could expand his power whereas Attila's western borders were up against an established presence in the form of the Roman Empire. It is likely that due to trade and the Treaty of Margus, Attila was probably richer, but in terms of size, his was the smaller part of the empire.

We now come to the year 440 AD. The Treaty of Margus had allowed various markets to open up, providing an opportunity for Attila to attack in force across the frontiers into Roman lands. There was no warning, no discussion, just brute force. Now we see the folk memory of the violence and cruelty of the Huns realised, but quite why Attila chose to do this is unknown. The Huns destroyed the cities and forts of Illyricum, Viminacium and Moesia. These were all near the Danube, the natural border between Roman and Hun territory, easily within striking distance for the Hun cavalry. Attila claimed that the Bishop of Margus had plundered his land and even raided some royal tombs. While this is not impossible, it does seem highly unlikely. The bishop was so terrified he would be handed over to the Huns that he betrayed his own city, which was razed.

This was not the Huns' first act of violence perpetrated on Roman soil, but it was the most devastating, and while they had previously attacked some of the migrant peoples and their towns, now Attila was attacking Roman settlements full of Roman citizens.

In 441, Attila and Bleda pushed further south to Singidunum (Belgrade) and Sirmium. It was likely they would have taken these areas regardless, but they were helped by the fact that that the attenuated Roman Empire had just removed its troops from the region to deal with Vandal attacks in North Africa. One can see the dilemma of the Roman Emperors: they could be brave in battle and effective administrators, but nobody can fight multiple wars on multiple fronts simultaneously.

Nothing was slowing down the Huns, and yet Attila stopped and proposed a truce, something that gave the Romans some needed breathing space. There had to be a good reason to stop. The best guesses are either an outbreak of disease in the Hun ranks (a common occurrence in all armies through the ages) or an attack to the east. Again, we will never know for sure, but it is a fair supposition to say that Attila must have had a very good reason to call off such a successful and devastating raid.

The truce didn't last long. Theodosius II called his troops back from the North African campaign, and in 443, the opposing forces met. Against all expectations the records show that for the first time in nomadic history, the steppe horsemen brought siege weapons to the fight. This meant that the attacking forces could only move as quickly as they could drag a battering ram. However, Attila would have had detachments of cavalry to screen his advance. As it was, the Romans lost every encounter. The settlements of Ratiara and Naissus (Niš) were captured and sacked. When the Roman army arrived, they found the houses burned and the men, women and children slaughtered. The Huns advanced as far as Gallipoli, within sight of Constantinople (although they stood no chance of destroying the double walls of the mighty imperial capital). Theodosius II hurriedly agreed peace terms that were punitive, as Attila claimed it had been the Romans (and not himself) who had broken the original treaty. There wasn't much the

Romans could do when the Huns effectively had a knife to their throats. There was an initial payment of 6,000 pounds of gold. The yearly tribute was tripled, rising to 2,100 pounds, and the ransom for each Roman prisoner rose from 8 to 12 solidi.

No sooner had the ink dried on the 443 peace treaty than the Huns were on the warpath again in the following year, but on this occasion Cassiodorus, one of the chroniclers of the age, was sent to Attila's court to negotiate another peace treaty. According to this, Attila was given lands and may also have been made a *magister militum*, the title other warlords on the borders of Rome had been given on the understanding that they were paid to protect the Roman frontiers.

Somewhere around this time (nobody thought to record the exact date) Bleda was murdered on the orders of Attila, who then became the sole ruler of the Hun Empire and now had at least double the number of men at his disposal to wage war. Of course, if the mission of Cassiodorus coincided with Attila's fratricide, it would explain the second peace treaty, as Attila had to secure his claims to the east before he could be sure his own generals were loyal. Any time bought by the Romans was vital, due to all the other crises and attacks they were facing. But the Romans were only delaying the inevitable. Attila had developed a taste for the conquest of Roman lands, and nothing the Romans had thrown at him had made him feel he was anything other than the supreme military power in eastern Europe.

In 447, Attila invaded the Eastern Roman Empire again, ravaging the areas he had attacked earlier in the decade. However, a Roman army was sent out to fight, and Arnegisclus met the Huns at what has become known as the Battle of the Utus (in Bulgaria). Little is known about the battle apart from the fact that Arnegisclus died in the fighting and that casualties were heavy on both sides. The fact that one of the leaders of a battle died shows how brutal the fighting must have been. No quarter was asked for or given, and while Arnegisclus may have died alongside thousands of his troops, Attila had suffered more losses than he was expecting. That seemed only to make him angrier.

From the Life of Saint Hypatius by Callinicus:

> The barbarian nation of the Huns, which was in Thrace, became so great that more than a hundred cities were captured, and Constantinople almost came into danger and most men fled from it... And there were so many murders and bloodlettings that the dead could not be numbered. Ay, for they took captive the churches and monasteries and slew the monks and maidens in great numbers.

It had been another successful campaign for Attila and his reputation as a fearsome warrior was now enshrined in Roman thought, but he had only just got going. It is tempting to think that this battle earned his epithet, 'Scourge of God', but while this may have been the sentiment at the time, it was only first referenced in a historiography of The Life of St Lupus written in either the 8th or 9th centuries, hundreds of years later.

So far, the devastation Attila caused had been largely in the Eastern Roman Empire. When the Huns had campaigned in the West it had been as mercenaries in alliance with Rome. The Roman Emperor at the time was Valentinian III, who had been born in the new capital of the Western Roman Empire, Ravenna. The port had existed for centuries and had always been an important city, but after Rome had been sacked multiple times and now with the rise of a new and potentially even deadlier threat, Ravenna was a good choice for a new capital. It was created as such in 408 when Uldin was at his peak of aggression. Rome could easily be surrounded and attacked, as the Visigoths proved in 410 and just a few years later, the Vandals in 455. Ravenna by contrast was surrounded by swamplands, terrain that cavalry would find impassible, and it had a direct maritime route to the more stable Eastern Roman Empire and Constantinople. On the one hand it was a very practical choice, on the other it was sign of how far the Western Roman Empire had fallen. Ravenna was not the new capital exclusively because of the Huns, but also in anticipation of the overwhelming barbarian attacks which would ensue.

Valentinian III had a sister called Honoria, who had had one of the most devastating strops in history. She resented the fact that she was having an arranged marriage to a Roman senator. We can condemn the patriarchy about its use of women as pawns in marriage alliances, but this had been the standard role for aristocratic women throughout history and was in no way a surprise for Honoria. Rather than marry the senator, she sent Attila her engagement ring. Honoria may not have intended a proposal of marriage, rather more a cry for help, but Attila chose to interpret her message as the former and accepted her proposal, asking for half of the Western Roman Empire for her dowry.

Quite what Honoria was hoping to get out of this is unknown. A Roman aristocrat would not have sought out a barbarian leader. (I am using the term 'barbarian' from the perspective of the Romans, and it is accurate as the term is Latin. The Romans simply could not understand all the new languages of these peoples. Frankish Gothic, Hunnic, etc., to the Romans they sounded like they were all saying 'baa, baa, baa', hence the term 'barbarian', which literally means people who say 'baa' – as opposed to the knights who say ni.) When Valentinian III discovered what his sister had done, it was their mother Galla Placidia who convinced him to exile rather than execute Honoria. There was also some frantic diplomacy with Attila to strenuously deny the legitimacy of the supposed marriage proposal. Attila, rather than descending immediately on Roman territory as might be expected, played the diplomatic game to reinforce his position. He sent an emissary to Ravenna to proclaim that Honoria was innocent, that the proposal had been legitimate and that he would come to claim what was owed to him. This established the legitimacy of his claims of conquest. Next, he needed a trigger.

In that same year (450) an unnamed Frankish ruler died, location unknown. What is known is that there was a succession dispute between his two sons. In short, Attila supported the elder while Rome in the guise of Flavius Aetius supported the younger. Attila threw the full resources of his empire into this campaign. This was not just a Hunnish army, but an army made up of his vassal kingdoms as well, including Ostrogoths, Alans, Burgundians and many more. Contemporary chronicles exaggerate his numbers as half a million strong. Whenever chronicles report an impossible number, it simply means there were far more men on one side than the other.

By 451, Attila was in Gallia Belgica (northern France/ Belgium), where he first attacked and captured Divodurum Mediomatricorum, known today as Metz (this has to be the longest name condensed into the shortest name in history). Next came Rheims where the Huns killed Bishop Nicasius before the altar in his church. Several other cities were allegedly saved by the fact that their bishops were pious men who prayed to God; what is more likely is that Attila was trying to find the Roman army rather than get bogged down in a siege that would leave his rear vulnerable to attack. More realistically, Bishop Lupus of Troyes (whose hagiography is the one that names Attila as the Scourge of God) is said to have saved the city by coming out from the walls and meeting Attila in person. Although this account was written much later and has echoes of the verifiable meeting between Attila and the Pope, it could have been a successful precursor to the main event.

In June of 451, Attila pushed further into Gaul (France), a move that forced the local Visigoth King Theodoric I to ally with Flavius Aetius, who had assembled a patchwork army of Roman and tribal forces. The two sides met at a battle that has many names, but the most common is the Battle of the Catalaunian Plains. The plains part is important. Had the battle been in mountains or had it been a siege, Attila would not have been able to use his horse archers to full effect, but on the plains he had everything he needed to bring the full might of his cavalry against a familiar enemy.

The Western Roman Empire had been wracked by civil war and invasion for generations, and so it would continue after this battle, but all the records emphasise the levels of slaughter and the size of the forces. This was clearly the largest and most important battle of the era. The night before, a large scouting party from the Roman side came across a contingent of Gepids (a Germanic tribe) on Attila's territory and a separate battle ensued. It was bloody but a stalemate was reached, and the remaining forces of both sides found their way back to their main armies. We are able to date these events accurately because Haley's Comet was in the sky at the time– seen by contemporaries as an omen of great import.

The start of the battle was delayed for reasons mentioned in Chapter 1, when Attila ordered the shamans to carry out rituals to divine the future. As animals were sacrificed and entrails were interpreted, the news was mixed. Attila would lose, but an enemy leader would die. This is not from western records but oral traditions, reinforcing how different the two cultures were at the time. So, Attila delayed his first attack until mid-afternoon, reasoning that if he were to lose, the gathering dusk would cloak his retreat.

The Catalaunian Plain rose on one side with a sharp incline to a ridge, a key feature that would prove important in the battle. Attila's first move in the afternoon was to take a position on the right of the ridge, Flavius Aetius took the left. The forces clashed and King Theoderic led his Visigoths to capture the crest of the hill. The approach would have been with shields as the Hunnic horse archers would have loosed a deadly hail of arrows on the advancing soldiers. Theoderic died in the melee. There are varied accounts of exactly how, but the key issue is the co-leader of the Roman forces was slain. However, the Visigoths didn't notice at this point and managed to push forwards and, for a change, outmanoeuvre Attila's personal guard. As dusk descended the battle continued and chaos ensued. Attila was forced to retreat to a great ring of fortified waggons (an indication that the Hunnic forces were not as mobile as they used to be and now had slowed their pace with infantry and a baggage train). Thorismund, son of King Theodoric and now the new king (although he didn't know it yet), returned to what he thought was his camp, but it turned out to be the Huns'. Fierce fighting broke out and only the arrival of Roman allies saved the now wounded Thorismund from the same fate as his father. Flavius Aetius was also separated from the main body of troops and camped with allies overnight.

When dawn broke over the battlefield on day two the Catalaunian Plain was littered with bodies and a forest of arrows. Both sides had suffered heavy casualties, but Attila and Flavius Aetius were still ready for battle, and their main forces were still willing and able to fight.

Aetius Flavius rallied his troops to besiege the temporary fort that Attila was defending. Meanwhile, Attila was resigned to his fate and ordered a pile of saddles ready to be burned. He did not want anyone to claim they had wounded or killed him and instead, was prepared to burn himself alive in a funeral pyre of saddles.

It was at this point that the Visigoths found their dead king. Thorismund was filled with rage and prepared to assault Attila's temporary fort. What came next is hotly debated, so let's consider the details such as we have and then take a look at the possible explanations. Flavius Aetius stopped Thorismund from carrying out the assault and allowed him to return to his lands to secure his crown before any other family members could act. This meant that the Romans had just lost a significant part of their army, which gave Attila more options than self-immolation.

Flavius Aetius had just lost all the initiative he had won at the cost of soaking the Catalaunian Plains in the blood of men. Why? Theory number one is he was playing a very long game and feared that if the Huns were completely wiped out, he would have no counterbalance to the increasingly powerful Visigoth kingdom. A second theory says he feared that a wounded and enraged Visigoth ruler assaulting a position would be futile and might bolster the morale of the Huns. Third, that after this he dismissed other allies so he could gather all the booty and later, the glory for himself. We will never know.

What happened at the end is a cottage industry of historical arguments, so sidestepping the controversy, the Huns and their allies retreated to their lands, enabling Flavius Aetius to claim the field of battle, one piled high with corpses from both sides. Undeniably, the outcome proved that Attila was not invincible. While it had not been his first setback, most of his other losses came from raiding forces trying their luck. This had been a major roll of the dice, with all his resources poured into one campaign, and while he had not been vanquished, he had not swept aside the coalition set against him. From the Roman perspective the rising tide of Hunnic attacks had been stopped. In two days,

Flavius Aetius had severely weakened two barbarian powers and had claimed a victory for the Romans. For a change, fighting with Attila had not ended with a humiliating peace treaty and tribute, although Honoria did fail to meet her fiancé.

The problem was that Attila had been chastened, not stopped. He returned to his lands, reorganised, and in 452 he invaded the Western Roman Empire once again, this time targeting Italy. Attila was still claiming the legitimacy of his invasion as the lands were his by right of an anticipated marriage to Honoria. Flavius Aetius was the man on the ground again, but unlike his confrontation with Attila on the Catalaunian Plains, this time he had only a small contingent of troops and stood no chance of winning a pitched battle against another Hunnic invasion force. After a strategic victory, admittedly with heavy losses, the Roman lands could no longer field an effective army; the Huns by contrast had in the space of a year rebuilt theirs.

Flavius Aetius set up a base of operations in the town of Aquileia. He was unable to stop the Huns crossing the Julian Alps, and now Attila was into the lowlands of northern Italy. People fled to the coast, to a swampy lagoon, hoping it would hide them from the rampaging Huns. It was here that they set up a small trading post that grew into a town and then into the city of Venice. Once again, a major piece of European history was the result of the violence inflicted by the Huns.

Flavius Aetius had already retreated from the area when Attila attacked Aquileia, and the Huns razed the city. Archaeological surveys show a catastrophic layer of destruction in the 5th century AD, and an attempt to rebuild a much smaller settlement a generation later, but there is a second (smaller) layer of destruction from the 6th century AD, when the Lombards destroyed it in 590. A few houses were added later, along with a basilica, but this once great city of antiquity is now just a church and fields.

Flavius Aetius did what he could with the men available and harassed Attila's army. This was no mean feat, as the Huns themselves were pre-eminent scouts and masters of raids. However, all he could do was slow Attila rather than stop him. Despite his considerable military talents, Flavius Aetius recognised his limitations and stuck to what he could do, rather than overreach himself.

At this point Attila stopped ravaging northern Italy and set up camp on the bank of the River Po (the largest river in northern Italy). Why? The answer as usual is uncertain. Flavius Aetius had harassed the Huns but not enough to warrant a halt. The most likely reason, which is the most common cause for any army to stop, was disease. In addition, in 451 there had been a terrible famine after the crops failed, so the Huns may have been unable to forage for enough food. This gave Valentinian III a chance to send an emissary to Attila. Perhaps it was time for another treaty.

Mantua is just south of the River Po and it was here that Attila met the three representatives sent by Valentinian III. Gennadius Avienus and Trigetius were both high-ranking and well-respected politicians; Pope Leo I was the third and more unusual member of the group. The Roman Emperor had sent the Pope as an ambassador to meet the leader of the pagan hordes. In the medieval era no king or emperor would have had such control over the Pope, and it shows how different the early church was (indeed, at this time the Pope was just one of five patriarchs, supreme church leaders). Leo would later get the epithet 'the great' and was the first Pope to receive this honour. The Eastern Roman Emperor Theodosius II was the first to call what technically was the Bishop of Rome by the far grander title of Patriarch of the West. This is a title that would continue to be used by popes until as recently as 2006. Yet in this instance he was sent as a mere diplomat and negotiator on the authority of the emperor. Who sent him has faded from history; the fact that he met the most feared warlord of the age has not.

And so, a legendary moment in history came to pass, and like many legends, the facts are thin on the ground. The fact that Leo met Attila is undisputed, but what the two men thought of each other is unknown. As stated earlier, there can be no doubt that Attila understood he was talking to a high priest of the Romans, a revered shaman, but any threats of God's wrath or any offers of baptism would have meant nothing to him. What little is known of the meeting does not credit Leo's diplomatic skills, it seems that Gennadius Avienus and Trigetius were the chief negotiators. Stories of Attila dismounting at the sight of such a magnificent holy man are later embellishments. There is a theory that Attila was aware of the fate of King Alaric, who had sacked Rome in 410 and died shortly after from a fever... or punishment by God. It is possible that he had heard the story, but as it did not stop the Vandal King Genseric from doing the same in 455, it is unlikely that it influenced Attila. What we know for sure is Honoria was not handed over to Attila, and Attila retreated north through the Alps, back to his territory. There does not seem to have been any wagons groaning under the weight of gold and silver paid as tribute. All of this implies that Attila was unable to push further south, which leads again to the conclusion that either his supplies were running low, or disease had broken out. It also seems that the new Eastern Roman Emperor had sent troops to bolster Flavius Aetius' troops, but how many and whether Attila was even aware of this is unknown. Regardless, the diplomatic mission, from Valentinian III's perspective, had been a staggering success.

Attila, however, had other problems. Theodosius II had died, and the new Eastern Roman Emperor Marcian decided that all tribute payments would be stopped. Attila started to plan a campaign to teach him a lesson. But first, a happy celebration, he was going to get married, again. Roman records at the time describe Attila returning to his palace where what happened next is set in a building. This is because from a Roman perspective, where else would a leader live? Attila had grown up in the traditional nomadic way, living in a tent, constantly on the move, following the herds. He may have conquered an empire, but throughout his life Attila lived in felt tents, opulently decorated yurts, but circular tents nonetheless. It's possible Attila had gone native and lived in buildings, but there is no evidence of this.

As previously stated, the steppe nomads were polygamous. Having multiple wives was a sign of status, and as Attila was the great chieftain, he needed a lot of wives. How many? Unknown, but it's safe to say more than anybody else. This shows that the failure to marry Honoria was hardly the greatest doomed romance the world has ever known, but instead, a purely political move by Attila to put a fig leaf of justification over his aggression towards the Western Roman Empire. Had the wedding taken place it would have been interesting to see what the sister of an emperor would have made of being bottom of the pecking order in the wifely hierarchy.

Attila's new bride was Ildico (a Germanic and not a Hunnic name) and all accounts agree she was a beauty. She was probably 18-20 years old, and by now Attila was in his late 40s (his birth year is not recorded). The wedding of a chieftain is an epic affair, with lavish entertainment, food by the wagonload and beer and wine by the barrel. After a legendary night of carousing, it was time for Attila to take his young bride to the bedchamber (or special tent for the nuptials) to consummate the marriage. And that's the last time the great warrior was seen alive. Instead, presumably pale and shaken, Ildico emerged alone because her new husband had died from a nosebleed and choked to death in a drunken stupor. This is from contemporary writers. That this young Germanic woman was the last person to see the greatest threat to western Europe alive meant that multiple legends sprung up. Most notably, Germanic and Scandinavian traditions claimed that she stabbed him to death to avenge the deaths of all her brethren the Hun had slaughtered over the years. The idea of a Delilah or black widow character, a woman who uses her feminine guile to slay the barbarian who no man could match with force is a very common and seductive narrative. But such an account just isn't there in the initial records. Instead, it's the more mundane truth that Attila had led a hard life in the saddle; he was middle-aged, and he was probably worn out from all the years on campaign. As it was, the man who had inflicted so much death and destruction died in bed, in the arms of his new wife. Not a bad way to go and much better than he deserved.

The problem now was that Attila's empire had centred on him. The Chinese emperors had their administration, the Romans had their civil service and generals, but the expanded Hunnic Empire existed due only to the sheer force of will and brutal violence of one man. Who had the right to succeed him? Who had the might to keep the empire together? But first, the man needed to be shown the honour he deserved (from the Hun perspective).

This is from the contemporary account by Priscus, preserved in the 6th century by Jordanes:

> Then, as is the custom of that race, they plucked out the hair of their heads and made their faces hideous with deep wounds, that the renowned warrior might be mourned, not by effeminate wailings and tears, but by the blood of men... His body was placed in the midst of a plain and lay in state in a silken tent as a sight for men's admiration. The best horsemen of the entire tribe of the Huns rode

around in circles, after the manner of circus games, in the place to which he had been brought and told of his deeds in a funeral dirge in the following manner: 'The chief of the Huns, King Attila, born of his sire Mundiuch, lord of bravest tribes, sole possessor of the Scythian and German realms – powers unknown before – captured cities and terrified both empires of the Roman world and, appeased by their prayers, took annual tribute to save the rest from plunder. And when he had accomplished all this by the favour of fortune, he fell, not by wound of the foe, nor by treachery of friends, but in the midst of his nation at peace, happy in his joy and without sense of pain ...

When they had mourned him with such lamentations, a strava, as they call it, was celebrated over his tomb with great revelling. They gave way in turn to the extremes of feeling and displayed funereal grief alternating with joy. Then in the secrecy of night they buried his body in the earth. They bound his coffins, the first with gold, the second with silver and the third with the strength of iron, showing by such means that these three things suited the mightiest of kings; iron because he subdued the nations, gold and silver because he received the honours of both empires. They also added the arms of foemen won in the fight, trappings of rare worth, sparkling with various gems, and ornaments of all sorts whereby princely state is maintained. And that so great riches might be kept from human curiosity, they slew those appointed to the work – a dreadful pay for their labour; and thus, sudden death was the lot of those who buried him as well as of him who was buried.

This is a Roman account, with all the omens removed, and although it most certainly has embellishments, something like this probably did take place. It is an interesting comment at the start that a warrior is honoured by ritual cuts to the face rather than 'effeminate wailings and tears'. Ritual scarring exists in many cultures in the world, so this was possible, particularly when there can be no doubt that Attila had been a unifier and enricher of the Huns. The grave diggers slaughtered at the end of the story were most likely slaves.

After the great leader was buried, what happened next was wholly predictable. Attila had ruled by violence through both demonstrations and threats, and he had committed fratricide to unify the empire. So, his three sons Ellac, Dengizich and Ernak went to war to win the ultimate prize. Some of the vassal peoples of the empire allied to overthrow Hun rule; others joined the warbands of individual brothers. Chaos reigned and civil war ensued.

A similar political situation was also playing out in the Roman Empire. Valentinian III had always been suspicious of Flavius Aetius, and the latter's continued rise in reputation only made that resentment grow. In 454, the general was in Ravenna going through the financial accounts with the emperor, who rose from his chair and laid all the empire's troubles on the shoulders of the one last effective general he had. Valentinian III drew his sword, as did his chamberlain Heraclius, and both struck Flavius Aetius. Valentinian III's blow to the general's head killed him instantly. Another high-ranking Roman, a friend of Flavius Aetius who had been passed over for promotion, sought revenge. About six months later, at the Campus Martius, the emperor was preparing for archery practice when two Huns approached him. They were Optila and Thraustila, both of whom had fought with Flavius Aetius and respected him. The two Huns attacked both Valentinian III and Heraclius. Optila stabbed Valentinian III in the temple, killing him instantly; Heraclius was dispatched just as quickly.

Flavius Aetius had been hugely popular and Valentinian III had made a lot of enemies during his reign. Nobody in Valentinian III's retinue lifted a finger to stop the assassinations, and now the Huns could claim an emperor had fallen under their blades (admittedly by court intrigue rather than in the melee of battle).

Jordanes writing a hundred years later speculated on what the clashes would have looked like. While not an eyewitness account, this succinct passage shows the genuine variety of peoples and fighting styles that existed inside the Hunnic Empire: '... the Goths fighting with pikes, the Gepidae raging with the sword, the Rugii breaking off the spears in their own wounds, the Suavi fighting on foot, the Huns with bows, the Alani drawing up a battle-line of heavy-armed and the Heruli of light-armed warriors'.

In 454 at the Battle of Nedao, most of the Germanic tribes shrugged off the hegemony of the Huns. The eldest son Ellac was killed in that battle and fighting continued off and on for another decade. For the peoples along the Danube, it would have been a terrible time as one warband after another was seen on the horizon looking for plunder, food or tribute. In 465, it appeared that the remaining two brothers, Dengizich and Ernak, had reconciled, as they sent a threat to Constantinople demanding tribute, or the Eastern Roman Emperor could expect raiding in Thrace once again. Emperor Leo I (not to be confused with the Pope) felt he could play for time and ignored the threat, so Dengizich moved to the Lower Danube in 465/6. Now Leo took the threat far more seriously and started to talk tribute.

Talks came to nothing, so in the winter of 467, Dengizichi crossed the frozen Danube. He had expected allied tribes to join him, but the mix of Germanic tribes and Scythians started raiding independently, showing that Dengizichi lacked the authority of his father. This war dragged on for two years, so none of the fast hit-and-run raiding of Attila. His son was bellicose but lacked the strategic ability, aggression and resources of his father. In 468, a Germanic alliance met the Huns at the Battle of Bassianae (in modern-day Serbia). It was a decisive victory for the Germanic peoples and the Huns never waged war with them again.

In 469, Dengizichi faced the German warlord Anagast (fighting on behalf of Leo I) in a battle so inconsequential it has no name or record of location. It was important only because Dengizichi was killed in it; he was decapitated and his head sent to Constantinople, a gift for Leo I. This meant Ernak was the last brother standing, and in complete opposition to everything his father stood for, Attila's son seems to have been happy with the lands he inherited and in no way threatened Roman territory. After that he faded from history; we don't even know in what year he died and whether his death was from natural causes or violence.

The Huns had been a significant military threat to the Roman Empire and its neighbouring peoples for 90 years. By comparison, the Tudor dynasty of England lasted just over a century. The Tudors had far fewer resources than the Huns under Uldin or Attila, and yet, while Hampton Court Palace stands as a testament to Tudor power, there are no structures that commemorate the Hun Empire. It is as if it has been deliberately erased from history, but that is not the case. These nomadic people lived in tents and traded for goods more than they made their own.

Staying with the Tudor analogy, Attila never ordered the construction of a Hampton Court not only because he lived life on the move, but also because with no central administration and no settlements, there was nothing permanent about the Hunnic Empire. It was glued together with violence and added nothing to the local sedentary populations. This meant that the empire faded far quicker than those based on city states, with all the buildings, goods and services associated with them. The overlordship of the Huns had not been a happy time for the subjugated peoples, so nobody wished to emulate them, nor was there much to emulate, except for their style of warfare.

The Huns in the East were never conquered by neighbouring Germanic tribes but, instead, settled, interbred with the local population and founded the state of Hungary. In the Middle Ages, the Christian kings of Hungary would chart their ancestry back to Attila with great pride. Over the years, Attila evolved from foreign devil to founding father, establishing a creation myth much like King Arthur in Britain (except, unlike Arthur, Attila actually existed). If the Huns were to have one legacy in Europe it would be the people. But in modern Hungary, the people do not speak Hungarian, they speak Magyar, and that is the name of the next group of Eurasian Steppe nomads ready to crash into Europe.

4

THE AVARS AND
THE MAGYARS

While the framework of this book is five great waves of conquest emanating from the Eurasian Steppe, it is of course a little more complicated than that. With the second wave of attacks on the West we are looking at two power bases of steppe nomads that came to have different names, the Avars and the Magyars. While the names are quite different, they are of similar origins. The reason for different names for what eventually became one people is the peoples they attacked. This is an example of history being written by the losers, where the vanquished try to describe an unfathomably different people, who apparently came from nowhere and descended like vengeful wraiths on the local population. So, to keep it simple I will refer to the group as the Avars, but mention Magyars on occasion to show mainly where settlements differed. Bearing in mind the end of the previous chapter, it is no spoiler to say that the remnants of the Avars settled in Hungary and spread their language, which has become known as Magyar.

By 470 AD, the Huns were a spent force from the European perspective. The Avars were first recorded in the Pannonian Basin (the last part of the Eurasian Steppe in modern-day

Hungary) about a century later in the 560s AD. Why they arrived in the West was a mystery to contemporary historians, but again, like the Huns, they appeared to arrive by no known animus. The previously mentioned Rouran Khaganate was an empire that stretched across the eastern Eurasian Steppe and at its peak covered lands north of modern-day China, including Mongolia and large areas of eastern Russia, as well as Uzbekistan and Kazakhstan. Khaganate is another word for empire, a European word used to stop this discussion becoming an impossibly exotic parade of words. The Rouran Khaganate was a collection of lots of different nomadic tribes. Its downfall came when there was an armed rebellion by a more bellicose tribe known as the Göktürks, who would later be known simply as Turks and who will be the third wave of invaders, discussed in detail later. It is also thought that remnants of the Hunnic Empire evolved to become another group from the steppe, the Tatars.

This breakdown of an empire which had ensured stability for over 200 years led to anarchy on the eastern Eurasian Steppe by the mid-550s AD. With warring tribes, raiding warbands and general hostility, it is unsurprising that some of these tribes felt their best solution was to get way from the war zone and head west. The timing of the collapse of the Rouran Khaganate coincides very well with the arrival of the Avars in the West about five years later. For a time, the Göktürks seemed to have actively hunted the Avars, which would imply that they had been on the wrong side of an alliance at some point. At this stage the need to head out of the heartlands of Göktürk power would have been essential and meant a fraught chase across a thousand miles of steppe grassland until the Göktürks broke off the attack. Most likely, as the new power in the old heartlands, they faced their own challenges and insurrections, and now the Avars were far enough away not to be a threat. This is all conjecture, but it's a reasonable piece of extrapolation from what can be proved. After that, the Avars would not have been heading to Hungary as quickly as possible (it is unlikely that this was a deliberate destination) but slowly migrating west over several seasons after they were out of harm's way.

It's worth considering that while the horse archers are the ones who get the coverage in the chronicles, they are not the only people who headed west. These were families, with their felt tents, herds of horses and yaks. Their falcons, children and way of life could be packed up within hours, enabling them to travel a dozen miles every day. This was not an army on the march, but a people on the move. The Huns and the Avars were people heading west to avoid a threat in the east, so the Huns and the Avars were probably the least warlike or powerful of the tribes in the power struggles on the steppe. And yet, when they arrived in Europe they were seen as terrifyingly proficient warriors compared to anything in the West.

A closer examination of steppe tribes in the sixth and seventh centuries throws up a number of peoples who get just a passing mention. What is clear is that by then the Eurasian Steppe was not a neutral area of nomadic families, but one of pocket empires of warbands, each one vying for supremacy over their neighbours. The Rouran Khaganate, rather than the Huns, may have been the inspiration, but again, to describe these tribal territories with the word empire implies a centralised bureaucracy and administration that simply didn't exist. A better description of what they were would be gangs. They were the dominant power that exerted control over any groups in their territory and were, as well, criminal enterprises employing extortion and violence that offered none of the security that those in an urban-based empire could expect. While safe harbour was the order of the day, these nomads knew that other peoples existed and that they might have to make their safe harbour over the dead bodies of sedentary peoples. It was a harsh logic from a pragmatic people.

One of the reasons the Avars are likely the least well-known group in this book is mainly because they appeared in Europe after the collapse of the Western Roman Empire but before the medieval era, during a period of few historical records. The second reason is that there is no central character. The Huns came first, but it's that fearsome warrior Attila who is remembered more than a millennium and half after his death. It's the legend of the man that is remembered even by people who have no interest in history. The Avars had no Attila, no Genghis Khan, nobody that caught the popular folk memory either as hero or villain.

The Avars arrived on the Hungarian plains in 560 AD, towards the end of the reign of the last great Eastern Roman Emperor, Justinian I, quite rightly remembered as Justinian the Great and the last to display what Roman power looked like. He built Saint Sophia, the largest church in the world until its conversion into a mosque in 1453. His General Belisarius recaptured huge areas of North Africa and Italy (including Rome) from various 'barbarian' tribes. With that level of central authority, success and effective military forces, the Avars, unlike the Huns, stood no chance of expanding into Roman territory. So instead of pushing south, they conquered the Slavic peoples of the north. It was the eastern Roman chronicles describing the conquests carried out by the Avars that revealed for the first time this new group of people called Slavs. The origin of the word is thought to mean people who speak the same language. However, it was their regular subjugation by Eurasian Steppe nomadic groups that was the derivation of the English word 'slave'. Much of modern Poland, Austria, Belorussia and Ukraine were part of the Avar Khaganate that had formed by about 600 AD. The list of leaders' names is fragmentary, making them more enigmatic.

At about this time, there was a delegation of Turks from the East to the Eastern Roman Empire where the Turkic messengers described the Avars as their vassal people, showing how they were still seen as subject people to the powers in Asia. With established Gothic kingdoms to the west, an Empire of Eastern Romans to the south, Turkic warlords to the east and frozen lands to the north, unlike some of the other groups explored in this book, the Avars were locked into place and, consequently, became the least nomadic of these nomad groups.

It would appear the first leader of the Avar Khaganate was Bayan I. His title was not king but chagan, or khagan or chakan, depending on which culture was spelling it. However, the fact that he ruled for more than forty years is suspiciously long and suggests previous unrecorded leaders. We know of Bayan I because there was a treaty between him and Justinian I, which stated that if Bayan attacked various groups in the area of Ukraine, he would be given gold and lands to settle for his troubles. Bayan I was able to carry out the task, and this was the foundation of the Avar lands, confirmed by imperial decree.

In 567, there was a war between two Gothic powers, the Lombards (at the time, they occupied land north of the Alps, but today, a region on the Italian peninsula is known as Lombardy) and the Gepids, whose lands were further east. The Gepids had sometimes fought with and at other times against the Huns a century earlier. The Lombards allied with Bayan I and the Gepids were crushed. The Lombard king captured and killed the Gepid king, whose skull was fashioned into a drinking cup (whether the Lombards or the Avars did this is disputed, but as the Lombards executed him, it would seem, on balance, more likely it was they who were the craftsmen). The Lombard king married the Gepid king's daughter and forced her to drink from the skull of her father. This story shows it was not just the Eurasian nomads who were capable of cruelty.

With the Gepid kingdom dismembered, the Avars seized the opportunity to move into the Pannonian Basin permanently.

During this completely forgotten war, two important events took place: First, the Lombards conquered northern Italy at a devastating cost to the Eastern Roman Empire, which will now be referred to as the Byzantine Empire. Justinian was the last Roman Emperor to speak Latin as his first language; from the time of his nephew and successor Justin II, all Byzantine emperors spoke Greek. Second, Justin II's forces captured Sirmium, an important town in Pannonia. This meant there were now Byzantine interests in Avar lands.

As the dust settled over the carved-up Gepid lands, Bayan I attacked Sirmium. Quite simply, he did not want a Byzantine

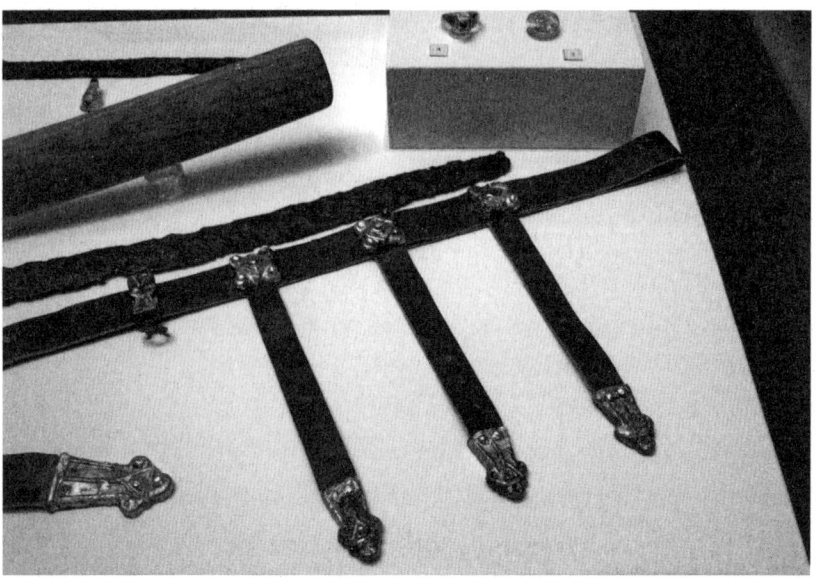

Above and opposite: Harness mountings and reflex bow from the Avar cemetery of Gyenesdiás, Zala County, Hungary. The cemetery was in use from *c.* 630 to the early 9th century. Of the 350 or so graves so far documented, about 20 burials were accompanied with a horse. (Courtesy James Steakley under Creative Commons 3.0)

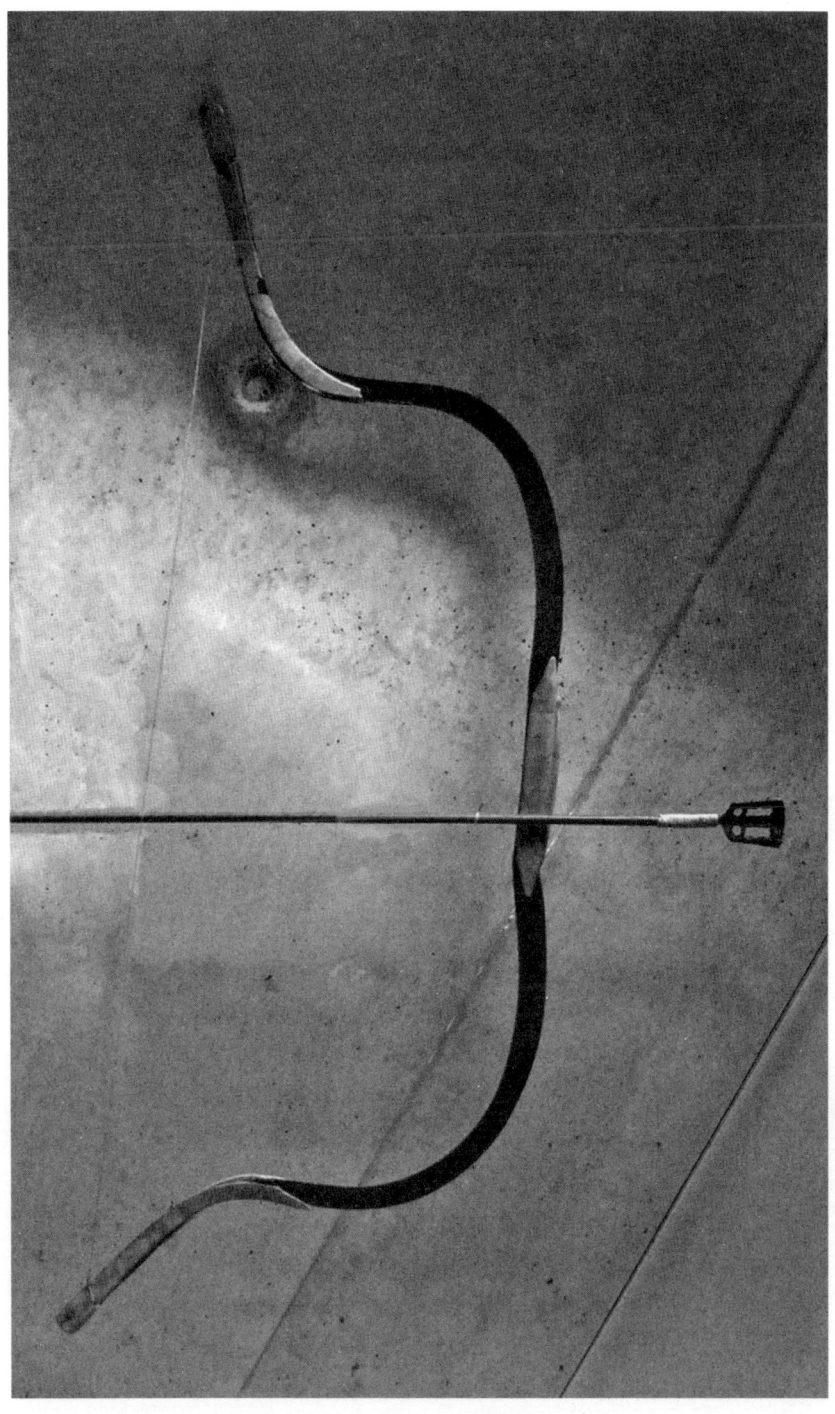

outpost in his newly won territory. However, as we have seen, while horse archers are formidable on a field of battle, they are ineffectual in a siege. The assault achieved nothing. In 570, the Avars moved into Thrace (just as the Huns had done). They raided and plundered, but the co-emperor Tiberius II (Justin II had suffered a mental breakdown, so while he was still alive, he recognised he needed a more capable man to carry out the day-to-day functions of leadership) raised an army and pushed the Avars back.

The Avars had failed in all their plans against Byzantium, so there was an uneasy peace for a time, after which Sirmium was besieged again. Bayan I, lacking any understanding of siege warfare, was reduced to using the simplest but slowest methods, surrounding the walls of the town and cutting it off from resupply. While his cavalry was unable to pierce the walls, hunger took its toll. The siege ground on for two years, but eventually Sirmium fell to the Avars. While the town had put up a brave defence, it was a sign of the waning power of Byzantium that Tiberius II was unable to send a relief army. The Byzantines would later face an existential threat from the third wave of steppe nomads, the Turks, but it was the Avars who signalled the start of this menace.

Time to pause and revisit the Silk Road to learn something more about the luxury textile it was named after. The production of silk (from the threads of the cocoons of the Bombyx mori moth) was a jealously guarded secret in imperial China, which had a global monopoly. Possession of silk was a sign of wealth, knowledge and power, but to be caught with a silkworm out of the high security areas of production meant execution. And yet despite the high security and extreme punishment, someone was able not only to get the secret to the Byzantine court, but to bring a viable collection of the Bombyx mori species. And where was the first area to start producing European silk?

Thrace. Just as China carefully guarded the secret, so, too, did the Byzantine Empire, but it had nearly been destroyed by the raiding Avars.

When the new Byzantine Emperor Maurice faced a threat to the north from the Avars and to the east from the Sassanids, he paid off Bayan I and managed to defeat the Sassanids, although this took years of warfare and drained the Byzantine treasury. Nevertheless, once he had accomplished this impressive feat he turned his attention to the Avars and by 599 had pushed them back across the Danube. Maurice was the first emperor in two centuries to campaign beyond the Danube into what was then Avar territory. Between the energetic Maurice and his highly competent General Priscus, the Avars were pushed further and further back. At this point the Avars looked like yet another barbarian kingdom on the hinterland of imperial authority. Bayan I had been successful but he was no Attila. Indeed, by 602, the Avar lands in the Pannonian Basin looked likely to comprehensively fall to Byzantine power. But just as things looked hopeless there was unexpected help when General Priscus revolted against Maurice. Priscus would eventually win the civil war, but it was this internal power struggle that saved the Avars. It was also around this time that Bayan I died. He was succeeded by Bayan II, followed by Organa, but so little is known about the successors there is even debate over their names.

In 617, the Avars launched an attack on the capital itself. They faced two serious problems: the apparently unbreachable double walls of Constantinople, and Emperor Heraclius, one of the last great and hugely successful warrior leaders of the empire. Despite failing to penetrate the great city's main defences, the suburbs outside the walls were plundered, with contemporaries claiming that a quarter of a million inhabitants were taken for slaves (an unlikely number, but even if it was just 10,000 that would still be a shocking sight).

Nine years later in 626, the Avars were back again to besiege Constantinople, this time with Sassanian forces. And once more Heraclius frustrated the attackers. The Sassanians were unable to bring siege weapons, nor could they craft any on site, and siege warfare was completely beyond the culture and customs of the Avars. Once the siege was lifted, Heraclius waged the very first holy war, supported by the church against the Sassanids, and brought down their empire in a spectacular string of victories (more about this in my book *Deus Vult*). At this time the Avars were so far on the fringes of history that even though they had allied with another empire to attack the very capital of the Byzantine Empire, we do not know the name of their leader, and in a number of chronicles their origin is confused, and they are referred to as Huns.

The Avars faced a new threat from the north when in 630, Samo united multiple Slavic groups who had all been harassed and forced to pay tribute to the Avars. He led this union against the Avars and managed to shrug off their authority. The exact origins of the Bulgarians are contested, but it seems that some were Avars or were at least people from the Eurasian Steppe who came under their authority. At the same time as Samo was rising up in the north, a Bulgarian leader called Kubrat was doing the same thing in the western parts of Avar lands. They attacked the Avars and carved out their own independent kingdom, pushing Avar influence ever further east.

After this sequence of events, it is possible to see why the Avars have not had the same folkloric tradition of groups such as the Huns or the Mongols. In some ways they were the least successful and the least mysterious of the waves of invaders coming from the Eurasian Steppe. But unlike some of those more famous groups, their staying power was greater. By the late 7th century, Samo and Kubrat had died. They were energetic but autocratic rulers and without them as the focal point of their kingdoms the Avars had a chance to reassert their own authority. What it meant for the rest of Europe was that the Avars were busy fighting in the hinterlands rather than attacking any of the major powers on the continent. Like the Bulgars (a group so reviled that emperor Basil II in the 10th century was called Basil the Bulgar slayer), the Avars were starting to evolve into another aggressive people on the hinterland of the Byzantine Empire.

Next, the Avars (under unnamed rulers) allied with the remains of Samo's Slavic lands and started attacking the fissiparous Bulgarian tribes. This Avar-Slav alliance consolidated their rule which stretched to the west from central parts of the Danube, into the Vienna Basin. It is in these new areas of conquest that archaeology starts to show the telltale signs of Eurasian Steppe nomad culture in burial finds from the late 7th and early 8th centuries. Among them are hair clips for the pigtails of the warriors and the classic cavalry weapon often called a scimitar. That symbol of these conquerors, the composite bow, has also been found. The reason for the rich burial deposits is that these people were still pagan (as were the Bulgarians and Slavs) and believed it necessary to bury with the deceased the things that might be needed in the afterlife. Europe at this time was mainly Christian, but its edges were full of different pagan groups, so from the Scandinavian north, through the Baltic states via the Saxons, down to the Hungarian grasslands, paganism thrived.

This expansion and consolidation took several generations, and by that time the Avars were threatening the Germanic heartland. The culmination of their westward expansion coincided with one the greatest leaders in European history, Charles the Great, known to history as Charlemagne. In the 19th century there was great debate among continental historians about whether Charlemagne was French or German. He was the first King of the Franks, and his family came from Frankish kings; his grandfather was Charles Martel (the hammer) who stopped Islamic expansion into Europe. But his capital was Aachen (in Germany) and he spent a large amount of time conquering and ruling Germanic tribes – so German then? In fact, he was neither. The countries of France and Germany were much later inventions. The best way to look at Charlemagne is that he was the great unifier, the most powerful ruler in the West since the earlier time of the emperors. When he died in 814, he directly ruled France, the low countries, Germany and northern Italy. Is it any surprise he was the first person in western Europe to be crowned emperor (on the very easy-to-remember date of 25 December 800) for more than 300 years. So just as Bayan I had the misfortune to be dealing with an Eastern Roman Empire during his lifetime, so, too, the Avars had the misfortune of dealing with the West just as a new empire was being forged under a hugely energetic and capable ruler.

From the perspective of the Avars, the conquest of the Bavarians (like the Saxons, it's hard to think of these tribal names as anything but German, but at the time they were pagans, outside of western European authority) and then the Kingdom of Lombardy, meant there was a new, highly motivated and capable enemy on their borders. Skirmishes began. We only have hints as to who started them and where they happened, but each side was testing the capabilities of the other, and a pattern soon emerged: if the Avars raided in small numbers, the Franks stood no chance of responding in time. In essence, the Avars caused the same problems for the Carolingians as the Huns did for the Romans, and as the Vikings would for Europe a generation later. Hit-and-run tactics in the age of the letter and horse meant a centralised authority couldn't find out where the attack was coming from and send forces in response in any timely manner. But when the Avars amassed too large a force, they were slower, giving the Franks enough time to raise a better trained force and win most pitched battles. Peace talks began; how seriously they were taken by either party is hard to say, but in 791, Charlemagne gathered a significant force and attacked from the west, while his son Pepin (now King of Italy) attacked from the south.

Both father and son did well and captured several towns (showing that while the Avars still fought as mounted archers, their lifestyle over 200 years had become far more sedentary). There was plunder to take home, but further advances were halted by disease, not of the men, but of the cavalry's horses, where as many as 90 per cent perished. This meant that Charlemagne and Pepin had no answer to the Avar cavalry and so (presumably) slowly made their way back to their own lands. Historian Carroll Gillmor identifies the disease as Eastern Equine Encephalitis, a highly contagious disease spread by mosquitoes. If Gillmor is correct it would explain why Charlemagne faced little resistance, as a pathogen like that would take no sides in war and was more likely to have disproportionately affected the Avars than the Franks. It took years to put in place the logistics and replacement horses needed to carry out a second campaign, and meanwhile, Charlemagne had an empire with its own problems to manage.

The recently conquered (but still independently minded) Saxons looked to the Avars for support and signed a treaty of alliance with them. This seemed like a wise move, but there was a complication: the threat of Frankish invasion had led to disunity in the Avar lands and civil war had broken out. Now the Avars were disunited and squandering their resources with infighting rather than trying to secure a unified front against a much more menacing foe. Several attacks were led by neighbouring Frankish lords in the intervening years, with mixed results. One potential assault never reached the Avar Khaganate as it was blocked by a Saxon uprising. Another penetrated so successfully that it seems to have captured the Avar treasury.

A second campaign began in 796. This time Pepin led the fight, aided by Charlemagne, who sent a major contingent from other parts of the empire. As shown by the previous campaign, cavalry was key and the reasons for this were twofold: first, as Charlemagne had been conquering vast areas of Europe, truly on a Roman scale, he needed the fastest troops possible, in other words he needed cavalry more than slow-moving infantry. While fighting the mobile light cavalry of the Avars, these forces evolved into a heavy cavalry, needing more armour to protect them, which gave them the advantage in a melee. Their protection consisted of a face helm and a padded woollen jacket called a gambeson, worn under a byrnie (later called a hauberk), a long shirt of chain mail armour. Second, these cavalrymen became the army elite, and as the conquests accrued somebody was needed to administer the new territories. These were split into benefices. They were rewards for the cavalrymen who had to manage, tax and protect the lands. Today, a heavy cavalryman who managed his own modest estate we would call a knight, a word that then had yet to be invented. But it shows how revolutionary Charlemagne was to have created a proto-feudal system and the definitive way to fight that would last for more than 600 years. It is also another reminder of the Eurasian Steppe nomads' impact on European society that the most medieval European of icons 'a knight in shining armour' was actually created in response to nomadic invaders.

It was precisely because of such innovation and resources that the Avars faced their most serious threat. The Franks moved into the Pannonian Basin from multiple directions and resistance by the Avars melted away. The winner of the civil war, the new Chagan Theodorus, met Pepin and sued for peace. A few tribal leaders resisted the new treaty but against such a foe were forced to head east to the edges of Avar lands. Once again, the Avar treasury (known as the ring) was plundered, giving Pepin a chance to return to Italy with glittering booty. The empty coffers also meant there were no funds for any resistant Avar groups to form a rebellion. This marked the end of the Avars as an active threat to Europe. To seal the peace treaty, Pepin did as his father had done to pagan subjugated peoples, he gave them the gift of Christianity.

Whenever a chronicle records that Christianity was brought to a people (this happened multiple times in Charlemagne's lifetime and later with the Vikings) there must be an accompanying note of caution. It's tempting to think that the subjugated people lined up for baptism, accepted Jesus and – hey presto – now the land was Christian. Of course, that is not how religion works. The reason pagan leaders accepted Christianity was simply because the Christian god had proved to be stronger than their spiritual overlords, and so a switch to the mightier deity made complete sense. It also meant, from a Christian perspective, that the treaties and peace talks were done in good faith, literally. Some people were systematically baptised and old temples would be torn down or reconsecrated, but it's fair to say that it would have taken time, certainly generations, for the old gods to fade away.

The year 796 can be seen as the end of the age of the Avars. Since they had first arrived in European records in the 560s, that means they were a menacing presence for more than 200 years (double that of the Huns), but they had never become the existential threat that Attila posed. The lands and peoples still existed, but as they became Christianised, they became yet another European Christian kingdom. But there is one more part of the story to be explored before we can move on to the third wave of Eurasian conquest.

In 804, the Avars were attacked again, this time by the growing power of Bulgaria. The Bulgarians conquered the Avar lands in Transylvania and southeastern Pannonia up to the Middle Danube, and many Avars became subjects of the Bulgarian Empire. Chagan Theodorus of the Avars, who as his name implies had converted to Christianity, died after asking Charlemagne for help in 805. This was a sign of how much had changed in the space of just a few years. Now the Avars were the victims and were unable to gather effective resistance to a new menace and turned to their imperial overlords for help. This was a plea from one Christian kingdom to another.

The Avar culture endured, but by now these nomads for generations had become farmers and settlers, living in towns and villages. The way they fought remained true to their heritage (and fundamentally different to that of western European powers), but the rest of the culture was now distinctively sedentary and Christian. Meanwhile, in the East on the Eurasian Steppe more groups began forming expansionist nomadic empires. There were the Khazars in central Asia (whose descendants would found Kazakhstan), the Cuman-Kipchaks (whose confederation stretched across vast swathes of the Eurasian Steppe for several centuries) and the Pechenegs. These were all nomadic groups, with their tents, bows, herds of horses, sheep, etc. They all had their individual names and unique cultural elements, which shows what a hugely energetic and vast area the steppe was, in that it could accommodate several empires simultaneously. In the north of Europe, the Scandinavians expanded their influence in Slavic lands, where they had founded Kyiv, originally a trading post that would have had goods brought in from local Slavic groups as well as being on the steppe and therefore attracting trade with the nomads, too. The Varangians or Kyivan Rus as they were known were starting to create their own fiefdom based on the town (and their Viking cousins from 820 moved on from raiding the British Isles to raiding continental western Europe).

In the middle of this swirling mix of expansion, raiding and tribute came the Magyars. Once again, we have a group pushed out of their home territories and forced westward to avoid conflict with more expansionist regimes. Many of the other groups (such as the Pechenegs) barely enter the written records of the day not because they didn't rule vast swathes of land (they did), but because their bases were far from the urban centres of Eurasia. They were faraway peoples of no interest to Chinese, Muslim or European writers. It is only the groups that were either forced or decided to conquer lands that had writing that became preserved in history ... which leads to an intriguing 'what if'. What if the Huns and Magyars, so feared in Europe, had been pursued further by their conquerors and those same conquerors had reached Europe?

The area on the steppe that they could easily reach, where resistance was weakest, were the lands of the Avars. The Magyars were there in the Carpathian Basin (the northern Balkans) by 860. In 862 Prince (and Saint) Rastislav of Moravia rebelled against the Franks and hired Magyar (also called Ungri-Hungarian) mercenaries in his successful attempt to gain independence. So we see a familiar pattern emerging: first the Huns, then the Avars and now the Magyars are used as mercenaries by the people that would then be on the sharp end of their arrows and blades.

By the end of the 800s, archaeological studies of burials show genetically Avar bodies in Magyar style clothing. This conclusively shows the integration of the two peoples and will become more important and more controversial when we come to the next wave of conquerors. The reality is that a sedentary population will always be larger than a nomadic one. The nomadic lifestyle is harsh, infant mortality is high, and the lack of nutritional concentration mean that populations cannot become too large or they all face starvation. Many Magyars arrived in Avar lands where there were simply far more Avars than Magyars, and over the generations the Magyars blended into the local population.

This era has been immortalised in the 13th-century *Gesta Hungarorum*, written 300 years after the events. This is a hagiographical account of the arrival of the Magyars. It is to Hungarian history what King Arthur is to British history and should be treated as a legend rather than historical fact. The critical element is the Magyars were led by seven chieftains:

Álmos, father of Árpád
Előd, father of Szabolcs
Ond, father of Ete
Kond, father of Korcán and Kaplon
Tas, father of Lehel
Tétény, father of Horka
and finally, Huba who doesn't get to be the father of anybody.

It is likely that the Magyars had a number of heads of families who formed the ruling elite, and the names are clearly of Turkic origin, but these pagan chieftains were turned into something more palatable for the European Christians of the 13th century. Other Hungarian chronicles agree that there were seven of them but then proceed to disagree about the names.

In the late 9th century, neither the Avars nor the Magyars wrote chronicles, and the rest of Europe had more important things to worry about than tribal migrations on the eastern edges of the continent. There are a few references to invasion, skirmishes and captured territory, but nothing that can be pulled into a detailed narrative. Instead, what is apparent is that over a couple of generations the Magyars replaced the Avars as the ruling elite of the Avar lands. Again, archaeology reinforces the merging of the two peoples and the Christianisation of the Magyars. From 895-1000, the area became known as the Principality of Hungary. From 1001, it was the Kingdom of Hungary. In its first fifteen years, it would overwhelm the

Fresco of Hungarian cavalry at the Battle of Augsburg. (Courtesy Sailko under Creative Commons 3)

Principality of Moravia, push the Bulgarians south and face three different armies sent from the West. The last one was met at the Battle of Pressburg in 907 and Augsburg in 910. They were decisive victories for the new state that secured its borders and sent a message to any would-be enemies that this new state in the heart of Europe was more than capable of defending itself.

While this was a European series of battles, fought between two Christian sides, the Hungarians demonstrated their origins through the tactics they used, tactics which have been mentioned before with the Huns, but which will be brought to their zenith of effectiveness later. They were all dependent on highly trained and efficiently organised horse archers.

Superior mobility enabled strategic and further tactical advantages. In essence, the whole army was capable of scouting and reconnaissance work. As such, multiple groups could be sent to multiple locations to scout out the terrain and locate the enemy. Their mobility made this far easier than it would be for the ponderous western European forces.

The scouting parties were also raiding parties, which created a psychological and logistical advantage. They were able to burn settlements to the ground, showing their overlords to be impotent to the Hungarian threat, and to plunder food, creating a scorched earth scenario, making it impossible for the advancing forces to resupply. Also, as the soldiers marched from one destroyed village to the next, their fear of the horse archers would only increase.

Tactically, mobility enabled two things: first was the ability to ride around enemy formations and shower them with arrows from all directions. The enemy couldn't engage if they couldn't get near the cavalry. Second was the feigned retreat, when the horse archers appeared to run away over the brow of the hill. The enemy army would break formation to chase down what they thought was a vanquished foe, only to realise the ploy was a trap. The cavalry returned in force and was able to pick off the now shapeless mass of enemy soldiers. All this required discipline and training, something that the Hungarians ensured was carried out.

The final strategy that the new Hungarian army used was patience. The army never rushed into a fight. Using modern military terms, all the above were pre-battle shaping operations, designed to get the enemy where the Hungarians wanted them and denuding their forces before the battle had even been fought. This enabled them to strike at the optimal moment.

This is a summary of the successful tactics deployed time and again throughout this entire era. From Attila to Babur, this way to wage war worked on multiple continents for more than a thousand years. But like any military strategy, it can be countered. The European heavy cavalry (knights) slowly evolved to use armour which was hard for the horse archers to pierce. If they were well organised and well led, and if the topography of the campaign area worked to their advantage, a charge from these lance-wielding forces could cut through the lightly armed and armoured Avars or Magyars.

Meanwhile, briefly mentioned above, the Cuman–Kipchaks had spread out over a massive area of the Eurasian Steppe. They were an example of a loose confederation of tribes that did not break into the territories of existing powers either in the East or the West, so they did not get a mention in the Carolingian or Chinese Imperial records. They were barbarians far beyond the horizon, an irrelevance, but there was one area where they settled which would make them famous – the Crimean Peninsula. Over the centuries this group would become known as the Crimean Tatars, and like the Huns, Avars and Magyars, they would intermarry with local populations whilst retaining the culture of pagan nomads. These people would still be making headlines in the 21st century.

The final point on this second wave of conquest is the one we started with. While the modern country is Hungary, the language is Magyar. Linguistic experts have carefully unpicked the language into its earliest component parts. The original Avars and later the Magyars would have spoken an Indo-European Turkic language, and while there are echoes of that in modern Magyar, the dominant influence is northern European and the modern language is from the Uralic language family. It is closer to Finnish than Turkish. So, while the country has a name derived from one Eurasian nomadic group and a language named after another, the language is far more local. But despite intermarriage and the passage of time and the fact that they were now sedentary rather than nomadic, the customs, history and the way they waged war remained very much part of their nomadic horse-archer heritage.

5

THE TURKS

No matter how fearsome the Huns or Magyars were, they were fundamentally groups pushed west by larger, more aggressive forces on the steppe. If they were the inferior martial force compared to other tribes, what would happen when those groups attacked sedentary populations? The answer came with the next wave. The Ural Mountains lie like a dagger striking across the Eurasian Steppe, a great range rising almost exactly north/south to the steppe that runs east to west.

So far in our story, the migrating tribes went west after reaching the Urals. The next group followed the range south, breaking not into Europe but the Middle East. This time the nomads were not fleeing anyone but were apex predators looking for prey. The problem with the word 'Turk' is that over the centuries it has become politicized. Today, two countries share the name. There is the Republic of Türkiye in eastern Europe and Anatolia, and then, thousands of miles to the east of that there is Turkmenistan (stan means 'land of' so it's the land of the Turkmen). But there are Turkic languages spoken in Azerbaijan and Uzbekistan, with similar cultural connections as far afield as Xianjiang province in China. For centuries in the West the nickname for the Ottoman Sultan was The Great Turk (more on this in the next chapter). Today, separating the history from the politics from the genetics is a very hot topic.

The Seljuk Empire began with Tughril, a Turkman chieftain in 1037. The empire would last in central Asia for 150 years. This obscure empire was huge, at its peak it covered 1.5 million square miles (3.9 million square kilometres). It was also the first time that an empire (rather than a group on the fringes, like the Hungarians) converted to a major religion; the Seljuks were not Christian, they were Muslim. As always with early conversion processes (such as the Romans to Christianity) it is important to exercise caution. Just because the rulers converted to a new religion and subsequently built appropriate places of worship does not mean their entire population would have shrugged off the old ways so readily.

Like the briefly mentioned Cuman-Kipchaks of the previous chapter, the Seljuks did not spring from sedentary societies, so their arrival in modern-day Iran or Iraq came as a huge surprise to the locals. As they conquered territory scattered with literate scribes, we began to learn more about this growing power.

By the middle point of the 11th century, nomadic horsemen began to raid on the edges of the Byzantine and Islamic worlds. Some raiders were hostile, some could be bought and used as mercenaries, others disappeared just as quickly as they arrived. The story of the early Seljuk Turks exists on the very fringes of history, and it's interesting that at a time when so much scholarship was going on in cities like Constantinople and Baghdad, very little was known about these nomadic peoples. But while their activity was in central Asia and on into the Middle East, some of their most famous clashes were against the old enemy of the Byzantine Empire and European forces now in the guise of crusaders.

1071 is the first important date in terms of the Seljuk impact on world history. This was the year of the Battle of Manzikert.

The Byzantine Emperor, Romanos IV Diogenes, understood a threat was coming, so he hired some of the meanest mercenaries in the world to bolster his considerable home-grown forces. The Normans were at their apogee of martial efficiency in the 1070s, so they were the first to be hired. Next up was the legendary Varangian guard, made up of Anglo-Saxon Englishmen and Vikings, who wore steel helmets and long suits of mail armour and who carried huge two-handed battle axes capable of cleaving a man from shoulder to waist in one blow. It is intriguing to think that both veterans and enemies of 1066 (Vikings, English and Normans) were potentially all fighting on the same side.

Romanos sought to fight fire with fire and had his own detachment of mercenary Seljuk horse archers. He had done everything right. He had mustered an army of about 50,000 (to put this into some perspective, at the Battle of Hastings neither side fielded a force of more than 7,000) and was ready to face Alp Arslan, the fierce warlord of the Seljuks. All Romanos had to do was find him.

Anatolia is like an oven in the summer, and Romanos had to cover hundreds of miles with a lumbering army. He didn't help matters by bringing a baggage train packed with luxuries and imperial comforts, which led to grumbling from the foot soldiers. And as usual, this western force lived off the land, meaning that the imperial army plundered whatever they needed, which led to hatred and bitterness on the part of the local populations.

Despite advice to hold in a key position, Romanos wanted to find this Seljuk army and end the Turkish incursions once and for all. Desperate to locate Alp Arslan, Romanos split the army in two and sent half off with the trusted and experienced General Tarchaneiotes. This was risky. Splitting a force is rarely advisable, but both armies were large and – in theory – more than capable of defending themselves.

Towards the end of August, Romanos arrived in Manzikert to find it empty of all troops. Had the battle already been won by his general? There was no time to find out as the familiar raids from the horse archers began again. Romanos sent out a detachment of cavalry to locate the source of these incursions, which resulted in the discovery of the entire Turkish force. Most of the cavalry was either killed or captured. As the skirmishing continued, Romanos must have wondered what had happened to his general.

When the two main forces finally met, it was obvious that Alp Arslan's army was considerable. By the 1070s the Seljuks had converted to Islam, which gave them access to diplomatic channels and, ultimately, troops from the major Muslim cities of the East. These weren't just Turks but also Syrians from Aleppo, among other allies. Alp Arslan sent envoys to talk peace, but Romanos wasn't interested. He knew he had everything to lose if he didn't stop the Seljuks then and there.

Worse was still to come. Many of Romanos' Turkic mercenaries felt they had more in common with Alp Arslan's forces than with the Byzantine army. On the morning of battle, Romanos awoke to discover many had switched sides. On 26 August 1071, Romanos led what remained of his army (still of considerable size) against Alp Arslan, and it was at this point that a number of hammer blows fell, almost all of them at the start of the battle. First, if Romanos was hoping for Tarchaneiotes to arrive on the field of battle, he was bitterly disappointed. His general had already been engaged by the Muslim army and crushed. No help was coming. Second, as soon as battle was ordered, the sizeable Norman mercenary contingent simply refused to fight. The Normans were not cowards, but they were shrewd and knew a lost cause when they saw one. Finally, Alp Arslan's strategy was the tried and tested (and eventually legendary) tactic of using the shape of the crescent for his horse archers.

As Romanos advanced, the Turkish centre would slowly retreat. Meanwhile, the wings of the Seljuk forces would creep around the flanks of the enemy in an attempt to surround them, all the time pouring arrow fire into the sides of the enemy troops. It didn't always work, but on this occasion it was textbook.

Romanos' forces were shattered and the fighting, while long and bloody (with the Varangian guard bravely defending the emperor in a last stand), did little to affect the ultimate outcome. It was a crushing defeat for Byzantium that would forever allow a Turkish presence in Anatolia.

When the emperor was captured by his mortal enemy, Alp Arslan put his foot on Romanos' neck and forced him to kiss the earth. After this, he raised the exhausted and blood-spattered emperor to his feet and asked him, 'What would you do if I was brought before you as a prisoner?'

There must have been a tense moment as Romanos thought what to say. He knew that the next words out of his mouth could well be his last. 'Perhaps I'd kill you or march you through the streets of Constantinople,' he replied.

'My punishment is far heavier. I forgive you and set you free,' said Alp Arslan.

As a peace treaty and ransom were negotiated, Romanos ate at Alp Arslan's side, but his comment was prophetic. When Romanos did return to Byzantine lands, he was forced into a civil war and was eventually blinded and deposed; his subjects treated him with less kindness than his enemy had done.

It is vital to understand that this defeat for the Byzantine Empire was to start the gradual and permanent transition of eastern Anatolia into a Muslim/Turkic area. However, it was still under recent new ownership when the First Crusade marched through the area just a generation later.

While Alp Arslan died at the hands of assassins in 1072, his trusted General Atsiz had been ordered south. He descended on

Jerusalem and starved it into submission. Being a relatively new convert to Islam himself, he had a deep respect for this holy city. However, once Jerusalem surrendered, he marched on Egypt where he over-extended his lines. He was defeated and retreated towards the holy city. Unfortunately, news of his defeat reached the population before he did, and he faced rebellion. He was a Turk and Turks don't take betrayal lightly. His piety evaporated. A gate was left open for him, and he and his remaining army poured in, taking out their anger and frustration on the inhabitants. It was the worst massacre the city had seen for many generations. Muslims, Jews and Christians all faced his wrath. The butchery was not religiously motivated, this was pure revenge. Atsiz was an equal opportunity slaughterer.

When the news of this massacre reached Europe, the story centred on Christian fatalities rather than on the more nuanced fact that a city had rebelled, and the warlord had exacted his revenge on the population as a whole; the Christian pilgrims had not been specifically singled out. However, this wasn't the only report of a Christian massacre at the time. In an entirely unrelated episode in 1064, Bedouins massacred five thousand German and Dutch pilgrims.

Since the roads to Jerusalem were generally safe for Christian travellers to the Holy Land, pilgrims always marched unarmed and had been doing so for centuries. It's important to highlight here that Jerusalem had been under Muslim rule for more than four hundred years, with little hostility aimed at Christian pilgrims, but now there had been two massacres in the space of a decade. While this was not the trigger for what became known as the First Crusade, it certainly added fuel to a growing fire of religious zeal.

So, in 1096 the (First) Crusade was preached at the same time as localised Seljuk power in Anatolia was fading. The empire couldn't exert power in the region; it wasn't on the steppe and the largely desert area was not a suitable place to send an army. Unsurprisingly, the situation descended into warring chieftains consolidating their powers in local towns and cities, and it was by sheer accident the First Crusade marched into this power vacuum. In 1097, the crusade, supported by the Byzantine Emperor Alexios and his army, had arrived at Nicaea, a key Byzantine city that had fallen to the Turks some fifteen years earlier. It sat on a lake and had become the capital city of the Sultanate of Rum, a fragment of the old Seljuk Empire. It was usually home to Kilij Arslan, who, despite his surname, was not a son of Alp (Arslan, or sometimes, Aslan, Turkic for lion, from where CS Lewis borrowed the name), but coincidentally he had been held captive by Alp Arslan's son. However, Kilij was the epitome of Turkish martial prowess and unbridled violence. This was a man who murdered his father-in-law, who had carved out a powerful domain from nothing and who had been instrumental in the eradication of the People's Crusade. He was a cold, calculating killer – and Nicaea was his prized jewel.

The crusaders tried surrounding the city, but with a lake on one side, that was impossible. However, some of the Turkish garrison sallied forth and engaged in the first proper battle of the medieval crusades. The Turks were hopelessly outnumbered, so after a brief skirmish, most retreated; however, a few had other orders and broke free from the engagement to ride out to the east to warn Kilij of the danger his capital faced. He arrived a few days later and the ensuing battle became a monumental cavalry engagement. While Kilij had underestimated the size of the crusader force, he fought long into the night trying to break the Franks and get to his capital. Eventually, and after a long and bloody battle, he was beaten back. The warlord knew a no-win situation when he saw one and retreated, presumably swearing revenge.

For the siege to work, the crusaders needed to block off the lake to ensure complete envelopment of the city. At this point Alexios arrived with his army and ordered a number of boats to be dragged across land and into Lake Ascanius. From the defender's point of view, this was checkmate. With their leader beaten back and the city now surrounded, it was better to negotiate peace than to allow an assault and a bloody sacking. However, rather than negotiate with Bohemund and his cohorts, Alexios got in early and sorted the whole thing out, much to the consternation of the crusaders. It was even done with a fake assault on the walls to make it appear as if the Byzantines had captured the city.

Once in, there was little bloodshed as Alexios wisely ensured that the crusaders could not come in more than ten at a time. He replenished their supplies and horses, and the crusaders left in high spirits after a relatively easy victory. On reflection, hadn't they promised to obey Alexios and return all the spoils of war up to the city of Antioch?

The crusade carried on further into the Anatolian hinterland, where temperatures in June and July regularly rise above forty degrees Celsius, and streams, rivers or even shelter are hard to find. By now Bohemund had become the de facto leader of the European crusaders and had split the force to allow an easier time of provisioning in such a sparse area. As they were now deep in enemy territory, this was a risky strategy, but there was no other realistic option. As soon as they left Nicaea in their various divisions, it became obvious they were being shadowed by a Turkish force.

Kilij Arslan had regrouped and created an alliance with the Danishmend's Emir (while this looks like 'Danish Men', they were actually another group of Turks who would normally have fought against Kilij but had recognised it was in their interests to destroy this crusader army). On 1 July, the Turks' occasional skirmishes and hit-and-runs turned into full-blown battle. The Battle of Dorylaeum was so-called because it happened fairly close to the ruins of this ancient city and should really have been called the battle-in-the-middle-of-nowhere. Kilij had chosen his spot well and as the crusader troops were now travelling in small clumps, it was the perfect place to attack the vanguard under Bohemund.

Bohemund ordered all the non-combatants to create a defensive camp and led the knights out to fight. This was the first time the Christian heavy cavalry was pitted against the light Turkish horse archers. In general, heavy cavalry should prevail, but if the Turks had room to manoeuvre then the knights could not make their superior arms and armour count. It was like a bull facing a matador. The Turks excelled at riding up close, firing arrows from their composite bows and hitting their target while at a full gallop. It was a classic tactic that Attila would have recognised. European mail armour was of only limited use against the piercing nature of arrows, and while their large shields and padded undershirts would have helped, some of the knights must have looked like hedgehogs by the end of the battle – the ones that were still alive.

Kilij threw everything he had at these invaders. His family members were now Byzantine captives, and as his reputation rested on marshal prowess, the loss of his capital would be his undoing unless he exacted an immediate and crushing defeat. In all the confusion, Bohemund and his knights were thrown back to the defended camp and surrounded. As the horse archers ground down the crusaders, the battle looked like turning into a massacre, but just as the camp's defences began to buckle, more crusader leaders arrived with their contingents of men and forced the Turks to break off their encirclement. As the day progressed, every time the Turks reinstated their dominance on the field, a new section of the crusader army arrived in the nick of time.

One of these was led by Bishop Adhemar of Le Puy, who arrived late in the day. He had been sent as Papal Legate (representative) on the expedition, but he was a hands-on military man when needed. In this situation he led troops into the Turkish camp and ordered it to be set on fire. After a day of being thwarted by continual reinforcements, seeing their camp on fire was the last straw for the Turks. They broke off and retreated. The crusade survived, but it had been a close-run thing. That they had been lucky was acknowledged by all involved, but why had they had good luck? This narrow escape was turned into a sign of divine blessing, that Jesus and the saints were looking after them and ensuring victory (although if God really had been protecting them, would he have allowed the ambush in the first place?) Regardless of the narrowness of victory, Dorylaem had been another victory and a further boost to the morale of the Christians.

The Turks had thrown everything they had at this army and failed. While raids continued, there were no more pitched battles as the crusaders marched through central Anatolia. But Kilij Arslan had left them a farewell gift: he had burned and destroyed as much as he could to ensure the crusaders got as little sustenance as possible, and it was this march that was to be remembered more bitterly than the earlier battles. Both men and horses were dying of thirst, while some knights were reduced to riding cows. Had the Muslims reformed and attacked them again, it was likely the crusade would have crumbled, but their two previous victories stopped any of the local emirs from doing anything rash.

Like their brethren in the West, the Seljuk Turks were now living a hybrid life. No longer did they sleep in tents on the endless grass ocean of the steppe, but instead now lived in an urban environment. However, the language and the way of war remained the same, as did their brutally pragmatic attitude to life and death. It is also worth remembering that the steppe could not sustain densely populated areas. As such, each of these groups faced the same issue, that of manpower. When we talk of the Seljuk Empire or Seljuk territory, there were parallels with the Roman Empire. The top officials, the overlords, were Turks, but the peasants working in the fields or the tradesmen in Nicaea were not. They could have been Caucasians or Arabs, maybe Christians or Muslims or Jews. Everyday life went on, only the face and name of the ruler changed. What the Seljuks had done was to make existing nation states, with all their infrastructure and cities preserved, their own, in the most successful expansion that had ever been seen.

At the same time this was going on, the Muslim world was experiencing what became known as its Golden Age. This was an era of breakthroughs in science, mathematics, architecture and medicine. By the time the Christians began fighting their way into this area, it was obvious which civilisation was the more advanced, and it wasn't the Christians. The important fact in all of this is that while the Seljuks in no way contributed to these advancements, their arrival did not disrupt this period of remarkable achievements. The era is generally believed to have lasted from around 800 AD to 1258 AD. The reason for the specific end date will be made apparent in Chapter 8.

Which brings us to Qiwam al-Dawla Kerbogha, generally referred to as Kerbogha. To simply summarise his career prior to the First Crusade, he was a general of immense talent who at times supported the right princes in the Seljuk court but at other times backed the wrong ones, which in one instance led to his imprisonment. His story could have been one from medieval France or England rather than being an echo of a warrior like Attila or Bayan I. He was an Islamic warlord with an ethnically different background, and his forces fought in the traditional way, with horse archers (like some of the previous empires) and an army bolstered with light infantry. What we shall now start to see is that because life on the steppe was harsh, if there was an opportunity to take some comforts, then who wouldn't? The Seljuks in the Middle East were, technically speaking, never ousted; it was more a case of their being absorbed into the general population.

Once the crusaders came to the periphery of the empire and targeted a city, Kerbogha was an obvious man to sort out the situation. The Siege of Antioch was perhaps the most outstanding moment in a campaign full of unbelievable and truly epoch-defining moments. The Christians didn't have nearly enough troops to surround the city, but it had fallen to treachery before. All that was needed was someone to open a gate in the dead of night and the city would be easy to infiltrate. However, nobody inside seemed willing to oblige, and the siege of Antioch would become a hideous stalemate. The crusade was too small to get in, and the garrison of Antioch was too small to defeat the Christians in battle, so the siege dragged on ... and on. The crusaders arrived in October 1097, just as the weather was starting to cool, which meant that many of the nearby crops had already been brought into the city. There was never a better time to bolt the gates and hope for a relief army.

In December, as provisions became harder to come by, the crusaders were forced to scavenge further and further afield to get food back to the camps. It was during one of these foraging missions that Bohemund and Robert of Flanders discovered a relief army, led by Duqaq of Aleppo. Duqaq and Rudwan of Damascus were brothers and had been fighting a civil war over the ownership of Syria when this strange western army arrived from Anatolia. Antioch was a great prize and anyone who could save it from the Christians would have the upper hand. Duqaq got there first, but the accidental discovery of his army before it had had a chance to reach the crusader camp was a disaster for him. This time the crusaders had the advantage of surprise and Duqaq was thoroughly routed.

This engagement showed the dangers of spreading the crusading army too thin in hostile territory. How long could their luck hold? Rudwan arrived later and met the same fate as his brother. This was the third Turkish ruler of considerable local stature to face a humiliating defeat at the hands of these strangers. Were they blessed by God? For the time being, the crusade was safe – as safe as you can be besieging a mighty fortified city.

Foraging parties, Byzantine food supplies, the occasional wagon train from Edessa, these were all essential lifelines to a dwindling effort. As 1097 turned into 1098, food stocks were dangerously low. It was noted that Peter the Hermit had travelled this far but was caught attempting to slink off, presumably thinking this crusade was in danger of becoming like the earlier one he had led. (Peter had led what was known as the People's Crusade, civilians only, a year earlier. It was wiped out completely by the Seljuks.)

Disease broke out and there was cannibalism. Why let a corpse rot when it could give life? Disease-ridden cannibals, intent on breaking into a mighty city, itching to have their revenge on the population had nothing to do with Jesus' teachings. This is what these Christian soldiers, allegedly fighting for God, had descended to.

The remaining Byzantine soldiers left with their general, and the weeks dragged on with no sign of capitulation on either side. Meanwhile, life in Antioch was also becoming grim. Their own food stores were running low, and the barbaric corpse-eating army outside its gates refused to leave.

In March 1098, there was some relief when a crusader fleet arrived with fresh troops and food, but all this seemed to do was prolong the agony as the help was not enough to tip the balance in favour of the crusade. Then in May, terrible news: Kerbogha had forged several alliances and could arrive at any moment. This was a very dangerous situation. The Christian army was physically weak; it could either stand and fight and face total annihilation or leave Antioch after all these months, with nothing to show for it.

Bohemund saved the day, but at a heavy price. First, he demanded he be given leadership of the crusade (Adhemar had always been the spiritual leader and remained so). The other nobles agreed. Second, he got them to agree that he, not Alexios, should have Antioch. This was easier to agree since all the Greek generals had left, and Alexios had not gone through the privations that everyone else, including Bohemund, had endured. Then he revealed he had been in talks with a man called Firouz, who was willing to betray the city.

There are several stories to explain why Firouz would do this, but the most convincing is that he had been discovered hording food, a crime punishable by death during a siege. So, to save his own skin, make a lot of money and, of course, stay on the winning side, he promised to open a gate on the 3rd of June, eight months after the arrival of the crusade at Antioch.

That night Bohemund ordered the army to march away from the walls to lower suspicions. Then, under the cover of darkness, the army returned, and Firouz, true to his word, let them in. The Christians quickly set upon the governor and all the civilians they could find. Thousands were slain, including Firouz's own brother. This is how the western Christians behaved on their first occupation of a Muslim city. To be fair, after eight months, the occupants could expect little mercy, but it was still savagery.

On the 4th, the crusaders realised that the garrison remained in its citadel, too strong to be attacked by them in their weakened state. On the 5th, Kerbogha arrived with his army, two days late.

He had tried, on the way, to defeat Baldwin in Edessa and had spent three weeks in the effort, to no avail. Knowing he had to move on, he finally did so, but the distraction at Edessa resulted in his arriving just a little too late to catch the crusaders outside the walls. Did this matter? While it is true that the crusaders were now behind the walls, the city was empty of food. All that had happened was role reversal, with the Christians now being the besieged rather than the besiegers. They were still weak and disease-ridden, and now they were facing a large, fresh army led by a veteran general.

Their initial victory was temporary. Morale collapsed; desertions rose. It seemed that Kerbogha might not need to fight to beat the crusaders. The next event can be seen either as a miracle or as a bit of theatrical hustling. Peter Bartholomew (not Peter the Hermit) had visions from Saint Andrew telling him where the Holy Lance (the spear that pierced Jesus' side during the crucifixion, hugely popular with knights as it symbolised both Jesus and war) had been buried in Antioch. He started excavating the church of Saint Peter and on 14 June a piece of iron was revealed, one which Peter confirmed was the Holy Lance. It was a miracle and a divine sign that God would let the crusade triumph over these insurmountable odds.

Adhemar of Le Puy, the official Papal Legate, was less than convinced by all this. But Bohemund desperately needed a break, so he enthusiastically paraded the 'lance' around the troops. The results were electrifying. Now they could all see tangible evidence that Jesus and the saints were with them. They could fight and win. But as so often in history, things weren't quite that neat. Before any rush to battle, Bohemund dispatched Peter the Hermit, who had been delivering some inspiring sermons after the fall of Antioch, to see if he could negotiate with Kerbogha's camp. He came back empty-handed, but the mission was a sign that he had secured a new position

Kerbogha at Antioch in 1098, a miniature from 1337. (Public domain)

of power within the crusade's council. More importantly, Bohemund would have happily negotiated his way out of the situation, rather than trust only in God.

On 28 June, the crusade took a huge gamble. It came out of the gates of Antioch, right in front of Kerbogha's army and formed up to do battle. Had the Muslims attacked as the crusade reformed its ranks, victory would have been assured, but from the Muslim point of view, things weren't that simple. As already stated, there was no central authority and the Fatimid (Egyptian) Muslim contingent of Kerbogha's coalition left as soon as the Christians formed ranks; not because they were cowards, but because victory would have made Kerbogha even more powerful than he was already. The Fatimids were far more worried about him than any threat from the Christians. It's a reminder that no side was completely united, and while it is natural to split things according to religious motivations, sometimes more earthly priorities got in the way.

Duqaq was also present at the battle, looking for revenge, but to have fought under his enemies' banners would have been deeply uncomfortable for him. So, from the Islamic point of view, the Christians were allowed to form up in battle readiness because of dynastic bickering. This was an army waiting to shatter. But the Christians knew none of this, so they explained it on a spiritual level. First-hand accounts, like the *Gesta Francorum* and others, make references to visions and images of the saints themselves, right there at the battle. Saint George (chosen because of his association with martial prowess) was seen to be fighting side-by-side with the flesh and blood men of the crusade. Unbelievably and against all the odds, the Muslims broke and fled, leaving behind them their entire camp. The concubines and servants were slaughtered, while the food and tents provided welcome relief for this army on the brink of collapse. It appeared that the exhausted, sick and starving Christians had vanquished what seemed an unstoppable foe.

At this point we leave the story of the First Crusade as it headed for Jerusalem and its capture in 1099 (in an orgy of violent bloodletting). The Seljuks became less involved, and it was the Arab Fatimids in Egypt who became the force most preoccupied with these Christian invaders.

Between 1100 and 1101, at least three major armies marched into Anatolia hoping to recreate the success of their fellow Christian knights. While some of these soldiers did make it to the Holy Land as much needed replacements, these expeditions were nowhere near as successful as those that had come before. Up until 1100, the Muslims had concluded that the crusaders were invincible and that whole new strategies would be needed to defeat them; but almost as soon as this sheen of invulnerability appeared, it began to fade, as later (mainly Germanic) expeditions perished in exactly the way the First Crusade should have done.

Kilij Arslan had lost vital prestige because of his setbacks against the First Crusade. He could not survive more failures. The Battles of Mersivan and Heraclea may have happened at different times, in different parts of Anatolia, but they were essentially a rerun of Dorylaeum – except this time the crusaders ran out of luck. Kilij had allied himself with Rudwan of Aleppo and showed these Christians forces what Muslim armies could do when unified. Harassing the slow-moving European forces with horse archers and choosing the site of battle to allow the manoeuvre of his lighter cavalry against the heavy armour of the knights gave Kilij the victories he so badly needed.

These new crusading armies, bringing desperately needed fresh troops to the Holy Land, were crushed. Just a year after the fall of Jerusalem, Islam was on the ascendency once more. These battles have been largely forgotten by everyone. Muslim historians don't tend to mention them because in the short term, they didn't change the status quo. After all, this was the start of the crusading movement in the Middle East, not the end. As for the European chroniclers, they were hardly going to spend too much time tainting the achievements of the so-called First Crusade by adding such a depressing sequel.

However, these forgotten crusading armies shed important light on just how lucky Bohemund and his company had been. Had Pope Urban II preached ten years earlier or later than he did, the crusade would have run into a relatively unified Muslim Middle East. It was complete chance that this armed pilgrimage stumbled through an area that was struggling to come to terms with dramatic shifts in power between the local warlords.

Marching across Anatolia in summer nearly undid the First Crusade not just at the Battle of Dorylaeum, but in the desperate march to escape enemy territory afterwards. Jerusalem was a very long way away from Europe, and the only way to get there was either by treacherous sea routes or a march over hundreds of miles of scorching desert, constantly harassed by Muslim horse archers. Crusading was expensive, dangerous and very time consuming.

It was this serendipity (from the Christian point of view), this blind luck and tenacity that had suddenly created from nothing a Christian sphere of influence in the Middle East, and these westerners were putting down roots. There was now the County of Edessa (the most northern and eastern state), the Principality of Antioch (land based around the city), the County of Tripoli (linking the area of Antioch to the lower and key kingdom) and the Kingdom of Jerusalem.

There was one last political change in the region at this time and that was the rise of the Hashashin, a sect led by Hasan-i-Sabbah. The term 'hashashin' is derogatory and means rabble, or in today's parlance, yobs, and was never used by the sect. They called themselves the Nizari Ismalilis; but the Arabic word hashashin has become the English word assassin. They were despised partly because of their assassinations, but also because as Ismailis, they were a separate sect of Islam, outside the Sunnis and Shias, so were often seen as the Islamic version of heretics. It is coincidence that the term sounds like the word hashish, and on that point the first job is to tackle a few myths about them.

Any secret religious society that goes around carrying out high-profile assassinations is likely to have some myths swirling around them. These stories were contemporary to the organisation and were created by both Muslims and Christians. Princes, warlords and generals of both cultures were targets for the Assassins, who often struck very publicly, using knives coated in deadly poison. However, most of the sources were written by people outside of (and often targets of) the Nizari Ismalilis.

My favourite myth (and one repeated by Marco Polo on his way to deal with the Mongols, the fourth group this book will explore) is that to recruit new members, young initiates were taken to a castle where they were kept in the outer gatehouse and fed hash cakes. When sound asleep, the men were transferred into the main castle, where they awoke to find themselves surrounded by lush gardens, dancing girls and plentiful food and drink. After a few days of luxury and indulgence, they were again slipped some hash and once in a stupor, returned to their starting point. When they awoke, they were informed by the Hashashin that they had experienced paradise, and in order to return, would have to follow orders and die martyrs to the cause.

This was an ingenious method of indoctrination and explained the fanaticism and single-mindedness of these hit men. It also explained their seemingly joyous response to being surrounded by the bodyguards of their high-profile victims and being rapidly dispatched to a better world. Of course, the modern reader will know it takes much less to brainwash young men into carrying out terrible acts of violence in the name of God.

The Hashashin embedded themselves in a string of castles in remote desert regions (mainly in modern-day Syria and western Iran). These were virtually impregnable as no army could realistically besiege such an arid region, and this allowed the group to spread terror from safe bases. (Their leader Hasan-i-Sabbah became known as the Old Man of the Mountains, and future rulers picked up the same title.) But they weren't the only ones in the assassination business in the Middle East at that time. Both the crusaders and the Muslim princes were responsible for their own fair share of murders, so the Hashashin's exact number of successful hits can never be known. In any case, because the sect was so secretive and because almost all our sources come from their enemies, it is hard to separate fact from fiction.

This aura of mystery and terror was exactly what they wanted, and while the Hashashin never deployed large armies or conquered vast territories, they were important players in the region for centuries. No person in power from Acre to Astrakhan was safe, a fact that will have affected the halls of power of the Seljuk Turks. Kerbogha wasn't felled by an assassin's blade, instead he died of old age in 1102. However, his last years were spent raising the new princeling Imad ad-Din Zengi, the founder of the Zengid dynasty, which would become a major force in the 12th century, reinforcing his reputation as a major power broker in the Middle East.

The fighting between crusader and Muslim was usually a multinational affair. The Middle East would regularly have had Turkmen mercenaries (sometimes the crusaders had them too), but the main Muslim forces, regardless of their exact ethnicity, fought in the style of the Eurasian Steppe horsemen. Light cavalry (usually mares) with a horse archer were the order of the day, and light cavalry meant minimal armour, perhaps a helmet and a circular shield, maybe with some leather armour. The emphasis was on speed and manoeuvrability; their ability to strike from a distance was their armour. The feigned retreat, followed by the encirclement of slower-moving western armies was the order of the day. By contrast, piercing the heavy armour of the European knights was easier said than done. Also, if the light cavalry ran out of manoeuvring room and the heavy cavalry (riding stallions) could focus their own might, then a charge by the European forces would annihilate the lighter-equipped enemy.

Without delving into the Mongols too early in this narrative, the Seljuk Empire came to an end because it was being squeezed from all sides. To the far south there were rising Muslim powers; to the west there were the Christians, and to the east there were the Mongols. Once again, a steppe nomad group was superseded by an aggressively expanding tribe from their own homelands, but this time there was nowhere to go. The Seljuks didn't have the mobility of the Huns or the Magyars. After a century they had become urbanised, their leaders fighting like nomads but living like Muslim princes. They had once been ethnically distinct, but a century of intermarriage meant that while they had family stories from the steppe, their day-to-day existence was that of a cosmopolitan Arab aristocrat.

Tribes and warbands of Turks still existed. As mentioned above, mercenaries were common on the field of battle, and this showed that not everyone had forgotten the old ways. The 1290s were a time of chaos in the Middle East. In modern-day areas such as Syria and Iraq there were two rival empires vying for power. To the south, with their capital in Cairo, the Mamelukes, fierce slave warriors who had overthrown the old regime a few decades earlier, held the regional power; to the north and east, the Mongol Empire of the great khans was in charge. And at this same time there was a third empire in play, the Byzantine Empire, which looked as if it had been all but wiped out by the Fourth Crusade nearly a century earlier. Even though their imperial title had been restored, what had once been the Eastern Roman Empire was now a shadow of its former self and was more indebted to the Italian trading powers than any imperial power in its own right. It certainly could not project its power into central Anatolia.

When, in 1289, the coastal city of Tripoli fell to the Mamelukes, there remained one last crusader city in the Holy Land, Acre, with its mighty walls, but that, too, fell to the Mamelukes in 1291. Contrary to popular belief, this was not the end of Christian activity in the Middle East. The Christians still held Cyprus and used it as a base of operations to attack Muslim shipping. In 1300, they achieved an amphibious landing and captured the small island fort of Ruad, just off the coast of Syria. While the gains were tiny, the Mamelukes were determined to stop any return of Christian forces to the mainland, and they threw their navy into the fray. Eventually, after several years of fighting and besieging Ruad, the Mamelukes recaptured it; but at the same time they faced another (and largely successful) invasion of Syria by the Mongols.

Enter Osman, a Seljuk Turk, the man who is seen as the founder of the Ottoman Empire. (His name is sometimes spelt Ottman or Othman, hence the term Ottoman.) The Seljuks had arrived from the Asiatic Steppe to the east but had been in Anatolia for several generations. Had Osman tried to establish his powerbase fifty years earlier or later, the political landscape would likely have been quite stable, so any attempt at building his own independent realm would have been quickly extinguished. Osman was the right man in the right place at the right time.

Practice drills illustrated in the Kitāb al-makhzūn jāmi' al-funūn ('The Treasure that Combines all Arts') believed to be a Mameluke work of the 1300s. (Courtesy Library of Congress)

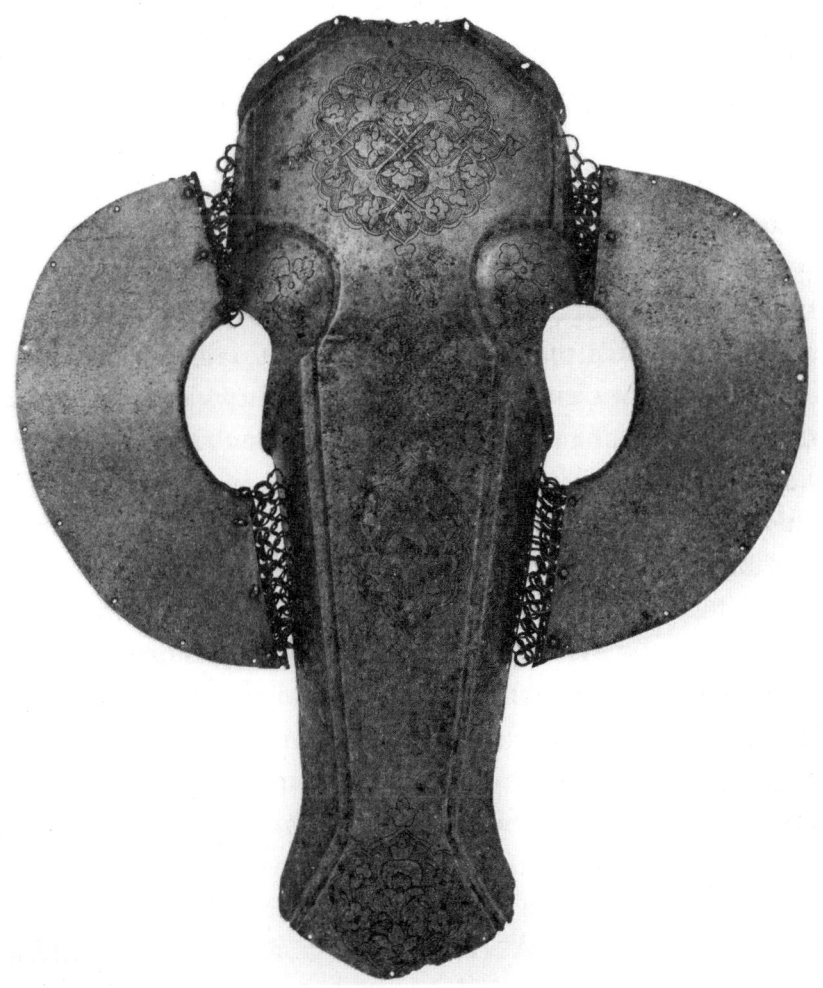

Later Mameluke horse armour *c.* 1450-1550 (Courtesy Metropolitan Museum of Art, public domain)

Nature abhors a vacuum and it's the same with power. Söğüt is a small town in western Anatolia. It wouldn't be a worth even a footnote in history if it weren't for the fact that it was here that Osman consolidated his power. Söğüt was the first capital of the Ottoman Empire, but it's quite telling that in its first 150 (or so) years, the empire had four different capitals. As the empire grew and controlled ever larger and more impressive cities, the old capital was left behind, and Söğüt was dropped as the capital as quickly as possible. The patriarchs of Osman's family were a succession of men who made no mark on history. Ertuğrul, his father, is known only because he is cited on the coins that Osman minted. No other contemporary power thought he was worth a mention.

Osman's grandfather, Suleiman Shah, managed to drown in the Euphrates in 1227, and that's virtually all we know about him, but his tomb became global news in 2015. After the breakup of the Ottoman Empire, his tomb ended up a few kilometres inside Syria, where there was an internationally recognised agreement that the tomb was technically Turkish territory. In 1974, when the area was due to be flooded, Suleiman's tomb was carefully moved to a new location that came under ISIS control in 2014/15. ISIS had shown nothing but complete contempt for history, and the Turks were not going to risk leaving Osman's grandfather's tomb to fanatics. So in February 2015, a Turkish military convoy technically invaded Syria (hence the news coverage) to remove the casket of Suleiman Shah.

Meanwhile, back at the very end of the 13th century, there is yet another example of a steppe nomadic group causing chaos at the expense of the local population. But this time there are differences: first, Osman was leading approximately 300 horsemen, the smallest group of any described so far in this book; second, and indeed amazingly, he founded the longest lasting empire of any of the Eurasian Steppe nomads. The next chapter will try to summarise more than 600 years of that empire.

6

THE OTTOMANS

The Ottoman Empire had humble beginnings. Osman's family had been in Anatolia for decades, but it was not until 1280 that he finally received the blessing of the more powerful Seljuk rulers to become a bey (chieftain) or head of his extended family after the death of his father. From then until he died in 1323/24, Osman greatly expanded the lands under his control, almost exclusively to the detriment of the ever-weakening Byzantine Empire. He must have calculated that he wasn't yet powerful enough to challenge the larger powers to the east, so he nibbled away at the Byzantine hinterland, and there wasn't much the Byzantine rulers could do about it.

They did try. In 1302, they sent a small army in an attempt to curb Osman's advances. The two sides met at the Battle of Bapheus, near the Byzantine city of Nicomedia. Osman's cavalry made short work of the smaller Byzantine force (helped by the judgement of the Alan mercenaries, who knew a lost cause when they saw one and didn't join in with the battle). Osman was very much a warrior in the mould of other great cavalry officers of the Middle Ages (like Genghis Khan before he won an empire), and for the next 300 years, sultans would regularly be seen in battle. But as the empire matured and later began to wane, the sultans began to shirk their duties on the battlefield.

It was Osman's successor who started the tradition of wearing Osman's sword, girded by his belt, at the time of his coronation. This was the Ottoman equivalent of being anointed and crowned in the West and was a reminder to all thirty-six sultans who followed that their power and status came from this legendary warrior and that they were martial rulers. This certainly rang true in the first half of the history of the empire. Osman's lavishly decorated sword and belt are the Ottoman equivalent of Britain's crown jewels, but it's doubtful that what is seen today (on display in the Topkapı Palace Museum in Istanbul) is what Osman held in his hand. Putting it simply, Osman was unlikely ever to have had such an impractical sword, but it could be that the original blade was later plated and embellished.

Osman was real, but in some ways he's another figure like King Arthur, the founder of a vision and a near mythical character. During his lifetime he was so unimportant that we have no contemporary sources about him. We don't know what he looked like; we have no proclamations extant from his reign. This was the Ottoman Dark Ages. Because there is such a dearth of information from this early period, many books about the Ottoman Empire spend most of their time exploring the empire in its heyday, from roughly the mid-1400s to the mid-1600s. While it is true that this was an era of remarkable achievements, to focus on this period gives a distorted view of the evolution of the empire. The rulers and events in the first 150 years of the story quite often get summarised in the first chapter, and things only get going with the siege of Constantinople in 1453, as if everything prior to that doesn't count. But to gloss over this century and a half does it a complete injustice as there were some significant events that fundamentally shaped the empire prior to that key moment.

So, while the early 1300s were the Dark Ages of the Ottomans, a little over a century later the empire was in rude good health, and with it came the desire to revisit the founder and give Osman a legacy. As a consequence, gleaning the real Osman from all the mythmaking becomes virtually impossible. Foundation myths tell something about the times in which they were created, like Rome with Romulus and Remus. And so it is that we come to the legend of Osman's dream. Osman had an ally in a local religious leader called Sheikh Edebali. They were obviously close because Osman married one of Edebali's daughters. According to the legend Osman went to Edebali for guidance and had a dream when he spent the night at the sheikh's house. The imagery varies but the key part is that Osman allegedly remembered that 'a tree then sprouted from his navel and its shade encompassed the world'. According to the dream, rivers began to flow and mountains formed. The account is suspiciously similar to the florid prose of a later Ottoman literary style that a 13th-century cavalry bey would not use.

When Osman asked Edebali what all this meant, his response echoes the Biblical account of Joseph and his dreams, a story which would certainly have been known to Islamic scholars. Edebali was apparently delighted with Osman's dream, declaring that it meant that Osman would be the founder of an extraordinary dynasty which, like the canopy of the tree, would encompass many lands. It was also, allegedly, this revelation that sealed the marriage to Edebali's daughter. So the story of the dream marks out Osman as a man with a great destiny. He was only a local warlord at the time, but the vision was clear: as his family moved from generation to generation and grew, so would his realm. The earliest reference to this dream is from around a century after the event is said to have taken place, and is undoubtedly a case of descendants adding lustre to an obscure ancestor. It is, however, a story that is still taught in Turkish schools and can be seen as similar to other apocryphal stories, such as the young George Washington being unable to lie about the cherry tree, or King Alfred burning the cakes.

Osman's powers during his own time were limited. He chose not to fight stronger Seljuk warlords in Anatolia and went for the easier pickings of the terminally ill Byzantine Empire. An example of his limitations is his attack and capture of the city of Ephesus. This once great and ancient city was well past its prime by the time Osman arrived in the early 1300s, but it was important as one of the last major Byzantine settlements left in Anatolia. Osman captured the city with relative ease, which was surprising (as will be seen again with the long siege of Bursa), but what was even more surprising was that it did not become part of Ottoman lands. Instead, it became part of the Emir of Aydin's fiefdom. In other words, it is likely that Osman was only part of the attacking army and that he didn't then have enough power to challenge the emir of a now obscure realm.

Another early legend about Osman is interesting because it has been forgotten. The tale concerns a disagreement between Osman and an uncle called Dündar, who wished to keep peace with a neighbouring Christian lord, but Osman disagreed. The argument turned deadly, and Osman shot Dündar with an arrow. While the story alludes to the growing power of Osman's forces that meant they could take on a neighbour who previously it had been thought best to deal with peacefully, it also portrays Osman as a man ruthless enough to kill close family members to get what he wanted. Again, this story is not contemporary to Osman and could be as contrived as the tale of his dream. This part of the Osman legend was dropped from later accounts of his life because it didn't portray Osman in a good light. No one knew then that the killing of an uncle would be a little local spat compared to the blood that would be spilt in the corridors of power in the generations to come.

Osman was married to two women (under Islamic law, a man could have up to four wives). This modest setup shows the Ottoman court had yet to create its famous harem, but as these already existed in other Islamic seats of power, it underlines the limited resources of the Ottomans at this time. Osman's first wife was Malhun Hatun and his second was Rabia Bala Hatun, the daughter of Sheikh Edebali. He had eight children with these women (seven boys and one girl; the ratio could be biased as the births of daughters were not always as carefully recorded as those of sons).

As Osman aged, his mind would naturally have turned to his succession. His eldest son, Alaeddin (son of Rabia), would have been the logical choice as the new bey of the embryonic Ottoman Empire, but the actual successor was his second son, Orhan (son of Malhun). Later on, the scramble for the throne led to bloodshed amongst the feuding siblings and sometimes resulted in civil war, but this was one of the most harmonious transitions of power not only in Ottoman history, but in 14th-century history in general. This story is roughly contemporary with Edward III's rise to power in England. By contrast, even though he was the rightful heir to the throne, his father (Edward II) was murdered, he had to be rescued from a Nottingham prison in a daring raid, and he had to order the execution of his mother's lover before securing the crown that everybody agreed was his to begin with.

Back in Anatolia, it seems Alaeddin recognised that Orhan was the natural born warrior, whereas he was more a man of learning who didn't fit the mould of the great warlord. He was, by all accounts, a pious man who was admired and respected by everyone. He personally paid for the construction of a mosque which, while small compared to the later great mosques of the sultans, is one of the earliest examples of Ottoman architecture still standing. So, while Orhan got on with conquering, Alaeddin became the first grand vizier, which means he was the sultan's chief advisor and oversaw the day-to-day administration of the empire. In modern terms, he was Orhan's prime minister, but in many instances the grand vizier was also a warrior and a pasha (general) who led campaigns. The title of Grand Vizier of the Ottoman Empire was to last until 1908.

While Osman had minted coins (one of the few contemporary pieces of evidence that he existed), they were little more than local copies of other coinage in circulation at the time. Alaeddin went substantially further. The monetary system was simplified and standardised, which helped trade because any realm with stable, reliable and quality coinage had the upper hand in trade negotiations. In addition to the monetary system, Alaeddin overhauled the army by creating and funding a standing army of regular troops. Anatolian warlords tended to run a completely martial realm, but as the Ottoman lands expanded, that traditional system wasn't going to work. Many of the new subjects weren't born horse archers, and it was recognised that to make the best use of the manpower available, greater use of infantry would be required and archers and their skills integrated into the army. While it was true that this army couldn't be as mobile and couldn't use the classic 'attack and feint' of the legendary horse archers of the era, it was larger and more flexible than before. The most famous warriors of the Ottoman Empire were the Janissaries, and while they were not formed until a generation later, it's worth noting that they were not cavalry but infantry, a marked departure from the traditional Turkic form of warfare.

In addition to revamping the monetary system and the army, Alaeddin introduced a third and perhaps most important reform in, of all things, clothing. This probably sounds odd, but right from the start the empire had a multitude of different ethnicities under the sultan's authority, and Alaeddin understood this was something to be encouraged and enhanced by the regulation of dress. Later western travellers to the empire would marvel at the kaleidoscope of colours and fashions worn by the empire's peoples, the different attires identifying the wearer as a Jew, an Albanian, a Greek and so forth. This was not to single out any group for discrimination but to provide a visual reminder that it didn't matter who your god was or what language you spoke, everyone in the empire lived under the authority and protection of the sultan.

What can be clearly seen here is that one generation in, the old ways are already fading away. Osman may have been a Eurasian Steppe nomad, but unlike the Avars, Huns or Magyars, he wasn't pagan, he was Muslim. Further, a generation into the growing power of the Ottomans, Alaeddin and Orhan were doing things that were beyond most previous groups. Minting coins, establishing laws, building a society – such provisions were based on urban living rather than the itinerant life of the steppe.

Our narrative is largely presented in chronological order, but the story of the Ottoman Empire intersects with the other groups yet to be discussed. So, while it's interesting that the power vacuum created by the Mongols gave Osman the opportunity to create his powerbase, it was another group's aggressive expansion that nearly destroyed it. This took place at the very end of the 1300s and will be discussed in Chapter 9. Suffice to say here, a small empire nearly didn't make it to a century, and the resulting conflict of vying interests led to more than a decade of civil war that nearly tore the Ottoman lands irrevocably apart.

Moving on to the middle of the 1400s, the Ottomans had a new sultan, Mehmed II, just 21 years old when he came to power (technically for a second time). He is known to history as Mehmed Fatih, Mehmed the Conqueror. By this time, it was obvious that the rather pathetic attempts of Osman to surround a city and take years to starve it out were a thing of the past. The steppe nomads had one strategy, the hit-and-run mode of warfare, and while they were the best in the world at this, that strategy didn't work against walled cities. The Siege of Constantinople in 1453 is worth exploring in more detail to show just how far these 'Turks' had come in 150 years.

Time to pause for a look at the ethnicity of the 'Turkish'/ Ottoman leaders. Virtually all societies at this time were patriarchal, which means that the women rarely get as much coverage as the men, and we know that these Eurasian nomads married local women. Today we would recognise that as mixing the gene pool, but back then any male child claimed the ethnicity of his father. It was important that the heir apparent came from the same stock as dear old dad. Except they weren't the same, and this was exacerbated by the Islamic tradition for Muslim rulers to have a harem.

As soon as westerners hear the word 'harem', the mind instantly fills with images of beautiful women in silk veils, lounging in lavish surroundings, gold trays piled high with exotic fruits. That's a western fantasy. Harem is specifically a Turkish word from the Arabic 'ḥaram', which means forbidden or sacrosanct. It was an area of the royal residence set aside for the exclusive use of the women (wealthy men of high position might also have had a harem in their homes). The royal harem, of which the one in Topkapı Palace is probably the most famous example, typically housed dozens of women; at its peak in the 16th and 17th centuries, there were about 300 residents.

The harem was the home of the sultan's mother, wives, daughters and other female relatives as well as the concubines (who were there purely for the sultan's pleasure). The power of the Ottoman court was based on a strict hierarchy, with the sultan at the top; the Ottoman harem was also a hierarchy, with the sultan's mother, the valide sultan, the supreme ruler. Wives were next in rank, and others followed according to how well they played the power politics of this all-female domain.

The women were guarded by black eunuchs (their emasculation guaranteed all children were the sultan's while, at the same time, they ensured that no man except the sultan had access to the women) and were served by other, lowly, harem girls. My favourite fact told during a tour of the Topkapı harem, is that even the cucumbers were mashed so the women only 'knew' the sultan, which is thorough planning.

These women were not 'Turkish' nor were they born Muslim. Although Islam does not forbid slavery, the Quran recognises it as unjust, and it is forbidden for Muslims to be or have slaves. It is for this reason that many serving the empire started life as non-Muslims but later converted to Islam in order to serve the sultan. For example, the Janissaries, the elite infantry of the Ottoman Empire were made up of men who had been offered/ captured as boys from across the Ottoman lands; likewise, the girls in the harem were Ottoman captives or Christians (often Greeks) brought in from the regions. A new arrival might not see the sultan for years, if ever. In the meantime, she worked as a servant and became well versed in harem etiquette, learning to dance, play a musical instrument or recite poetry. If she caught the sultan's eye and became a favourite, a gözde, she would learn how to please the sultan in the bedroom. This was an opportunity which might mean that she could bear a son and become the mother of the next sultan – a role that came with considerable power. As a result, the competition was fierce and the intrigue was intense, but the reality for most of the women was, at best, harem work or, at worst, seeing your son murdered as another woman schemed to get her son on the throne. While harem life meant a life of luxury and ease for some, it was also a gilded cage, one that had a dark side and showed that women were just as ruthless as men in the pursuit of power, position and wealth.

Let's consider the implications of every sultan's mother being a European. It meant that after a few generations, the sultans simply didn't look very 'Turkish'. Some sultans had blue eyes, and there are records of some dying their fair beards to look more 'Turkish' (the hair on their heads was covered by their turbans). At the empire's pinnacle under Suleiman the Magnificent in the 1500s, the sultan (sometimes referred to as the Grand Turk) was ethnically about as 'Turkish' as the King of England.

For generations, when the new sultan was proclaimed, all the other male children in the harem were strangled (in other words, all the new sultan's brothers and half-brothers) to ensure the line of succession was pure and unchallenged. Did the justification begin when Bayezid strangled his own full brother on his accession? Did the civil war between brothers in the early 15th century give further impetus? The answers are unclear, but it is safe to say that the Ottomans took 'survival of the fittest' to a whole new level. During the later periods of the empire, the sons of the sultan lived in the harem until they were sixteen, when it was considered appropriate for them to appear in the public and administrative areas of the palace. The Topkapı harem in Istanbul, which was where the harem was based for most of the empire, was, in essence, the private living quarters of the sultan and his family rather than just a pleasure palace.

Like all empires, the Ottoman lands were multi-ethnic polyglot communities with a variety of religions the locals were free to pursue (although non-Muslims had to pay a tax). In short, by 1500 it was hard to find anyone in the whole empire, including in the sultan's own palace, who was ethnically 'Turkish' in any meaningful sense. Today this is a highly contentious issue, with representatives of the Republic of Türkiye getting very angry when 'Turkishness' is questioned. They like to think that there is a dotted line from the deeds of the sultans to today's republic. Meanwhile in Europe, complete ignorance about this society has led to everyone being described as a 'Turk', whether they are ethnically a Syrian Arab merchant, a Kurdish sailor or a Serbian Janissary. A strange mixture of ancient prejudice and modern nationalism has made this a headache for the modern historian.

The last Byzantine Emperor, Constantine XI, who by the mid-1400s ruled only Constantinople and the hinterland around it, looked to the West and to the same prize as many emperors had done before: the reunification of the Christian churches and a chance for the Pope to claim victory by doing so. Nicholas V was the Pope at the time and he genuinely wanted to help Constantinople. However, Europe was in its usual divided state, and with two recent devastating defeats at the hands of the Ottomans, there was little appetite to assist. On 12 December 1452, the Catholic and Orthodox churches were reunited, but it didn't last twelve months. Nevertheless, given the previous 400 years of acrimony, it was a remarkable achievement even if the preaching of a crusade ultimately came to nothing. Pope Nicholas V ended up sending a small fleet to aid Constantinople, but it was never going to be enough to tip the balance of power. Interestingly, Mehmed II wanted the city but not the bloodshed. This can be seen by the fact that his ambassadors approached Constantine with a generous offer: in exchange for the surrender of Constantinople, the emperor's life would be spared, and he could continue to rule in Mistra (southern Greece) as a vassal. His reply has been preserved by Sphrantzes: 'To surrender the city to you is beyond my authority or anyone else's who lives in it, for all of us, after taking the mutual decision, shall die out of free will without sparing our lives.'

The two sides had now fixed their positions. Constantine XI wisely spent what little time he had stockpiling food and repairing the mighty walls which were over twelve miles long, with many layers. They were a wonder of the age but expensive to maintain. He depended on Venetian and Genoese assistance, along with the city guard, to defend the walls, but his meagre revenues couldn't possibly stretch to an entire mercenary army. Surprisingly, a few of his soldiers were ethnic Turks who stayed loyal to the end. While Constantine XI did everything he could, the situation was a painful reminder of just how much the power of the Byzantines had shrunk. It's estimated that Constantine XI had 5,000-7,000 fighting men in this final siege.

Meanwhile, Mehmed II had managed to amass an army and a navy of around 100,000. He had seventy ships at his disposal (some were war galleys, others were transports) and the magnificent new siege guns (which came with their charges already mixed by munition experts, meaning that their firepower was far greater than anything at the disposal of Murad II). The mightiest cannon, named 'Basilica', was twenty-seven feet long and able to fire a 600 lb stone ball over a mile.

Let's pause here for a reminder that the Ottoman force was not the same thing as a 'Turkish' force, an example of which is a Hungarian named Orban, the cannon expert who built the Basilica. The Janissaries were by now around 10,000 strong, and none of them were ethnically Turkish. Also, spare a thought for the Serbian Prince Đurađ Branković. He had been one of the Christian leaders at the Battle of Varna, fighting against Murad II, and had been one of those who paid to repair the walls of Constantinople. Now he was on Mehmed II's side as a vassal subject. It was 1453 and time had run out for the Byzantines.

Constantinople, like its emperors, wasn't what it used to be. At its peak, under the 6th century AD Emperor Justinian, it had a population of half a million people; by the mid-15th century that number had dropped by around 90 per cent to approximately 50,000. Contemporary chroniclers reported that there was now farmland inside the walls of this once great city, but none of that took away its lustre as a prize. Ever since a Hadith had targeted Constantinople, the Islamic world had obsessed over it; its capture had been a goal for centuries. But that world was not the only one to have the city in its sights. Bulgaria, Serbia, Rome, Venice and Genoa would all have loved to have taken this prize, but by 1453, the only power with any real chance of cracking its impregnable defences was the Ottoman Empire.

Very few moments in history are well remembered across continents. The Battle of Hastings is legendary in Britain, but most Italians have never heard of it. A number of key initiatives, critical battles and pivotal moments have been mentioned in this book, and yet, unless they are part of your country's history (or you have a special interest in that part of history), most are obscure to the wider world. The 1453 Siege of Constantinople, however, is so famous that almost everyone has heard of it. 'It's when the Turks beat the Greeks and kick-started the Renaissance' would be a fairly standard description of what happened, and while almost everything in that sentence is wrong, it's a testament to the impact of this siege that it is widely remembered even in our modern world.

And so we come to the siege itself. Accompanied by his bodyguard, Mehmed II arrived in sight of the walls on 5 April; his army and navy had been arriving for days. It is generally agreed the siege started the following day, when the first thing Mehmed did was to make certain that all outlying fortifications were his. They were easy enough to mop up and ensured that there would be no flanking attacks or unexpected raids from these strongholds. This was an eminently sensible tactic from a sultan who had turned twenty-one just days earlier.

While his army was carefully manoeuvring and taking control of the outposts, Sultan Mehmed ordered his siege cannons to start the laborious work of grinding down Constantinople's defences. The Basilica, while fearsome, did have two drawbacks: it took three hours to load, and 600-lb stone balls aren't scattered about the place. The defenders had sufficient time to patch up the damage and used barrels of earth to plug the gaps. These acted as shock absorbers, reducing the impact of the cannon balls and greatly decreasing their effectiveness. As the siege wore on, people came to see the awesome sight of the Ottoman army, in all its glory, attacking the most famous city in Christendom. It was the Italians who pointed out to the Ottoman gunners that to keep firing at points of the wall which had already been damaged was folly. Instead, it was better to fire at different points, grouping every three shots into a triangular formation so as to ensure maximum impact and better chances for breaches. Thanks to this advice from the Christians, the siege cannons were able to work more effectively. Constantinople itself had cannons on its walls, but they were smaller than the Ottoman guns and, as the walls had never been designed to be used as gun emplacements, they often broke free from their positions and even damaged the walls as a result.

Mehmed II wanted to encircle the city as tightly as possible. Constantinople was a triangle, with one side facing land and the other two flanked by water. The Genoese area of Pera (also known as Galata), on the other side of the northern body of water known as the Golden Horn (an inlet running off the Bosphorus where it meets the Sea of Marmara), contained the landmark Galata Tower in an area that had grown up alongside

Constantinople over the centuries. During the siege the Genoese were nominally neutral, but there was a problem with that position. The standard defence to protect Constantinople from being surrounded (and which had been deployed by the time the Ottomans arrived) was to run a great iron chain from the walls of the city across the Golden Horn and over to Pera. This closed off the channel. On the day that a few Venetian ships came into view, they were not low-profile galleys, but high-sided cogs, large medieval merchant vessels. The cogs had been lashed together and not only carried much needed supplies but bristled with crossbowmen. Mehmed II ordered an intercept. Despite the fact that the Ottoman sailors had to clamber up the high sides of the Venetian vessels under withering fire from the crossbows, they carried out their orders with bravery. The battle lasted most of the day, with one side and then the other gaining the advantage. Onlookers cheered as everyone watched the drama unfold. Mehmed II was so engrossed that he waded into the water and called out to his men to keep fighting. However, after a long and desperate clash, the Venetians managed to get to the great chain and were admitted into the Golden Horn. It is said that Mehmed II pulled out parts of his beard in sheer frustration. After such a humiliation, the sultan demanded that the Genoese lower the chain as it was clearly showing favouritism to the Byzantines. The Genoese very politely refused.

What happened next seems like the stuff of legend, but all the chronicles agree that these events really did take place. Mehmed II ordered a shallow ditch to be dug around Pera to the Golden Horn. The ditch was lined with greased planks and some eighty (yes, eighty) of Mehmed II's warships were hauled across land and launched into the Golden Horn. In the history of the dozens of sieges carried out against Constantinople, no one had ever thought to do this, let alone successfully execute such an audacious piece of engineering.

The defenders were horrified when they saw Ottoman ships in the Golden Horn. They barely had enough troops to man the landward walls, so to stretch their forces even thinner in order to garrison the (longer) seaward wall was a terrible blow. Constantine XI and the Venetians agreed a plan to immolate the Ottoman navy with fire ships, but the news got back to the Ottomans, who were waiting for them. The counterattack failed completely. As a sign of his immense displeasure Mehmed II ordered that the forty Venetian survivors be impaled on spikes opposite the walls so the defenders would have to confront the meaning of their defeat. Constantine XI showed equal cruelty by taking his 260 Ottoman prisoners onto the battlements, where he had each one beheaded in full view of the opposing army.

A point about this siege, commented on by all contemporary accounts, was its sheer noise. Cries and shouts were nothing new, but the largest arsenal of cannons ever yet fired caused a persistent cacophony, and all of this was enhanced by the Janissary band. Thunderous drums, blaring horns and clashing great cymbals added to the sound of the siege.

As well as the activity going on at the walls and on the water, Mehmed II had yet another tactic up his sleeve. Tunnelling had been used in many sieges to undermine walls and cause a breach when the foundations failed. The multiple tunnels Mehmed had ordered were dug by Serbian mining specialists, but amongst the volunteer defenders of Constantinople was a man by the name of Johannes Grant. There's some debate over whether he was German or Scottish, but he wasn't Greek or Italian, and he was very good at counter-mining. Some half a dozen Ottoman tunnels were broken into and, after intense and claustrophobic underground fighting, were destroyed by Greek fire. For about a week in mid-to-late May, Mehmed was frustrated again and again as his supposedly secret plans to breach the walls were continually thwarted. It was during this period that he sent an ambassador to meet with Constantine XI, an event that tends to be ignored by both Turks and Greeks. It is better in the story telling to have one side obsessed with capturing the city at any cost and the other fighting bravely to the last man, rather than seeking a possible escape from martyrdom. The fact of the matter was that both Mehmed II and Constantine XI were men with a genuine understanding of the situation. From Mehmed II's point of view, the siege was eye-wateringly expensive, and while he now had his ships in the Golden Horn, the walls still had not been breached. The siege could still fail.

Fortifications are sometimes referred to as defensive multipliers. For instance, a well-constructed tower might mean that ten men could fight off one hundred, so each defender would have a multiplier of ten. Considering the numbers at this siege and the fact that Mehmed II had brought cannons into play, a new technology the walls of Constantinople had never been designed to withstand, it was a testament to the strength of the walls and to the courage of its defenders that it took such Herculean efforts to overwhelm a comparatively tiny garrison.

As a result of this round of talks, Mehmed's ambassador reported that Constantine was prepared to offer everything the sultan could want: all the outlying fortifications would be recognised as Ottoman and the amount of tribute would be increased (leaving Byzantium forever pauperised), but the one thing he could not relinquish was the great city itself. He could not – would not – be the emperor who lost the city. The talks showed that even after the execution and torture of captives, even after all the gold and blood so far expended in the siege, both sides were still willing to try and find a diplomatic solution. It was reported that even some of the Ottoman generals wanted a peaceful solution and urged their sultan to take the deal. There was no blood lust or religious zeal in the strategy to capture Constantinople, but everything except the city itself was a deal that fell crucially short for Mehmed. For him the whole point of the siege was to end the anachronism that was Byzantium's existence in the middle of the Ottoman Empire. The talks came to nothing.

By 26 May, Mehmed and his war council were planning what they hoped would be the final assault, which began around midnight on 29 May 1453. The first troops sent in were the Christian contingents, composed of Serbs and Bulgarians. They were supported by the Azaps, poorly equipped Turkish soldiers. In essence, Mehmed II was sending in the cannon fodder to soak up the initial resistance from the garrison on the walls. These attacks were conducted to the sounds of the Janissary bands playing their intimidating war music. The attacks centred on the city gates and the few breaches in the walls that the cannons had made in the preceding hours. Some of the attackers made it past the walls but were pushed back. As was only to be expected, the fighting was fierce and vicious. Amongst the attackers was Ulubatlı Hasan. He was one of the many Anatolian (Turkish) chieftains who, instead of paying tribute, brought soldiers to the fight, similar to the role of knights in feudal Europe. Hasan was lightly armoured and armed with a scimitar and circular shield, but most importantly, he carried a standard and was the first man to plant Mehmed II's flag on the city's walls. His bravery and daring showed that the walls of Constantinople were not unassailable and inspired his men to follow. Hasan, however, was hit by multiple arrows and crossbow bolts. He fell, but his actions and sacrifice added fresh resolve to the attackers, while also demoralising the defenders.

The trickle of Ottoman forces pushing through the breach turned into a flood. The walls fell; the siege had ended in success for the Ottomans, but the final assault was staggeringly brutal. Eyewitness accounts talk of blood flowing in the streets and bodies (of both attackers and defenders) bobbing 'like melons' in the waters around the city. Mehmed II had promised his men three days of plunder, a standard practice of the age after a city had been defeated and was designed to encourage the residents to surrender without the fight. Unfortunately, on this occasion, treasure was not enough, and the conquering Ottoman soldiers massacred thousands; many more were captured and later sold into slavery. It is alleged that when Mehmed II saw the scale of the carnage and destruction he said, 'What a city we have given over to plunder and destruction.'

In the last hours, Constantine XI was seen fighting on the walls. He was a brave man who had very little and faced a united enemy with almost infinite resources. Had he handed over the city without a fight, he would have become a pariah. Instead, he is now an unofficial saint in the Greek Orthodox Church, and many legends have sprung up around him. It was said there was a prophecy that Constantinople would be founded by one Constantine and lost by another (which is true, but the legend post-dates 1453). Another legend says that an angel rescued Constantine XI by turning him into a marble statue and placing him in a cave near the Golden Gate, where he waits patiently to be brought to life to win back the city for Christendom. This is why he is sometimes called 'the marble emperor'. The name of Constantine was used as a rallying cry by Greeks during their war of independence with the Ottoman Empire, and he is, unsurprisingly, a national hero in Greece. He was a courageous man who died a martyr but, ultimately, he lost. Constantine XI was both the end point to the thousand-year history of the Byzantine Empire and (arguably) the full stop to the Roman Empire.

The siege took about eight weeks, a remarkably short amount of time, especially considering that this was one of the most difficult sieges in history. It is also a salient reminder of how things had changed. When Osman besieged the Byzantine's major city of Bursa, he had no siege equipment and could only wait it out. It took nine years before they eventually captured that city. Now the descendants of those warriors had the most technologically advanced siege weapons in the world and had captured a most prized city in less than nine weeks. The empire had come a long way from the time of Osman.

Because its impact was felt in so many different ways, the importance of this siege cannot be overstated. The Byzantine emperors were considered to be Greek by the rest of Europe; however (and somewhat unexpectedly), the Byzantines were proud of their Roman heritage, and even though they had been using Greek as the lingua franca for about 900 years, the emperors still called themselves 'Roman' emperors and also 'Caesars'. When this Christian 'Greek' Orthodox capital fell, the other great centres of Orthodox Christianity, Kiev and Moscow, picked up the baton. In fact, about eighty years later, the grand princes of Moscow changed their title to the more exalted Tsar, the Russian for Caesar. There was no way that they could have taken such a title had the Byzantine Empire still existed. The Ottoman sultans also added Caesar to their list of titles after 1453.

The repercussions did not end with changes to the Orthodox church and the transference of titles. While gunpowder had been around for centuries, cannons of the size and in the numbers used in this siege had never been used before. Mehmed II's victory was the first time in history that gunpowder was seen to have played a key role in the outcome. Indeed, because of the widespread deployment of cannon, the idea that a high stone wall could stop an enemy attack became obsolete in that year. Mehmed II had shown that cannons had overtaken traditional siege weapons and that a stone wall, however well built, could be broken down quicker than ever before. From now on designs such as star forts (so-called because they looked as if they had star-like points) and low, earth-filled walls were built to absorb the shock of siege cannons as the new weapons made obsolete the more medieval forms of attack.

As the city's conqueror, Mehmed II now owned all the great buildings inside it, and none was greater than Saint Sophia, known as Hagia Sophia. In the early 6th century AD (about the same era as the Avars), Byzantine Emperor Justinian wanted to build a new church in the ruins of an older, smaller structure. What rose out of the ground was the largest ancient dome ever built and a structure that would not be matched for over a millennium. For nearly a thousand years, this was the world's largest church, a record that's still unbeaten. Hagia Sophia was the pinnacle of late antiquity architecture and a reminder that the early Byzantine Empire was every bit a match for the fallen Western Roman one.

This is a story that ranks not alongside that of someone like Attila, but a completely different one, one of a brand-new society, with a navy and artillery, something well beyond the needs, resources or technology of any other group so far mentioned in this book. The Ottomans had fully evolved away from the world of the Eurasian Steppe nomads to become a great Eurasian Empire, although ironically, one that did not cover any of the traditional lands of their ancestors. Indeed, jumping ahead about a century to the mid-1500s, the Ottoman Sultan Suleiman conquered Hungary. This was not framed as brother attacking brother or the rightful conquering of homelands. It was naked aggression against a European kingdom – might is right.

From the time of Mehmed II to Suleiman's reign, the Kingdom of Hungary either fought directly or backed proxies against the expanding Ottoman Empire. It was a zero-sum game that took more than a century to play out. In 1521, Sultan Suleiman arrived at the walls of Belgrade, the Hungarian fortress town that had withstood all previous Ottoman assaults, but this time, after the walls were undermined and the population had withstood weeks of withering cannon fire, it fell in just over a month. As a result, Belgrade became a key mustering point for Ottoman forces heading west. The Hungarian King Louis II tried to retake the town by amassing a huge army of around 60,000, but in his haste to build an overwhelming force he forgot about supplies, and the army disintegrated due to lack of food and pay. Events culminated five years later in the summer of 1526 with the Battle of Mohács. This was to be the last stand of the Hungarian kingdom, which had amassed an army of around 20,000, while Suleiman had more than double that number. Louis II also had thousands of heavily armoured knights clad in plate mail armour, and their horses, also encased in steel, were the medieval equivalent of tanks.

This campaign was not only an indication of Suleiman's military strength, but of his diplomatic skills as well. The Ottomans were now threatening the eastern borders of Habsburg power, and as the Habsburgs were the enemies of France, the French King Charles V had signed the Franco-Ottoman alliance in 1525. The concept of 'my enemy's enemy is my friend' is a good summary of why European states made all kinds of alliances, but a Christian king brokering an alliance with a Muslim sultan was seen as shocking at the time. Even so, this alliance in one form or another, was to last for almost 300 years. (One of its first practical outcomes came a few decades later in 1553, still in the time of Suleiman's reign, when a joint Ottoman-French armada successfully attacked the Genoese-held island of Corsica in the western Mediterranean. This meant that Suleiman would face no crusade and had no reason to fear a unified European army marching to the aid of Hungary.)

Because it had been raining, the two sides at Mohács (in southern Hungary near the River Danube) did not clash until early afternoon. Suleiman sent in his lightly equipped Rumelian (from what was essentially the Balkans and part of northern Greece) troops, which were quickly routed by the Hungarian heavy cavalry. However, as the Rumelian soldiers retreated, the cavalry was lured into contact with the Janissaries, whose muskets could pierce armour, and the noise sent the horses into a panic. Chaos ensued, so much so that some thought, incorrectly, that the battle was over. The Hungarians, however, must have fought on even after it became apparent that they had lost as we know Louis II only left the battle as darkness was falling (this was in high summer). During his retreat he fell from his horse into the river at Csele and drowned in his heavy armour.

Louis II had chosen to fight a battle with less of everything, hoping that obsolete heavy cavalry could withstand musket and cannon fire. He paid for his folly with his life, and that of many of his troops. Meanwhile, Suleiman was so unimpressed by the size of the opposing force at Mohács that he remained there for a few days, assuming he had only beaten the vanguard of a larger force. He was, for a time, unaware that what he had faced was the best Hungary could muster and that its king lay dead in the river. Once he realised that the path was clear to Buda and its twin town across the Danube, Pest (they were not unified until the 19th century), he lost no time advancing on the two. Suleiman plundered Buda but, due to ongoing local uprisings, didn't finally occupy it for fifteen years, in 1541. The Battle of Mohács destroyed the Hungarian monarchy and opened the gates to the rest of the kingdom. After such an emphatic victory, it was only a matter of time before Hungary became an Ottoman territory. Before the end of his reign, Suleiman would besiege Vienna (unsuccessfully).

Suleiman's list of titles reflected the hugely diverse nature of Ottoman heritage:

'Sultan of the Ottomans, Allah's deputy on earth, Lord of the Lords of this world, Possessor of men's necks, King of believers and unbelievers, King of Kings, Emperor of the East and the West, Majestic Caesar, Emperor of the Chakans of great authority, Prince and Lord of the most happy constellation, Seal of victory, Refuge of all the people in the whole entire world, the shadow of the almighty dispensing quiet on the Earth.'

In my book *The Sultans* I concentrated on titles that reflected either a European level of prestige (such as Caesar) or ones that were to do with religion (such as 'Allah's deputy on earth'). What I did not go into was 'Emperor of the Chakans of great authority'. As mentioned earlier, back in 562, Bayan I was described as ruling the Avar Khaganate, however his title was not king but chagan or khagan or Chakan. In other words, buried in the middle of perhaps the most awesome list of titles any ruler has accrued is a reference to the old ways; the Eurasian Steppe title is there as an echo of the origins of this empire. However, that title was not the most important one and was never used on its own.

Here we return to the thread that links all the groups discussed, the Silk Road. One advantage of the pan-Asian Mongol Empire was that for the first time there was a central authority to provide the peace and stability needed for trade to prosper. When the empire did break up, large areas remained relatively stable. There might be Mongol hordes in the northern and eastern territories, but in what is modern-day Iran, the Safavid Empire ruled and further west, the Ottoman Empire was in charge. By the time of Suleiman, virtually all the western trade routes of the Silk Road were under Ottoman control. The Black Sea would eventually become 'an Ottoman Lake', with all surrounding lands under its authority, and any merchants arriving there would have to work with the Ottomans. Further south, from the Caucasus to the Safavids, all was Ottoman territory.

The Ottoman Empire might be remembered for its aggressive expansion and various famous battles, sieges and wars, but its real success was in trade. The diverse nature of the empire (think about the different cultures of places like Serbia, Armenia, Iraq and Egypt) meant that internal trade was hugely profitable. Various sultans ordered a network of caravanserai, the hostelries and resupply points for traders on the move, and pumped into this were the goods coming along the Silk Road. All of this was far more complex than any previous steppe nomadic group could have organised.

But the reality was that the time of Suleiman was also the time of the waning of the Silk Road's importance. With the discovery of the New World, trade attentions and fortunes were turning to the west, far beyond the powers of the Ottomans or their Christian trading nemesis, Venice. Both were simply too far east in the Mediterranean to be part of the land grab in the Americas. Instead, previously parochial powers on the world stage came to the fore, principally Spain, Portugal, France and Britain. Some of these powers (along with the Dutch) would also begin heading east via the horn of Africa and on into the Indian Ocean. The Silk Road lost its monopoly, and while a shorter route to the East than a maritime voyage from Spain, a ship could carry more goods faster. By the 1700s, most of the trade on the Silk Road was dominated by Armenian merchants, and Armenia was part of the Ottoman Empire, now a shadow of its glorious past. Everything in the East was starting to fade and fray as the European powers came to global dominance.

Shortly after Suleiman's reign, Crimea and the Crimean Tatars came under Ottoman control as a vassal state (they had previously been vassals of the Mongols). This period is a rare example of a time when the sultans leaned into their ancient heritage. The Great Khan of the Crimea was then still living in much the same manner as that of the traditional steppe nomads, and the Ottomans referred to the Tatars as 'brothers', even though their sultan was living in a palace in a great city. Their languages were similar but everything else was different, even the way they waged war. Once absorbed into the Ottoman forces, the Tatars were used as irregular scouting troops to carry out raids and reconnaissance in force. The advantage for the Great Khan was that with the Ottomans he could do more than he could have done on his own and was able to plunder further afield into new lands. For the sultan it meant he could sow fear and confusion in an enemy heartland with no cost to his core troops.

The Tatars were pivotal in 1683 during the last great threat to central Europe at the second siege of Vienna. It was in this year that Sultan Mehmed IV attempted the one major conquest that had eluded Suleiman the Magnificent: the capture of Vienna. If the Ottomans succeeded, it would shatter Habsburg power and credibility. It would also ensure dominion over Hungary and the Balkans as they would simply be too far away from Christian support.

Vienna was a prime target and now that Belgrade was in Ottoman hands, this city of the Holy Roman Empire, ruled by the Habsburgs, was once again within striking distance. With the Danube running through it, the city was the perfect location for trade to flow in and out of Europe from the Black Sea. But the Ottoman intent to strike Vienna was known for about a year beforehand, giving the city time to gather a coalition to fight the imminent Ottoman threat. Apart from their failure to keep their plans secret, Ottoman preparations were foolproof. Nobody underestimated the task ahead of them, so when the army marched out it was over 100,000 strong, far larger than any army the European powers could put in the field. When the Ottomans arrived and set up camp, it was so large and the tents were so well ordered that some onlookers thought the Ottoman plan was to set up a rival city beside the old one. It seemed the Ottoman numbers were so many and the camp so magnificent they would win through sheer scale.

While the Ottomans set up camp, the Crimean Tatars headed further west, raiding and pillaging and generally making life miserable for those who lived in a wide swathe around the capital. While this was plunder for the Tatars, it was also an opportunity to scout the countryside to see if there was a relief column on its way. There wasn't. Leopold I, the Holy Roman Emperor, did not have the power to protect his own subjects, and he 'bravely' left the city before the besieging army arrived. One of his generals further weakened the city by moving 20,000 men to Linz. Leopold may not have been in Vienna, but the marvellously named Count Ernst Rüdiger von Starhemberg was there as the commander of a 15,000-man garrison, which was effectively outnumbered 7 to 1. With his emperor having fled the city, von Starhemberg had every reason to sue for peace and save his own skin, but this was a man in his forties, a seasoned veteran who had fought in multiple conflicts. Von Starhemberg had the experience and the energy to conduct a vigorous defence and counted on his Polish-Lithuanian commonwealth allies to provide a relief force before his defences crumbled.

Von Starhemberg did everything he could prior to the siege. He added about 50 per cent to his forces' numbers by equipping volunteers to become a militia, and it turned out that gamekeepers from the local forests were excellent snipers. He also had taken the logical, if draconian, measure of demolishing many of the houses and buildings outside the city walls. This allowed a clear field of fire from his more than 300 cannons targeting any oncoming Ottoman assaults. Grand Vizier Kara

Mustafa Pasha countered by ordering his forces to dig long lines of trenches directly toward the city. He also had great earthworks erected, man-made hills so that Ottoman artillery could fire directly into Vienna.

Suleiman had failed at the first siege mainly because of abysmal summer weather. His siege cannons got bogged down in mud and the weather continued to be uncooperative, which meant that his bombardment never reached the intensity needed. Kara Mustafa Pasha was aware of this and did everything he could to protect his troops from enemy fire while also ensuring that there were enough good firing positions to grind down Vienna's defences. Von Starhemberg had anticipated that the Ottomans would try to undermine the walls, so in various likely positions he had tree trunks buried in the soft ground to hamper the advance of the Ottoman sappers. The whole siege was a series of moves and countermoves.

While von Starhemberg had been able to stockpile food, Vienna was a large city with a significant population, and Kara Mustafa Pasha was able to surround it completely, ensuring there was no way they could get additional supplies, either by land or the River Danube. As days turned into weeks and weeks became months, the defenders were slowly starving. When Kara Mustafa Pasha tried probing the defences with frontal assaults, it was usually at night. The constant bombardment, mixed with night-time attacks and little food, led to exhaustion on the part of the defenders. Men collapsing through fatigue and malnutrition became so common that von Starhemberg ordered any soldier found asleep on watch to be shot where he lay.

In an attempt to disrupt the Ottoman assault, there were multiple night-time attacks from the defenders. The first one achieved complete surprise and slowed Ottoman preparations. Fires were started and various Ottoman stores and mines were set alight. But after that, the Janissaries were waiting, and with each new sally forth from the walls the raids steadily became less successful and more costly in defenders' lives. One defender reflected the frustration at the zeal of the Ottoman siege, saying, 'It is beyond the powers of human comprehension to grasp ... just how obstinately the Turks defend themselves ... It is easier to deal with any conventional fortress and with any other army than with the Turks.'

In early September the Ottoman sappers were working to position their mines of gunpowder to explode and create breaches in the walls. Von Starhemberg countered with moves by his own sappers to intercept the Ottoman tunnels as they reached the walls. (It was common practice for tunnellers to stop occasionally to listen for any tell-tale sounds that might indicate a nearby enemy tunnel. Sometimes they broke into each other's systems, leading to vicious and claustrophobic close-quarter fighting by candlelight.) By 8 September, despite von Starhemberg's best efforts, some of the lower outer walls had fallen into Ottoman hands, but there were good reasons why the defenders kept fighting. An honourable one was that if Vienna fell, it would be used as an Ottoman base for further operations west, just as the fall of Belgrade had been a launch site into Hungary. A less noble but more immediate motivation was the fear of a massacre. The atrocities of the Thirty Years' War (between fellow Christians) were fresh in minds, and the knowledge that the Ottomans were more than capable of massacring an entire population would have been something in the minds of everyone in the city.

Then a miracle – or a disaster – depending on the point of view. The Crimean Tatars had not been scouting the areas around Vienna as they should have been and had failed to spot a huge relief army before it swooped on the Ottoman camp. The Ottomans had grown complacent in their defences over the eight weeks they had been in situ. The Siege of Vienna turned now into the Battle of Vienna as an army of over 50,000, a mixture of Holy Roman and Polish-Lithuanian forces, descended on the Ottomans. The battle started in the most spectacular way imaginable when King John III Sobieski led a gigantic cavalry charge down the slope towards the Ottoman camp. He was at the front of his 3,000 Winged Hussars, cavalrymen wearing plate armour and full-face steel helmets (at the time this was an anachronism, but John had learnt that the heavy armour worked well against the Ottoman light cavalry). Each one of these men had a metal frame with large white feathers on his back. The Hussars looked like a flock of steel birds swooping down on the enemy, the sight of which inspired the allied army to charge straight through the panicking Ottoman forces. John's Winged Hussars, plus the thousands of other allied cavalries charging into the fray, made this the largest (recorded) cavalry charge in history. Thousands died; thousands more were captured.

Kara Mustafa Pasha had been badly let down by his allies, who had recognised a lost cause and didn't even engage in the final battle, despite the fact it had been the job of the Tatars to ensure nothing like this could happen. Kara Mustafa Pasha was able to escape with a portion of the army, but Vienna was to remain eternally out of reach of the empire. On his return to Belgrade, Grand Vizier Kara Mustafa Pasha was strangled on the orders of the commander of the Janissaries. It had been the Ottoman Empire's worst ever defeat in a single battle, and the leader of such a disastrous campaign could not expect to survive the consequences. King John III Sobieski's spectacular cavalry charge became a legend. It was said afterwards that he had played on the words of Julius Caesar, but rather than saying, 'Veni, vidi, vici' (I came, I saw, I conquered), he changed it to, 'Veni, vidi, Deus vicit' (I came, I saw, God conquered).

The king and his soldiers had first look at the spoils in the Ottoman camp, and they were wondrous. Kara Mustafa

Pasha's tent (along with some others) is still in a Polish museum where it is occasionally put on display. The grand vizier's tent is a stunning example of the use of textiles, with intricate geometric patterns woven in vibrant colours. Such detail in a campaign tent would have seemed extraordinary to the Christian onlookers who initially saw the Ottoman encampment as a potential new city.

Many books have been written about the significance of this siege and the final Battle of Vienna, said to have changed the face of Europe. No longer would central Europe fear Ottoman invasion; now it was the turn of the sultans to see an erosion of their power in Hungary and the Balkans. That much is true, and it is also true that the siege was followed up with other major Christian victories, but it is easy to read too much into events with hindsight. The siege was a close-run affair, and had the Tatars done a better job of scouting, there would not have been a surprise cavalry attack. The simple fact is that most of the areas under Ottoman rule in 1683 were still under its rule in 1783. The consequences made a significant difference to Hungary, which would forever shake off its Ottoman overlords, but it had always been a bit of a hinterland, positioned as it was between two empires and never a docile subject under Ottoman governance.

There was a second Battle of Mohács in 1687. The first battle had been an emphatic victory for Suleiman and opened Hungary to Ottoman domination. The second battle happened in roughly the same place, but this time the outcome was the exact opposite. It was an overwhelming defeat for the Ottomans and closed the doors on any further attempts to recapture Hungarian land. The new Grand Vizier Sarı Suleiman Pasha fled the field of battle fearing for his life. His fears were well-founded, and when the remains of the army caught up with him, another grand vizier's life was cut short, another small tragedy in a sea of many. The army was now in revolt. It had suffered defeat after defeat; its losses had been substantial.

As can be seen in the second siege of Vienna, the Ottoman Empire had evolved far beyond its humble origins. Mehmed IV may have shared the name with the great conqueror of Constantinople two hundred years earlier, but unlike his namesake, he sent his grand vizier to do the actual fighting. It's safe to say the great warlords of the steppe such as Attila, Genghis Khan and Tamerlane would not have been impressed. Also, while there were trappings of the exotic around the siege, basically the same tactics and tempo used in the Thirty Years' War a few generations earlier or the War of Spanish Succession a generation in the future were the ones used at Vienna. It was a typically European campaign and not something that shared any DNA with the Huns or others from the steppe (with the possible exception of the raiding carried out by the Crimean Tatars). It is ironic that to western Europe the Ottomans seemed exotic when they were really just another European power, albeit one with resources that spread onto two other continents. However, as briefly mentioned above, internal tensions in the empire were increasing. The health of the empire depended on military successes, and it was under Mehmed IV that we start to see the irreversible decline of Ottoman martial success. This was not unique in Europe. Britain had seen the execution of its king in the 1640s, and almost exactly a century later it would see a successful revolt by its colonies in America.

Revolution in France came shortly after, and from the embers of the Terror that followed came the export of revolution and of wars of conquest that would eventually follow under the banner of an artillery officer by the name of Napoleon. The attempts to curb the later Emperor of France are broken up by historians into wars of coalition to show the changing alliances during this roughly 25 years of war. There was a total of seven coalitions with the usual European names such as Prussia, Austria and Britain, but a key member of the second coalition was the Ottoman Empire, which played no small part in Napoleon's decision to invade British Imperial India and hit the British Empire where it really hurt. Unfortunately, he decided to invade India via Egypt (it makes a funny kind of sense but ultimately failed). This meant much of the fighting in the late 1790s was happening in Ottoman territory. Napoleon wrote from Milan in August 1797:

> The time is not far off when we shall see that in order to destroy England we must seize Egypt. The death of the vast Ottoman empire obliges us to prepare for measures to conserve our trade in the east.

A key part of this story started when Napoleon landed unopposed in Alexandria. (Nelson, for the only time in his career, had been outmanoeuvred.) In 1798, Alexandria was a small town of no strategic significance, but that wasn't the point. Napoleon was ahead of his time in the then more or less non-existent field of public relations, and he understood that this success would make for a good story back in Europe. He knew that when the newspapers reported that he had landed in Alexandria, the educated classes would recognise the name as a place where pharaohs and Roman emperors had once walked, and he knew they would be impressed. Napoleon was a great general, politician – and PR guru.

Napoleon also espoused some remarkably progressive (if politically expedient) views on Islam. At the time, Islam in western Europe was synonymous with decades of violence (a taint that lingers in some quarters to this day). So, to have Napoleon state that the Prophet Muhammed was 'A great man who changed the face of the earth', would have gone down well with the local population. His proclamation to the Egyptians was remarkably conciliatory in tone and begins:

> People of Egypt: You will be told by our enemies, that I am come to destroy your religion. Believe them not. Tell them that I am come to restore your rights, punish your usurpers, and raise the true worship of Mahomet. Tell them that I venerate, more than do the Mamelukes, God, His prophet, and the Qur'an.

On one occasion he even dressed as a local by putting on a turban, much to the acclaim of the crowd. This was another PR stunt to get the locals onboard, but first he had to humble the local army, which meant fighting the Mamelukes. The cavalry that faced Napoleon at the legendary Battle of the Pyramids was, much like the backdrop of the ancient pyramids, a splendid relic of the past. Apart from their carbines and muskets, the Mameluke cavalry that fought on that day would have been familiar to Osman 500 years earlier. The Mamelukes were resplendent in their brightly coloured silks and plumed helmets. Their weapons were inlaid with mother-of-pearl or ivory. History was in the air, something Napoleon emphasised when he spoke to his troops, saying, 'From the heights of these pyramids, forty centuries look down on us.' It was East versus West; it was the new tactics of France against the traditional bravery of the Mamelukes, but the one thing Napoleon took great pains to emphasise was that this was not Christian versus Muslim. Even though his forces were in Egypt, and later Syria, this – most emphatically – was not a new crusade.

At this time in the West there was a standard tactic to deal with the dangerously mobile cavalry of the enemy forces. Napoleon ordered each of the five divisions of his army into hollow rectangles, with cavalry and baggage at the centre and cannon at the corners. The men stood in multiple rows. All had fixed bayonets and as one line of men reloaded, they were covered by another line that could fire. The square shape of the divisions meant that the Mameluke cavalry had no way to flank the French. The Mameluke's Murad Bey had split his forces, and he was with the thousands of cavalry on the French side of the Nile, next to the town of Embabeh, with thousands more infantry behind its impressive walls. However, another ten thousand of his infantry watched uselessly from the other side of the Nile during the course of the day. Although they were in the wrong place at the wrong time, it was unlikely they would have tipped the battle to the Mameluke advantage.

Murad Bey let the French sweat under a scorching sun and didn't attack until 3.30 in the afternoon. When the attack came it was instantaneous, ferocious and a sharp lesson to the French about what the skilled Mameluke horsemen could do. However, despite the bravery and the exquisite costumes, they were no match for superior tactics mixed with cold steel and hot gunfire. The cream of the Mameluke forces was gunned down. Men screamed and horses whinnied as the sand of the desert turned red with one pointless charge leading to another ineffectual attack by Murad Bey's men. By the end of the day, Napoleon's force of 20,000 had suffered just twenty-nine fatalities. The French surveyed the carnage of the battlefield as thousands of brave Mamelukes lay dead or dying on the sands of Egypt and in the streets of Embabeh. For both Murad Bey and Selim III, 21 July 1798 had been an unmitigated disaster. Napoleon was now in charge of Egypt.

Napoleon's time in Egypt and the Levant makes for a great read, and it is hard to stop getting misty-eyed as all the different cultures and locations get trotted out; but in reality, this endeavour was a horribly expensive long shot. When Napoleon finally conceded he was getting nowhere, he set sail back to France and abandoned his troops in the process. Once the imminent threat had gone from the borders of the now crumbling empire, Selim III declined to participate in the rest of the campaigns against France, but for a time at least, the Ottomans had been recognised as a European power.

In the north the Ottoman Empire had been losing ground to a new rising power, Russia. The Crimean Tatars were absorbed into Ukraine, only to be savagely ethnically cleansed by Stalin in the 20th century. There is an alleged letter that is often attributed to the Zaporizhian Cossacks that berates the Ottoman sultan in the foulest possible language; it's safe to assume it's a fake, probably from the late 1700s. Nobody has found the original letter, which was sent from many different dates in the 1600s to a variety of sultans. The point of the letter was to show Russia's growing political confidence, so while it is a fascinating read, remember that no sultan ever saw it.

The increase in clashes between an expansionist Russian Empire and a weakening Ottoman one led to the Crimean War. When France, Russia and Britain flexed their muscles, the Russians sent their army and navy to invade Ottoman territory.

The Crimean War of 1853-56 was the first major European war since the Napoleonic era. It took many powers by surprise, with Austria and Prussia thinking a diplomatic solution could be found while real fighting was going on. Indeed, the confusion around the war has led to its misnomer. It's called the Crimean War because the Crimea is where most of the land battles took place, but there were naval engagements in the Baltic Sea, the Balkans, the Black Sea, the Pacific (against eastern Russian territory), and there was fighting in the Caucasus, too. At the time it was referred to by most combatant nations as the Russian War, which is probably a better name for it.

Field Marshal Ivan Paskevich and General Mikhail Gorchakov marched an 80,000-strong Russian army into the Danubian

Principalities of Moldavia and Wallachia. These had been under Russian 'protection' for decades, and now the dithering around Christian rights gave Russia the excuse it had been seeking to invade these areas and seize control. But Russian logistics were still behind the times, and within months the army was less than half its original size as men deserted or died of disease. Omar Pasha led a small column of Ottoman troops towards the Russians and managed to push them back, but the victories were minor ones. The best that could be said for the Ottoman forces was that they didn't collapse.

In Russia there are sixteen days of Military Honour (some are national holidays) every year to commemorate multiple victories over many centuries against many enemies. The Battle of Sinop is one of these days, although when compared to other great clashes (such as that against the Mongols in their prime or the siege of Stalingrad), it does seem to be an overreaction to a fairly forgettable naval engagement, remembered, if at all, for the fact that it was the last battle involving fleets of sailing ships. But it was a comprehensive Russian victory.

The Ottoman fleet was anchored in Sinop Bay (on the northern coast of Anatolia, so the first battle of the Crimean War was hundreds of miles away from the Crimean Peninsula) and was protected by shoreline forts. Russian Admiral Pavel Nakhimov led his ships into the bay under fire, and his crews skilfully lined up to engage the Ottoman vessels. Nakhimov was so precise in his orders that his warships covered the entire harbour with interlocking fields of fire. While the ships on both sides dated from the old era of sail, the artillery onboard the Russian ships was the new Paixhans guns, and they were nothing like the usual cannons. The cannon had, for centuries, fired solid projectiles: cannon balls, canisters of ball bearings or chain shot. These new guns were the first naval cannons to fire shells, explosive rounds that did damage not just from the projectile, but from violent chemical reactions that caused explosions. The Russian guns simply blasted the opposition wooden ships to splinters or set them on fire. All but one Ottoman ship was sunk or run aground.

The Crimean War in Britain is remembered as a mainly British affair. It acknowledges that the French were also fighting and that there were some Ottoman troops acting as stretcher bearers ... or something, but it was largely about 'the thin red line' and the historic clashes, such as the Battle of Balaclava. This was not the case. While British efforts were considerable and British forces fought bravely and suffered through horrific conditions, some 200,000 British servicemen fought in the war, compared to 300,000 Ottoman troops and 400,000 Frenchmen (Sardinians also joined in because they wanted to keep France happy; their small number of troops acquitted themselves well). This meant that nearly a million allied troops were moved around a continent (with some naval assets in the Pacific) against more than 700,000 Russians. It was the clashes in the Baltic that were the most worrisome for Russia. Saint Petersburg was then the capital (not Moscow) and was as vulnerable as Istanbul to a potential maritime invasion.

There were naval clashes in the Baltic and an epic siege in the eastern Anatolian city of Kars, but the focus was the Siege of Sevastopol, which rumbled on for a year. The port was able to receive regular supplies and, at one point, had more than 400 cannons on the walls, ready to make life hell for the besiegers. Like the Crimean War itself, the siege is remembered in Britain as a largely Anglo-French affair, but the Ottomans were there with a force of 60,000, twice the British numbers. Vladimir Kornilov and Pavel Nakhimov (the hero of Sinop) led the defence of the port. Kornilov was to die during battle, but the two navy men proved to be as talented on land as they were at sea. Most of the well-known battles of the war such as

Balaklava are born of the defence of the supply lines of the allies as they besieged the port.

The Treaty of Paris in 1856 can be seen as the agreement that re-established Ottoman power. The empire had been on the slide for 200 years and in the last 50 or 60 had become an embarrassment. The treaty was a humiliation for Russia, which lost its political influence over the Danubian Principalities as well as the areas around the mouth of the Danube that had once been Ottoman territory. The Black Sea became a demilitarised zone, neutralising the Russian fleet, and islands in the Baltics were also demilitarised. The city of Kars was returned to the Ottomans. Britain recognised the importance of the Ottoman contribution to the war and made Sultan Abdülmecid a Knight of the Order of the Garter, the highest honour Britain could confer. In contrast to a stance that had prevailed over centuries, the West was now trying to make the Ottoman Empire feel like part of the western powers, which it was. While by no means an equal partner or even a key power, it had much to offer the West: a counterbalance to Russia, access to the eastern Mediterranean and the Black Sea trade routes as well as influence on two continents. The sultans, for so long seen as 'other' and leaders to be ignored, were now players at the table of global diplomacy.

The First World War brings us the death throes of the Ottoman Empire. We are now so far away from the foundations laid by Osman at the time of the Crusades and the Mongols as to be in a different world. Aircraft, tanks, radio, cars, steam trains and machine guns are just a few advances in technology completely beyond the imagination of anyone at the time of Osman.

There is film footage of Ottoman subjects getting on with their daily lives in Istanbul. No other group discussed in this book could produce anything like it. Mehmed VI (the last sultan and with none of the dynamism displayed by his namesake Mehmed II) was formally deposed in 1922. This means that there are probably a few old souls still alive who were born as subjects of the Ottoman Empire who could, in theory, read this sentence.

This period was the only time in the history of the empire when the sultan was not in charge. Just before the war there had been a coup, and the empire was now ruled by a cabal known as The Three Pashas in a kind of unofficial acknowledgement that the Ottoman Empire was dead. The name 'Ottoman' Empire was apt. For more than 600 years the same family had ruled the empire, and every single ruler came from that same dynasty; sons, brothers, uncles, all came from the line of Osman. Every time there had been an uprising or revolt, whether the sultan was mad, bad or dangerous, it simply never occurred to anyone that the sultan should be replaced by anyone other than a descendant of Osman. There is no equivalent to this anywhere else in the world. So, given the empire's history, it is surprising that it was the pashas, not the sultan, who conducted (for better or worse) the empire's role in the war. The Ottomans were not on the winning side in the war and they paid the ultimate price with the dismemberment of their lands.

By the end of the war, many of the lands that had once been part of the empire had already become countries in their own right, for example Greece and Egypt. But after the war Britain and France carved up the Middle East to create new countries such as Kuwait and Palestine. The rump of the empire was turned into a brand new, never-before-existing state called the Republic of Türkiye, founded in 1923 by a man known as Atatürk (Father Turk). A man with no Turkic DNA (he was born in modern-day Greece) forged the identity of this new republic not based on Islam (he was a secularist), but on an ethnic identity. To this day the motto of the Republic of Türkiye is 'How happy is the one who says I am a Turk.' Turkish citizens are Turks, regardless of DNA ethnicity, and they are the blood brothers of Attila or Genghis, no matter what the science says.

This has taken us well past the events of all the other chapters in this book, but that is the story of the Ottoman Empire. It was a remarkably long-lasting civilisation that does not get the credit or interest it deserves. It will appear again as it is part of the story of some of the other steppe nomads. The empire evolved far beyond anything Osman could have foreseen, and events allowed it to expand and flourish for centuries, however, just like every other empire in history, after the rise comes the fall. (My book *The Sultans: The Rise and Fall of the Ottoman Rulers and Their World, A 600 Year History* about the Ottoman Empire, unsurprisingly, provides a much more detailed history than can be provided here.)

7

TEMUJIN

After the Ottoman Empire took us all the way into the 20th century, it's time to return to the Middle Ages. The Seljuks had expanded into the Middle East in the 11th century, but now we move to the 12th century and the birth of Temüjin (I have anglicized it to Temujin), which was so unexceptional we know only that it occurred sometime in the twelve-year period from 1155-67. This is no disrespect to Temujin. Just like Attila or Osman, he was born into a society that had neither scribes nor a culture of literacy and writing. The life of Temujin is perhaps the best argument in all of history that 'history is written by the victors' is demonstrably not true. It is the case with every group discussed in this book that there is far more documentary evidence written by the losing sides than the victors. While we can assume this gives a distorted view, many of the excesses are corroborated.

There is, however, one exception to this: according to *The Secret History of the Mongols* (completed shortly after the death of Temujin) Temujin was born clutching a blood clot in his fist, the sign of a great warrior, and it was believed that his clan, the Borjigin, were the descendants of the union between the semi-divine blue-grey wolf Börte Chino and

Gua Maral, a fallow deer. In another account Temujin's mother was impregnated with him by a ray of light. These stories conclusively prove two things: first, the Mongols had little expertise in obstetrics, and second, clearly everything from *The Secret History of the Mongols* is designed to enhance the reputation of one of the most feared men and civilisations in all of history.

The reality is we know nothing definitive about Temujin's early years, but what we can glean from the legends is that while his father was the Borjigin leader, he had the misfortune to be born into a tribe whose influence was waning. It cannot be overemphasised that life on the steppe was harsh, which led to a brutally pragmatic culture of hunt or be hunted, whether by man or beast. The strong preyed on the weak and his clan had become weak.

When Temujin was the ripe old age of eight, his father strengthened the family's position by arranging his marriage to a child bride from a neighbouring tribe. And now a brief aside on child brides, which today we find shocking and regard as, at best, child exploitation. This is to misunderstand the medieval world. When a European king married a twelve-year-old princess it had nothing to do with sexual preferences. Phrases like 'they lay in the wedding bed' are symbolic. They would literally lie in a bed, fully clothed, to show they were now husband and wife; it was a ritual intended to cement an alliance, usually linked with peace treaties or trade agreements. The marriage was a way to seal the deal, and pre-pubescent brides were kept well away from a mature groom's bedroom because even with the limited medical knowledge of the time it was recognised that sexual intercourse at such a young age would likely cause harm. So, while the opening line of this paragraph was flippant, these marriages were a time-honoured, globally recognised means of unifying two separate parties, each of whom had something to gain from the union; there was nothing unusual about the practice.

Temujin's bride-to-be was the similarly aged Börte, the daughter of an Onggirat chieftain, whose tribe was on the rise. This was an opportunity for the Borjigin to gain a powerful new ally, but because the Onggirats were more powerful they had the upper hand in the negotiations around the marriage, and so it was decided that Temujin would stay with his bride's family to work off her dowry. In essence, Temujin was not only an honoured guest and son-in-law to the Onggirat leader, but he was also a hostage; the Onggirats could keep an eye on the boy and raise him in their traditions to create a strong connection. It was a plan that worked for everyone.

However, on his return journey home, Temujin's father came across a band of Tatars. While they were old enemies, the steppe tradition of offering food and shelter to travelling bands was invoked. Unfortunately for Temujin's father, the Tatars recognised their old enemy and poisoned his food. Before he died, he managed to send word back to Temujin who was with his mother.

Temujin was just a child and was not of an age to lead the Borjigin. It seems (and it must be remembered that most of this comes from legendary sources) that because their chieftain had died with no obvious successor, virtually all the clan members left to follow a new leader, and it was at this point that Temujin's mother stepped into history. Uelun Ujin was a remarkable woman who should be better known. She did everything she could to keep the Borjigin from leaving, pointing out that they would only have to wait a few years before Temujin was of age, but her pleas fell on deaf ears, and this mother of several children now had to fend for herself and her family alone on the steppe.

Before continuing the story, let's unpack the poisoning of Temujin's father. While modern historians talk about Seljuks,

Tatars and Mongols, along with a dizzying array of more obscure tribes, the circumstances around the poisoning show once again what a culturally and linguistically homogenous civilisation the Eurasian Steppe nomads were. The idea that strangers should show hospitality to strangers was something assumed by Temujin's father, and the fact the Tatars played along shows they knew the rules. More importantly, as the Tatars were the enemies of Temujin's clan, they were obviously from a competing tribe, and the outcome might have been different had Timujin's father not had the bad luck to be recognised.

Uelun Ujin was in a critical situation. The children were too young to hunt and she couldn't do it on her own, so she was reduced to finding wild berries and millet and eking out the most basic of foods, some of which had to be stored to get them through the cruelly cold winters when nothing grew, and any surviving vegetation was under thick layers of snow and ice. Her only other option was to seek out nearby groups and hope for hospitality, but welcoming such a family meant extra mouths to feed with no benefits. As Uelun Ujin's husband's fate had shown, not everyone played fair.

This was the toughest time in Temujin's life. Battles can be won, blades can be blocked, arrows can miss, but hunger is implacable. For a few years the family was on the brink, but things gradually improved as Temujin and his brother Behter grew and learned how to hunt, a skill that saved them from starvation. The boys were stepbrothers: Behter was older and therefore had a better claim to the tribal leadership because of his age. But Temujin was the son of the favoured wife Uelun Ujin. According to Mongol custom, Behter could marry Uelun Ujin and become Temujin's half-brother and stepfather simultaneously – the ultimate in sibling one upmanship.

As time passed, the rivalry grew, the tension increased and the arguments between the brothers intensified, but there is no record of what triggered the final showdown. One source says it was an argument over the spoils from a hunt, but whatever it was, at some point in their adolescence Temujin killed Behter. Apparently Uelun Ujin scolded Temujin for the fratricide, but there was nothing to be done. Life went on. While the group now had to be larger than just Uelun Ujin and the two boys, it probably numbered less than twenty (this is an author's guess, nobody knows). Such a small group was highly vulnerable to any form of aggression by any other tribe on the steppe.

During Temujin's adolescence there would have been multiple incidences of capture, escape and hiding from unfriendly war parties. Names such as Jamukha, Sorkan-Shira and Bo'orchu appear as friends willing to risk severe punishment by hiding Temujin. All these men and their families would be greatly rewarded for their loyalty as fate finally began to smile on Temujin. Why did these people help a loner prince who had fallen on hard times? There was nothing in it for them. The answer must be that Temujin had charisma; there was something about the boy who was slowly becoming a young man, a one with a certain energy and charm, someone who had drive, ambition and vision that got people's attention. They liked what they saw.

In many respects Temujin's early years summarise the life experience of every Eurasian Steppe nomad so far described. Life was a fight for survival not just against nature, but against belligerent tribal groups as well. He had survived through sheer force of will and with the help of one of the most pragmatic mothers in history. He valued loyalty and kinship, and all of this would be there in his motives and actions later in his life.

As his name garnered recognition of competence and fairness, small groups began to join him. What had once been a tiny family unit was now growing into a small tribe. Once his position had stabilised and improved from the near starvation of his youth, he went back to the Onggirats to marry Börte. Apparently her chieftain father was delighted that Temujin had survived, and Uelun Ujin was given a black sable cloak (a highly prized and valuable gift) as a wedding present. This cloak was quickly given as a gift to Toghrul, a warlord who had allied with Temujin.

However, shortly after the wedding, a raid by an enemy tribe caused the substantial destruction of Temujin's camp. Even worse, they captured Börte. Temujin used his newfound power with allies to get Jamukha to lead a mighty army of 20,000 horsemen into enemy territory and not only win the military campaign but return Börte to her husband. The only problem was that she was pregnant, and she had been away too long for it to have been Temujin's. So, when Börte gave birth to Jochi her first son, Temujin simply declared the child to be his. The only person to bring this up in the future was Chagatai, Börte's second son, who was definitely Temujin's.

Jamukha had brought Temujin great success, and over the next few years their bond became even stronger ... right up until the point where they were in open war with each other. In 1187 their two armies of equal size met at Dalan Baljut where Jamukha comprehensively beat Temujin. He lived to fight another day, but over the next decade he faded from the story of the major powerbrokers on the steppe. It's important to know this as it shows that his gifts were not supernatural and that he could rebuild after a setback; it also shows the generals he picked stayed with him and remained loyal.

In this lost decade, where was Temujin and what was he doing? It seems likely that for a time he headed south into Jin territory (that of a northeastern Chinese dynasty) as a vassal or mercenary leader. The Jin appear to have used the Mongols in the same way the Byzantines used the Seljuks: to boost their ranks and have access to the mobile horse archers as irregular units that could carry out reconnaissance in force and ambush enemy units as they marched.

In 1196 Temujin and the Jin waged war against the Tatars (the same tribe that had killed Temujin's father) who were threatening Jin territory. By now Temujin was leading a battle-hardened group of warriors and the campaign was a success (which also helped his ally Toghrul). They had licked their wounds and learned from their mistakes, whereas Jamukha had not learned from his victory, he had been a sore winner. He had beheaded enemy captives, desecrated corpses and boiled 70 prisoners alive. Consequently, defectors began to come over to Temujin's side. What had seemed like a decisive victory for Jamukha now looked like the beginning of the end of his reign.

Temujin and Toghrul were now acting together, with Toghrul the loyal junior partner. This alliance enabled them to achieve a winning streak against various other groups and tribes on the Mongolian Steppe. Flushed with success and seeking to cement his position, Temujin proposed that his son Jochi marry one of Toghrul's daughters. The proposal was for a typical marriage alliance, however, as the legitimacy of Jochi was always in question and despite Temujin saying Jochi was his son, everyone knew he wasn't, and Toghrul took offence. Temujin had overreached and it led to open hostility between the two. Once again Temujin suffered a defeat, this time at the hands of Toghrul at the Battle of Qalaqaljid Sands in 1203. Temujin's son Ögedei was wounded in the battle, and it was a decisive victory for Toghrul.

Only a few paragraphs have passed since the story of Temujin's birth and childhood, so it is worth noting that we are now into the 1200s, and Temujin is about forty. He has now spent over two decades in the saddle as a warrior. He has built a fearsome reputation, but twice now, when he was on the cusp of major domination of the Mongolian Steppe, he has lost a crucial battle. On both occasions it was at the hands of a previously loyal ally. It was by no means game over for Temujin, but after his time in exile, he couldn't afford another body blow to his reputation. His generals were still loyal to him, but as Toghrul and Jamukha had proved, loyalties can change. The shifting allegiances of the warbands of the steppe nomads, and the fissiparous nature of alliances is perfectly demonstrated in the early story of Temujin.

Temujin was down but not out, as he gathered the leaders of his warbands and declared union with them. This became known as the Baljuna Covenant. Temujin swore to lead wisely, and the generals swore to be with him to the end. Every one of these men delivered on their promise and this moment, after his previous serious defeats, is often seen as the start of his apotheosis into a legend. This is, of course, using hindsight, but it is to the credit of these men that they remained loyal when other allies and companions had not. It is also worth pointing out that these groups were a mixture of faiths. There were many pagans present (Temujin was one of them) but Nestorian Christians, Buddhists and Muslim groups were there, too. Temujin's oath transcended their faiths which was an important way Temujin would rule moving forwards.

Months later, Temujin was able to attack Toghrul when his defences were down. Earlier the number of 20,000 was used to describe Temujin's army when it was led by Jamukha. Now the number was 8,000, showing how badly mauled his forces had been at their previous encounter. The battle lasted three days, illustrating how fierce the fighting was and how Temujin had no option but to win. Both sides would have been well aware of their enemy generals, their temperaments, styles and tactics. Both sides would have relied almost exclusively on the light-mounted archers that had been waging war on the steppe since the time of Attila. Eventually, Temujin prevailed and although Toghrul managed to escape he was cut down a few days later by a warrior who was unaware of his status. Temujin had won.

A year later, in 1204, Temujin finally faced his childhood friend and turncoat Jamukha with his Naiman allies at the Battle of the Thirteen Sides (the battle has multiple names, I picked the most intriguing one). Temujin won the day here, too, and this time his nemesis was captured at the battle. There are two completely contradictory accounts of what happened next, so all we can say for certain was Jamukha was executed. The Naimans (the final group in the Mongolian Steppe region to resist Temujin's authority) were brought into his forces with various marriage alliances which made them partners and not subjugated people. Temujin sought to be a unifier, at the point of a sword if necessary, but violence was never his first option. He was open to including different ethnicities and religions, but loyalty and reliability were first and foremost. Join and you would be enriched; resist and you could expect to be crushed. It was the way of the steppe written as an imperial doctrine, because Temujin had created an empire. It had been centuries since this region was unified, and unity was what made it one of the most feared martial powers in Asia. Now Temujin was their leader, and like a coiled spring, he was ready to burst out of the confines of his home territory to seek, quite literally, pastures new.

However, there were loose ends to tidy up before that grand vision could be implemented. In 1206, there was a kurultai (a great gathering of all the chieftains) at the source of the Onon River, and it was here Temujin was given a new title. He had unified the clans and now had a battle-hardened and disciplined army at his disposal. He was truly the universal ruler, the Genghis Khan. Even though Temujin was his name, he is remembered by his title, and it is important that his full title be used because abbreviating it to, say, just Genghis sounds like it's a first name. Using 'Genghis' only would be using half a title and not even the right half; it would be like writing King of... without knowing the rest of it.

What we now begin to see is the massive expansion of an empire that would consume the rest of his life and would rival that of Alexander the Great in terms of the speed of its creation, and surpass it in the size of his conquests and the length of his rule. Alexander conquered huge swathes of Asia, but his conquests broke up the moment he died. Not so for Temujin, a man whose progeny would lead to the most widely spread Y chromosome in the world. Putting it simply: more people in the world are descendants of Temujin than any other man on the planet.

Genghis Khan did something that no previous group in this book had the vision to do; he reorganised society and communal links. Looking back at the Avars or the Huns, power was all about the ruling family and their various clan ties. This had led to civil war, and it was under this umbrella that Genghis Khan had tasted the bitter fruits of betrayal and rebellion. Temujin had become the universal ruler, the Genghis Khan, when he no longer organised his army by tribes or ethnicities but by melding them all into one regimented army, led by the best general for the job. Naimans, Turkmen, Mongols and others rubbed shoulders in the ranks; age-old enmities and blood feuds were diluted in a great host.

Genghis Khan's revolutionary vision shaped the whole of society for the advancement of the empire. Never before had a civilisation been created solely for the sake of conquest. Many had previously conquered, but their conquests had been because of success, not the main goal. If small, disorganised tribes in the past had terrified China, the Middle East and Europe, what would happen when a man with a vision and a highly disciplined fighting force rode onto the stage of the known world?

The first area of attack was a region so remote it barely gets mentioned in the history books, but Siberia is a gigantic area that accounts for over 75% of modern Russia and is about 30% larger than all continental Europe. If the Eurasian Steppe was sparsely populated, Siberia was even less so. Like the Eurasian Steppe, Siberia had its own nomadic tribes, although they had to adapt to more extreme weather conditions. However, during the brief Siberian summers, the region was a vast ocean of grassland which provided the nomads with an abundance of nutrition for stock (and even a brief farming season) and room to manoeuvre as well.

Led by Jochi (the first son of Genghis Khan), the Mongols attacked swiftly and decisively, and the local leaders quickly capitulated. This victory not only secured the Mongol homelands from any potential attack from the north, it also gave Genghis Khan access to their grain and fur trade as well as to their gold mines.

Next to be targeted were the nomadic tribes to the west of the Mongols. While on paper these people would know the tactics of the Mongols and fight in the same way, their armies were structured in the old way and proved to be no match for the new system that Genghis Khan had created. While in central Asia the Mongols swept into the kingdom of the Qara-Khitai, who quickly capitulated. This was the first sedentary population to submit to the Mongols, and in contrast to what was to come later, there was little violence.

Throughout this era both Uelun Ujin, Temujin's mother (who lived until 1210), and Börte, Temujin's first wife (who died a few years after him) acted as advisors. They were included in discussions about strategy and their opinions carried weight.

When Genghis Khan was on one of his many campaigns, these two women worked to keep the great Khan's immediate family running smoothly. Uelun Ujin obviously didn't want a repeat of the fratricide she had witnessed, and Börte, as the first wife, was the supreme authority amongst the ever-increasing harem that a steppe nomad leader would always acquire. Both of them did an excellent job and were highly regarded by their male peers.

So far, those conquered had been peripheral groups. None of them are well known or discussed in the history books, but it was sensible to secure the steppe regions bordering the Mongol heartlands so that they were now surrounded by vassal states. Now that they were strategically secure, Genghis Khan could focus on the real prize, China, which lay to the south.

The first place to feel the brunt of the Mongols' assault was territory that at the time was undergoing consolidation. Western Xia (now Xinjiang) was ethnically and culturally similar to the steppe nomads rather than to the Han Chinese and, at this time, separate to the Jin dynasty. The Jin depended on border walls (parts of which would later become the Great Wall of China), forts and walled cities. Genghis Khan had been in these lands and knew it would be better to delay any attack and go for easier pickings. Western Xia was largely flat and open and depended on the Gobi Desert (more than a million square kilometres of bleak terrain) to deter any aggressors. While merchants on the Silk Road may have, at times, crossed it, no army had. The logistics involved in trying to keep soldiers fed and watered as they marched through the desert were seemingly insurmountable. This natural barrier was a better deterrent than any man-made fortification.

Unfortunately for the population of Western Xia, Genghis Khan's forces were extremely motivated and well prepared, and after some raids into their lands which provoked little resistance, Genghis Khan personally led a full-scale invasion across the Gobi Desert into the Western Xia heartlands, making this one of the greatest flanking manoeuvres and surprise attacks in history.

It was this remarkable manoeuvre that led to the assumptions of some concerning the speed of the Mongolian forces. As previously noted, an army consisting solely of cavalry can obviously traverse territory faster than infantry, but not by a factor of ten. The Mongols did not have magic horses that were capable of galloping for hours on end. The attack on Western Xia was a lightning attack only in the sense that it came from a completely unexpected direction and managed to outflank the opposing forces. It had less to do with speed and more to do with imaginative leadership and logistics.

Men can't fight if they are starving or dying of thirst. Arrows cannot be loosed if there are none in stock. Much of world history, the rise and fall of powers and the successes in war can be traced back to effective logistics – or the lack of them. As the famous Chinese tactician Sun Tzu wrote in *The Art of War*, 'The line between disorder and order lies in logistics.' It is not an exciting topic, but key factors rarely are. Weather and sanitation have done more to upend the plans of great generals than daring raids or last-ditch cavalry charges.

Genghis Khan was ambitious and innovative, but to get an army across a desert he needed to be resourceful, imaginative and detailed in his planning. Medieval forces traditionally lived off the land and the Mongols were masters of that on the Eurasian Steppe, but a desert (hot or cold) has very few resources and certainly nothing approaching sufficient food and water for a large quantity of men and animals, an army.

Genghis Khan's logistical planning has not been preserved, so there are no details to discuss, but it would have meant meticulous attention to detail and the tight control of supplies along with cast-iron discipline in the army to avoid expending supplies prematurely. This aspect of his campaign in Western Xia is a vastly underappreciated but key component. Genghis Khan wasn't just brave, innovative and vicious, he was a master tactician as well.

Once past the Gobi, the Mongol invasion force faced no immediate opposition. It had arrived apparently from nowhere and made steady progress towards the capital, Zhongxing. However, a huge Xia army blocked his path, resulting in a stalemate that lasted for two months. These events show the effectiveness of the tactics Genghis Khan used to move through the Gobi Desert. If the Xia army was large enough and well organised enough to block the Mongols near the capital, had it known that the Mongols were coming at them from the desert, the stalemate might well have happened at the border where Genghis Khan might have been forced to use up precious manpower on the fringes of enemy territory. As it happened, Genghis Khan carried out the classic tactic of a feigned retreat. The Xia forces fell for the trap and were destroyed in a rain of arrows. Now Genghis Khan faced his greatest test yet: could he conduct a successful siege, something he had no experience of? While his horse-mounted archers were lethally mobile on a battlefield, they were all but useless against city walls.

Genghis Khan's first ploy was to use simple battering rams prepared for the purpose. However, any military engineer will tell you that while the gates were made of materials far weaker than those of a wall, they have a 'kill zone' in front of them, with overlapping fields of fire from all kinds of projectile weapons, including gunpowder (invented a few centuries earlier). After fruitless attempts to storm the capital, the Mongol leader decided he would 'brute force' the problem in a different way and had his army redirect the nearby Yellow River (whether this was to deprive the city of water or to flood it is a little hazy). It worked for a time, but either the Mongols were not good enough engineers or Xia forces sallied forth from the city and broke down the Mongol dams; in either case, Genghis Khan's plans were scuppered when the Mongol camp was flooded. Genghis Khan had tried everything he could reasonably have been expected to do in his first siege, but it had failed, and he was forced to retreat from the capital.

Nevertheless, at this point, apart from the walled city, Genghis Khan had complete control of the Xia lands, and with no chance of reforming his army, the Xia emperor was a prisoner behind the walls of his own capital. The emperor had no option but to surrender and broker a peace treaty. His daughter, Char, was married to Genghis Khan, and a year later in 1211, the Xia emperor was overthrown by his nephew, who may have rebelled against his uncle but didn't dare rebel against his Mongol overlords. Now, for the first time, the Mongols had a major area of urban development (rather than minor settlements in central Asia) under their command. The Mongol Hordes had had setbacks during this campaign. but the outcome was a glorious success.

The same year that Western Xia fell to the Mongols, a new Jin emperor came to the throne. The Jin Empire was in northern and eastern modern China and had recently been at war with Western Xia. They had diplomatic connections to the steppe nomads through Genghis Khan, who, when he was known as Temujin, had served in their ranks with his forces. Because of the often-strong connection between the Tatars and the Jin, the Jin claimed overlordship of the eastern Eurasian Steppe. In 1210, a delegation arrived at the court of Genghis Khan to proclaim the ascension of Wanyan Yongji to the Jin throne. This was not the usual declaration of a new emperor as was custom; now the ambassadors demanded the submission of the Mongols as a vassal state, recognising Jin authority over their lands. A decade earlier and they would have got their way, but now with the Mongols unified under one energetic and effective leader, the rules had changed. Some members of the Jin inner circle knew of these changing circumstances, and some Jin high court officials defected to the Mongols and urged Genghis Khan to attack the Jin lands. But Genghis Khan knew that a silver tongue could disguise less than noble intentions. He had been betrayed by his blood brother, so he was not going to take at face value the word of a few Chinese turncoats.

Upon the arrival of the Jin ambassador demanding submission, he allegedly turned to the south (where the Jin were located) and spat on the ground; then he mounted his horse and rode north, leaving the stunned envoy choking in his dust. Genghis Khan's court gave the Jin ambassador an offensive message for their emperor, one so insulting the envoy dared not repeat it upon his return to the Jin court. The Mongol leader's defiance of the Jin envoys was tantamount to a declaration of war between the Mongols and the Jin Empire.

Once again, Genghis Khan assembled a formidable army and marched south. This time, however, he did not cross a desert, but instead broke through parts of the Great Wall. At the Jin emperor's disposal were 800,000 infantry and 150,000 elite cavalries. The Jin forces easily dwarfed the Mongol army, but because they were spread over hundreds of miles of wall, at any one engagement the Mongols were likely to have the numerical advantage.

The Jin chancellor sent troops to reinforce the defences along the Great Wall in order to prevent the Mongols from advancing further south. But Genghis Khan had learned the importance of attacking on multiple fronts and from directions that were not expected. So he ordered his third son, Ögedei (who had long ago recovered from his earlier wounds) to attack the Jin western capital, Xijing (modern Shanxi) with a separate force; by doing this, he would divert and cut off any Jin reinforcements. This completely successful attack allowed Genghis Khan to advance with the main Mongol army to attack the Wusha Fortress and capture the Wuyue camp. When this was achieved, the Jin frontier forces were neutralised and the Mongols penetrated the Jin heartlands, meeting with little resistance. The Jin did not expect this line of attack and were completely outmanoeuvred and outfought by the Mongols, who followed the classic pattern of infantry in poor formations being picked off mercilessly by horse archers. It was a complete rout for the Jin: their general was killed and most of the Jin army was wiped out. The Mongols rested for a month before moving towards Yehuling.

The new Jin general realised that by spreading his forces he would be on the back foot in every battle, so he abandoned three cities to concentrate his men. He also used the mountainous terrain to his advantage, surmising correctly that the Mongols would not be able to use their cavalry effectively in such conditions. In every respect, this was a wise strategy, but unfortunately, the Jin hadn't counted on the morale, leadership and sheer tenacity of Genghis Khan. While it was true that the mountains forced the Mongols to dismount and fight on foot, their bows worked just as well dismounted. Add to this that the size of the Jin detachments was more of a liability than a strength in the narrow valleys and bottlenecks of the rugged terrain. The Mongols rained down arrows on the Jin forces and the infantry died in their thousands. A messenger was sent to talk peace terms with Genghis Khan, who managed to get the emissary to defect to the Mongols and give away the various locations of Jin forces.

The campaign was rapidly turning into a rout for the Jin forces. By August 1211, a Mongol general had managed to kill a Jin general and wipe out his entire army, and it was said that dead Jin troops were spread out for a hundred miles. After that, the chief Jin general rallied the remains of the forces in the region and did the smart thing by surrendering. The element of warfare that Genghis Khan had not mastered was siege warfare, so he concentrated his men at Huihe Fortress. Unfortunately, as the stragglers were still arriving, they came under attack by pursuing Mongol forces in October 1211. The Mongols might not have been able to break down the walls, but they could surround a fort. With thousands of men needing to be fed, the Jin could not last indefinitely, so they left the safety of their walls and fought Genghis Khan in what would be a three-day battle. Genghis Khan personally led 3,000 horsemen on a cavalry charge towards the enemy while the remaining Mongol forces followed behind. The entire Jin army was annihilated while the chief Jin general barely escaped alive. On his return to the imperial court, he was, unsurprisingly, replaced. He had not been incompetent; he was simply up against one of the most famous and most talented warlords in history.

After the final battle of 1211, the Jin Emperor Xingsheng was assassinated by a general in the central capital, Zhongdu (modern Beijing). He took control of the city and vigorously defended it during a four-year siege conducted by the Mongols. Here we see once again that during their early periods nomadic empires were highly effective in wiping out enemy forces on the field of battle, but when it came to sieges, their only tactic, due to the limitations of their technology, was to starve the enemy. In the surrounding lands, things were even more desperate for the Jin peasantry. As mentioned earlier, since the nomadic lifestyle precluded any concept of farming the Mongols had no idea what these peasants were doing grubbing around in the fields. They appeared to be useless and filthy so best to kill them, all of them. The death toll was not recorded, but it would have been in the hundreds of thousands.

Conditions in the capital became insufferable, and the residents of Zhongdu were forced to resort to cannibalism before they finally decided to surrender. The Mongols allowed the Jin dynasty to retain control of Zhongdu but forced them to pay an annual tribute of 500 men, 500 women and 3,000 horses (a reminder of how important the horse was to the Eurasian steppe nomad). In the summer of 1212, Emperor Xuanzong of the Jin Empire abandoned Zhongdu and relocated the capital to Bianjing to the south. This was seen, correctly, by the Mongols as a display of weakness, which encouraged them to continue their conquest of the Jin dynasty. The siege had undeniably slowed down Genghis Khan, but now, for the first time, two areas of China were vassal states to the Mongols and not the other way around. It was already apparent that Genghis Khan was the most successful steppe nomad chieftain of all time; but he wasn't done yet.

While the Mongol leader was in China, various clan members and advisors were left to run things in the heartlands. Not everyone was incorruptible and Qorchi was an example of the that rule. He had been appointed as a governor over some of the defeated tribes on the steppe. While he wasn't cruel or disloyal, it seems he liked the perks of the office (particularly his ever-expanding harem) to the neglect of his job and all the boring admin work involved in governing. This wouldn't have mattered except that his corruption caused the tribes to rise up in revolt after taking him prisoner and, perhaps a little more personally, killing General Boroqul, one of Genghis Khan's most trusted and effective generals.

Revolt was unacceptable. If people capitulated quickly and paid their tribute, they could expect to go about their everyday lives free of interference. But to rebel, to go back on your word, meant a swift and merciless punishment. The rebels rallied around Kuchlug, a Naiman prince (the last group to stand up to Genghis Khan) who managed to antagonise not only the Mongols but also the Muslims in the areas he now controlled.

Kuchlug was a strict Buddhist (apart from all the peace, love and forbearance) and was determined to forcibly convert the local Muslims. So Kuchlug succeeded in angering Genghis Khan (at a time he was ordering the massacres of hundreds of thousands of peasants in China) and creating real resentment in the local population, the only ones who could offer him support. It's safe to say that Kuchlug was not a military genius.

Jochi (Genghis Khan's eldest son) was sent to mop up the areas that were not under Kuchlug's rule and did so with all the efficiency of his stepfather ... I mean father. (No point in antagonising the ghost of Genghis Khan.) To lead the main attack, the Mongol leader selected Jebe, a man who had had a typical career in the Mongol army. He had originally fought against Temujin but came over to his side and remained loyal for the rest of his days. Jebe was reliable and knew exactly what Genghis Khan expected in retribution.

While the story is only going to end one way (the shattering of the enemy army and the decapitation of Kuchlug), it should be noted that Jebe was not a thoughtless brute. As his forces travelled through Kuchlug's territory, it was explained to the locals that the Mongols had a culture of religious tolerance. There was a mix of all the main religions plus traditional followers of shamanistic spiritualism in the Mongol Empire, so the locals could be good Muslims with nothing to fear. In every possible way, Kuchlug failed, and he paid the ultimate price, but what is interesting is that while the Mongols have a reputation for winning their military clashes, on this occasion they won the diplomatic argument, too.

Quashing the rebellion meant that the entire eastern part of the Silk Road was now under Mongol control. Consequently, so long as tolls were paid, there was no trouble, and Mongol patrols meant that banditry in the area faded away to virtually nothing. This was a boom time for trade along the Eurasian

Steppe, but from there the routes headed into the Khwarazmian Empire.

In the early 13th century, the Khwarazmian Empire was spread over most of central Asia. Parts of Georgia, most of Iran, Afghanistan, Kazakhstan, Uzbekistan, etc. were all included in this vast and powerful empire, which at the time was the largest Muslim empire in the world. It was about the same size as western Europe. It had started forming in the late 11th century at the time of the Seljuks, and the two empires shared a border further west. While it was huge, it was relatively young, just over a century old, and its real growth had happened within living memory. So, by the early 1200s, it had never been wealthier or more prosperous. What its ruler Shah Ala ad-Din Muhammed II couldn't have known at the time was that it was all about to disappear. The shah was hugely powerful and tremendously pampered. His fawning followers described him as the new Alexander the Great and he believed the hype.

The only vexation was his problem neighbour, Genghis Khan. The bone of contention was the merchant caravans along the Silk Road. It seems the governor of the Khwarazmian territories that bordered the Mongol Empire feared that a fifth column might be lurking amongst the peripatetic merchants and used this to justify an attack on a caravan where everyone was killed. The Mongols sent emissaries to see what had happened and they were also killed. At that point Shah Ala ad-Din Muhammed II sealed his fate. The meaning of the saying 'don't shoot the messenger' is obvious, but it also implies that even messengers from enemy territories should be allowed to pass unmolested, as the communication was needed. It was an outrage that could not go unpunished, and the Mongols were the masters of such unambiguous acts of violence.

In 1219, Genghis Khan sent an army of at least 150,000 (the whole of western Europe at this time would have had difficulty scraping together an army of that size) and descended on the Khwarazmian Empire like the hounds of hell. When the city of Urgench had the audacity to hold out against the Mongols, they were eventually punished with one of the worst massacres in human history.

It is now worth pausing to take a look at the cruel logic of Mongol massacres. Genghis Khan's enormous army of 150,000 was composed mainly of men of military age from the sparsely populated steppe. They were not just a military force, they were Genghis Khan's people. As the steppe was so vast it was vital that even this enormous army not be spread too thinly. If, for instance, he needed 5,000 men to keep a city loyal and there were, say, 15 sites that needed this kind of oversight, it would mean that half his army would be deployed to supervise already conquered territories. But if the Mongols massacred the entire population of a rebellious city, news of the atrocity quickly spread so that when the Mongols arrived at the next city, the gates were flung open and everyone capitulated. The tactic was incredibly cold and brutal, but the logic was inescapable.

One after another, the cities of the empire fell to the Mongols. Ala ad-Din found out the hard way that he was no Alexander the Great and spent the last few months of his life being chased across Asia by Mongol scouts led by Genghis Khan's stalwarts Jebe and Subutai. They never quite got to him, but the once-great shah died of dysentery, a broken man, on an island in the Caspian Sea. His only remaining possession was his cloak, in which he was buried by his handful of loyal followers. He went from being one of the richest, most powerful men on the planet to a deposed and destitute ruler, who saw his empire go up in flames. The Mongols did their best to erase him (and his empire) from history, which is why there are no surviving images and why you've probably never heard of him. The Persian chronicles of the time put the death toll at a little over 5 million. As usual, modern historians take issue with the veracity of such statements, and more sober assessments put the death toll at a likely 1.25 million. Either way, the sheer ruthlessness of the Mongol military machine was breathtaking, and the slaughter was on a scale never before seen in human history.

Some historians challenge the perception that Genghis Khan was a great military leader as some of the Mongols' greatest achievements were not carried out by him. I think that is missing the point. Very rarely does a leader fight in every battle in a war. In fact, one of the signs of a great leader is the ability to delegate and find the right people to carry out the necessary roles. In that respect Genghis Khan was one of the best, and it was during the attack on the Khwarazmian Empire and the hunt for the shah that Jebe and Subutai conducted one of the greatest campaigns in military history, It was known as the Great Raid and it took place from 1220-1223.

To understand more about this campaign, we need to be aware of the distances. From the central Mongol heartlands and the emerging capital of Karakorum all the way to the edges of the Khwarazmian Empire was about 2,000 miles. The initial attack on the empire was a virtually unprecedented manoeuvre for one campaigning season, and it is facts like this that lead to phrases like 'the Mongols swept across central Asia'. Well, they travelled unopposed because they were in friendly territory, but again, they didn't have winged horses that could travel at the speed of motorbikes. This was simply steppe nomad people doing what they had been doing for a thousand years, heading in a specific direction, living off the steppe, plus raiding once they were in enemy territory. But when the Great Raid is discussed, it should be remembered that about two-thirds of the distance travelled was undertaken just to position themselves to attack the Khwarazmian Empire.

A look at a map of Jebe and Subutai's journey as they hunted down Muhammed II, who was obviously heading away from the Mongol forces, makes it apparent that the route forced the two Mongol generals ever further west. By the time they reached the southern shores of the Caspian Sea, having completed their mission, another 700 miles can be added to their travels. Therefore, while the rest of the raid was to take them into uncharted territory (from their perspective), they had done most of the journey before even starting their pursuit of the shah. For this campaign the Mongols numbered around 20,000, a reconnaissance in force from their perspective, but a major army when compared to the forces they would face.

Fortunately for the Middle East in 1222, the two generals skirted along the northern border of what is modern Iraq and headed into the Caucasus. The first country they attacked was Georgia, a nation that thus far had been spared any raids by the Eurasian Steppe peoples. King George IV of Georgia thought that the Mongols might be Christian allies when Subutai marched some of his forces in front of a series of Georgians holding crosses, but it was just a ruse meant either to lull the Georgians into a false sense of security or to assess the size of the forces they faced. A pitched battle quickly followed.

The Georgians fought in the European manner, with infantry and heavy cavalry (knights). As mentioned in the chapter on the Seljuk Turks facing the First Crusade, if the heavy cavalry had been able to charge into the Mongols the invaders would have been badly mauled, and the Mongols were a long way from their homelands and any possibility of reinforcements. But it was here that Jebe and Subutai showed why Genghis Khan had chosen them, and even though they were in unfamiliar lands, up against a never-before-seen enemy, they conducted a masterclass in Eurasian Steppe nomad tactics. They lured the knights out with a classic feigned retreat, and once they were separated from the main army, they surrounded them and made short work of them with a blizzard of arrows. Then they turned to the infantry, which had no chance to outmanoeuvre or outrun the light Mongol cavalry. They were also annihilated.

The Mongols would go on to plunder Georgia as they passed through the shattered kingdom. The Georgians hastily pulled together another army, but it was also destroyed. When bad weather arrived, the Mongols wintered in Dagestan (the modern-day part of Russia in the Caucasus), where they were reliant on local guides who showed the Mongols nothing but contempt and led the Mongol army through the most difficult terrain in the most arduous passes. What enemy armies failed to do, mother nature compensated for. The troops were exhausted and with winter weather worsening, the Mongols had no option but to halt. This pause allowed the neighbouring territories to create alliances as old enemies united against this new and extremely dangerous threat.

Now the Alans, Rus and even Kipchaks were allied. All were other branches of the Eurasian Steppe family and, consequently, used the same bows, rode the same horses and used the same tactics as the Mongols. Jebe and Subutai pushed on along the northern coast into the Crimea, where they met another branch of their steppe family, the Crimean Tatars. From there, they entered Novgorod, the Slavic state which would eventually evolve into Belarus, Ukraine and western Russia. There they raided around the outskirts of Kyiv before finally heading east. When Mongol ambassadors were sent to the Prince of Kyiv, they were executed. (It was never a good idea to execute Mongol emissaries, as the prince would discover.)

It was around this time that the Mongols met the great coalition of forces designed to wipe out this menace from the East. Some of the forces opened dialogues and critically engaged the Mongols separately. Had the coalition stuck together, they might have overwhelmed the Mongols, but by means of clever diplomacy on the part of Subutai, the Mongols fought and beat each one in turn, with enough time to recover in between clashes.

In May of 1223, the coalition caught up with the Mongols and the battle of Kalka River followed. The numbers are not known, but as the Mongols started with 20,000 men in 1221, it had to be fewer by then. The allied forces outnumbered them exponentially – 60,000 would seem a reasonable guess. Despite the river, the Mongols still had room to rush towards the enemy and then fall back in a classic feigned retreat. It was by means of these push/pull tactics that the Mongols separated the Rus forces from the rest and destroyed them – but not without a major sacrifice. During this period of manoeuvre, Subutai had to decide whether to defend his rear guard and face potentially overwhelming odds or sacrifice the rear guard to give the rest of the army time to reposition and carry out a clean attack on the now separated Rus force.

Subutai chose the latter, which must have been difficult for him, because Jebe was leading the rear guard. It was wiped out and its general was killed. Now Subutai had all the space and time he needed to launch a counterattack. What happened next was novel. He would charge his forces at the enemy, pouring volley after volley of arrows into the enemy ranks as they went. Sometimes these surges forwards would be real charges into the enemy ranks, but at other times, just before contact, the Mongol cavalry would wheel around and head back. It was a type of choreography never before seen by the coalition forces, and they simply didn't know whether they should hold rigid formations to resist the physical charges, making them an easy target for archers, or separate and reduce casualties from missiles but be more vulnerable to a frontal assault. Only an army as disciplined, as well trained and as well led as the Mongols in the 1200s could conduct such complex tactics in the chaos of a battlefield.

While the loss of Jebe was a bitter blow to the Mongols, their casualties were light overall, and most importantly, the coalition was annihilated. And the Prince of Kyiv who killed the ambassadors? Dead amongst piles of his own troops. The peoples of the West had thrown everything they had at the Mongols and nothing had worked. Then, most terrifyingly of all, they disappeared over the horizon to the east, leaving nothing but death and destruction in their wake. Subutai successfully brought the largely intact army back to the Mongol heartlands, having made a roughly 6,000-mile round trip and having vanquished every foe he had faced. This was a unique achievement in history. Even in the modern world, with trucks, trains and aircraft, no other military force has carried out such an audacious reconnaissance in force.

Meanwhile, after shattering the Khwarazmian Empire, Genghis Khan found that while it was no longer a threat, it wasn't falling into line. Consequently (and cunningly), he simply moved the borders of his territory further east. The point had been made; there was no need to overextend, particularly in a land that he had made a charnel house. This disengagement in central Asia allowed him to refocus on the much richer prize of China.

By returning to central Asia, the Mongols had given the Jin and the Western Xia the opportunity to rebuild their forces against an inevitable second wave of invasion. In 1222, that invasion began with Genghis Khan (now at least in his 60s) leading a mighty force that would fight both the Jin and the Western Xia. A few years into the campaign Subutai returned to the side of his leader, now a man who had seen Kyiv was fighting in areas south of Beijing.

Genghis Khan was not necessarily always looking for battle and plunder. As many times as he fought, he would also send out envoys to see if there was a possible diplomatic solution. When negotiations took place, they were not a one-way street of dictation or intimidation. The Mongols knew they had a much smaller population compared to China, but wherever there was resistance the violence inflicted was terrible. Nobody will ever know the number of deaths caused by the Mongol Empire, but if modern historians estimate 1.25 million dead in the invasion of the Khwarazmian Empire, which happened over roughly a year, then it is likely a similar number, if not more, would apply to China, if only because the Mongols were in China for longer. This has led to some very strange modern interpretations of these horrifically violent events. In 2020, the Carnegie Institution for Science's Department of Global Energy published a paper which extrapolated that so many had died, the deaths might well have scrubbed as much as 700 million tonnes of carbon from the atmosphere by allowing forests to regrow on previously populated and cultivated land. This led to Genghis Khan being dubbed a 'green ruler'. While this may raise a wry smile on the face of the modern reader, the true colour of Genghis Khan's rule was red, and with 2 or 3 million (maybe more) dead as a result of his campaigns, the fact that greenhouse emissions declined would have been cold comfort.

The campaigning went on, cities fell, civilians were slaughtered, Jin and Xia armies were crushed. Nothing could stop the Mongols. In the winter of 1227, Genghis Khan was injured in a fall from his horse, and as he was still on campaign, his injuries did not have time to heal. Despite his fading health, the great leader encouraged his men to push on until they were once again at the walls of Zhongxing, the capital of the Western Xia. He was determined to capture the one city that had eluded him before he returned home to recover. But as the siege wore on, his health deteriorated, and in August of 1227, Genghis Khan died. His death was kept secret from the Xia authorities and from his troops. The siege must continue; it was what he wanted. The city did indeed fall the following month, and at that point it was revealed to the Mongol army that their beloved Genghis Khan was dead.

The cold, harsh logic of the multiple massacres inflicted on civilian populations was, to use a modern phrase, nothing personal, it was just business. But now Genghis Khan was dead, and he had died while the city before them resisted. What happened next was nothing like the usual massacres carried out by Mongol forces; this time it *was* personal. This time it was revenge. The brutality inflicted on the people and buildings of Zhongxing was shocking, even in comparison to the violent excesses already described. What happened at Zhongxing showed what the Mongols could do if they were angry. On every other occasion, if I have written of an obscure location, I have put in brackets where it was in terms of a modern-day country, or I have given the old name for a city that exists today. Not so with Zhongxing. The aftermath of this defeat resulted in an unsurpassed orgy of death and destruction. While the bodies of the dead were piled high, there were also references to cruelty and torture. The city itself was razed. Nothing was left to remember the insolence of these people as the great Genghis Khan was dying in his yurt outside its walls. These people were made to feel the pain of the mourning army in what was one of the most horrific events in world history.

But no amount of bloodshed and destruction could change the fact that Genghis Khan was dead. The entire Mongol army left Western Xia, and the warriors became pall bearers on one of the largest and longest funeral ever. The death of Genghis Khan was so important it has been seared into the cultures of many, accompanied by many myths. There are for example other accounts of how the great Mongol leader died. One chronicle reports Genghis Khan's death by lightning – the scourge of God, scourged by God. Another tale tells of the Xia princess betrothed to Genghis Khan, who, on their wedding night killed him by castration. The reality is that by 1227, Temujin was an old man, possibly in his 70s, and yet he was still on campaign, a hard life even for a man half his age. The fact that he had taken a fall from his horse must be true, as it is embarrassing for someone who was virtually born in the saddle. And while, technically, nobody dies of old age, for a man who had lived a life that hard, it was a minor miracle that he lived to such a ripe old age.

Then there is the matter of his burial. Genghis Khan was the first great khan of an empire that would continue to grow for generations, so the tomb would have to be suitably impressive. It has never been found. Like Attila, the legends that swirl around the burial and the attempts to keep the location safe are known to be exaggerations. Taking away the more fanciful stories (but with some shocking facts yet to come), Genghis Khan was buried on or near the sacred Burkhan Khaldun peak in the Khentii Mountains. This was in his ancestral heartlands and was a site he had already marked out for his burial. The reason for the vagueness of the location is that the mountain itself became a prohibited zone and was off-limits to all but his elite guard. The exact location was still known a couple of years later when one of his sons ascended to the throne in 1229, and the grave was honoured with three days of offerings, and not just animals; thirty maidens were also sacrificed. This was a rare example of human sacrifice in Mongol funerals, but compared to the millions of deaths Genghis Khan had ordered in his lifetime, this was nothing.

His burial site remains a mystery, but he is everywhere in Mongolia today. The airport in the modern capital city of Ulaanbaatar is named after him. In 2008, there was a giant 40-metre-tall statue of him erected as a mausoleum (without the body). His stern face is printed on the larger notes of the Mongolian currency. His alleged birthday is also the first day of winter and a national holiday in Mongolia. Brands of vodka are named after him. He is a world-famous figure, a name of which the modern country of Mongolia is incredibly proud.

Meanwhile, after Genghis Khan's unanticipated death, the question of who would rule the Mongols came next. There were four sons: Jochi, Chagatai, Ögedei and Tolui. This was a new empire and there were no rules or precedents. It was obvious that Chagatai would never let Jochi (the eldest but the illegitimate one) become ruler. Jochi and Tolui were the better generals, but they were regarded as brash, and there were concerns that Tolui's principal wife was a Nestorian Christian and might have had some missionary zeal, anathema to the Mongol concept of religious tolerance for all the faiths under their authority. So Ögedei became the frontrunner. He was known for his heavy drinking, and while he had fought on multiple campaigns (even getting wounded in one battle), he wasn't in the same league as the other sons. Saying that, he came with none of the baggage of some of his brothers, and most importantly, he was well liked by everyone. He also had at his disposal excellent generals, so in 1229, Ögedei became the second great khan. It was Tolui, however, who enshrined the procedures for succession, critically including that all military operations must be halted as all military leaders must return to the Mongol homelands to declare the new Mongol khan.

So, Temujin the man underwent an apotheosis from a real human being, who had to endure all manner of challenges and setbacks, to the legendary Genghis Khan, universal ruler, founder of a mighty empire and unifier of the Mongol clans. A generation later the following quote was attributed to him by the Muslim scholar Ala-ad-Din Ata-Malik Juvaini in his History of the World Conqueror. Whether he really said it or not, it perfectly encapsulates his self-confidence and the knowledge of the fear he had instilled in the hearts of the neighbouring rulers:

O people, know that you have committed great sins, and that the great ones among you have committed these sins. If you ask me what proof I have for these words, I say it is because I am the punishment of God. If you had not committed great sins, God would not have sent a punishment like me upon you.

8

THE MONGOLS AFTER
GENGHIS KHAN

With Ögedei now installed as undisputed ruler in 1229, the Mongols could once again go about their business of conquest. Ögedei may have become the new great khan, but his brothers had been given vast areas to rule over in the horde system, where each area was tied to a family member and each horde was named after a colour, so in this case there was the White Horde and the Golden Horde. These may seem exotic, but strip away all the latent orientalism, and the best way to think of a horde overlord is as the equivalent of a prince or governor of a territory. Although ultimately loyal to the great khan, day-to-day they were autonomous rulers, raising taxes, hearing legal cases (or at least their courts were), and many of these men were still going on campaign.

While Genghis Khan the man was irreplaceable, he had created an incredibly positive legacy for his successor. Military training, effectiveness and leadership were at an all-time high. All areas of the empire continued to be efficiently managed, which meant that while the title on the door of the office had changed, it was still business as usual.

Chormaqan was a great general who had risen through the ranks under Genghis Khan. Under orders issued by Ögedei, he was sent west where his goal was to secure modern-day Afghanistan and Iran and head towards the Caspian Sea. In other words, he was to return to the smouldering remains of the Khwarazmian Empire and ensure everyone stayed in line. As both the Soviet Union in the late 20th century and NATO forces in the early 21st century discovered, Afghanistan can be a tough nut to crack. There is a local saying, 'Afghanistan is easy to enter but hard to leave.' While this has been the case for western powers (starting with the British Empire in the 19th century), it was not the case in earlier times. Alexander conquered and co-opted the locals in the space of one campaigning season.

It was the same for Chormaqan. He worked his way through the arid plains and mountainous foothills with iron discipline, and the locals fell into place. From there he continued through the Eurasian Steppe, moving into Iran and heading towards the Caspian Sea. The Mongols had been here before and had conducted horrific massacres. Nobody dared resist. Genghis Khan's plan to establish the Mongols as a merciless force worked and their reputation preceded them. There were a few fights, but they were little more than skirmishes. After all, this Mongol army had shattered the army of the Khwarazmian Empire in its prime. What chance did the survivors have now? Muhammed II was dead, and his successor was deposed with little fuss in 1231 after the few remaining cities that had not declared their loyalty fell. The Mongol Empire, with minimal effort and bloodshed, had expanded even further and was now firmly in control of Asia all the way to the Caspian Sea.

Meanwhile in Jin China, things started badly for the Mongols. Their first invasion in 1229 was met by a well-organised Jin defence force. When the Mongols attempted to besiege the city of Qingyang (central China), they were surprised by an army in the field (the Mongols normally had scouting parties carrying out reconnaissance in the hinterland, so why they hadn't picked up on the Chinese force is unknown). The Jin did all the things the Mongols would normally do: they outflanked them and attacked with elite cavalry. The siege was broken and the Mongols were forced to retreat. Ögedei was furious. He dismissed the general and brought back Subutai to run the conquest of the Jin Empire, but Subutai didn't return in time to take control of the 1230 offensive, and this, too, was a Mongol defeat. Then in 1231, Subutai and Tolui (the fourth son of Genghis Khan and Ögedei's brother) met the Jin at the Battle of Daohuigu. The Jin forces had carried out a scorched earth policy to ensure the large Mongol army could not live off the land. This gave them fewer options as they moved forwards and had to rely on a logistical line stretching back to their conquered territories. When the Mongols met the Jin army, the Jin were in the fortified Tong Pass. At this point the Mongols faced a siege, which was not their preferred way to wage war. Initially, Subutai planned to circumvent the Jin forces entirely, but when they were attacked by a second, smaller army already in the field, the Mongols faced threats from one army in a defensive position and another army attempting to outflank them. Tolui and Subutai were experienced enough to know that they had been outmanoeuvred. When battle was engaged the Mongols had no option but to retreat and head back through areas already denuded of supplies. The Mongols suffered heavy casualties and now had suffered three defeats in as many years. The Jin were fighting back.

The first failure could be blamed on poor leadership, but with generals such as Subutai and Tolui in charge, that argument evaporated. Was this a sign that the divine power Genghis Khan had instilled in his people had disappeared with him, and with that, their chances of success had also disappeared? Or might it have been something a little less prosaic, that the Jin had learned through bitter experience how to counter Mongol tactics? While this change in the Mongol fortunes on the battlefield was not due to the disappearance of divine backing, it is fair to say that the Jin had learned and adapted after years of experience, but they weren't infallible either. In 1231, the Mongols attacked again and finally took the regional capital, which had been the lynchpin of the Jin defence to the north of their remaining lands.

The Mongols now moved quickly to the next major city. When they appeared with no warning, the garrison panicked and fled to Henan Province to the southeast, abandoning the civil population in the process. Tolui and Subutai, with their superior movement and discipline, decided to use a three-pronged attack on the Jin in the East; this was near the realm of the Song, the other dynasty ruling part of China at the time. The Mongols could only deal with one power at a time, so for the moment, the Song were largely ignored.

The Jin capital was Kaifeng and the idea was to attack it from north, east and west. The western force was under Tolui, who headed furthest south before homing in on the capital. When Jin scouts alerted their general to the Mongol movements, he led a colossal army of 200,000 to annihilate Tolui's forces. It has been said that Chinese and Russian histories are the same as everyone else's, only a lot more people die. This is an example. The equivalent English ruler at this time would have been Henry III, and he would have been impressed by a force of 12,000. That any Chinese dynasty could call to arms so many soldiers is a testament to the richness and organisation of the Jin. However, the Mongols had their own scouts, and realising the Jin had prepared an ambush, Tolui sent a small force along with a baggage train as a juicy target, only to wheel his main force around and to the south, allowing him to attack the Jin from an unexpected direction and achieve complete surprise. Despite the fact he had far fewer men, it was an intelligent and well-earned victory.

By the time Ögedei arrived with reinforcements, territory near some of the major cities in the Jin regions had been conquered, scoured and claimed. More Jin attacks came, but the momentum was with the Mongols once again, and soon they were back at Kaifeng, where Ögedei and Tolui fell ill. Ögedei just needed time to recuperate and, assuming his brother would also recover, left before Tolui's death to continue oversight of the Kaifeng siege. It is to Ögedei's credit that when it came to delegation, he knew his limitations and allowed more successful generals to show him what they were capable of. For example, by the time of his death in 1248, Subutai had been on 20 campaigns and won 65 pitched battles, a record that is hard to rival.

By this time the Jin were exhausted from fighting the Mongols, so the Jin emperor reached out to his bitter rival, the Song emperor, to ask for supplies, stating correctly that if the Jin Empire fell, the Mongols would turn their military might on the so-far-unaffected Song. The Song refused. The Mongols had not threatened them, and the enmity between the Jin and the Song was a long and bitter one. This would not be the first time that old rivalries blinded leaders to the greater, newer Mongol threat.

The Mongol siege of Kaifeng lasted for just over a year. There were attempts at peace, but it didn't help that some Jin luminaries assassinated the Mongol emissaries. For the population of Kaifeng, the siege became a nightmare. On the other side of the walls lurked an ever-present and inescapable danger, but on the inside, there were three other threats just as lethal: First, plague broke out (due to poor sanitary conditions, sieges often resulted in pestilence). Then as the weeks wore on, the people began to starve. No matter how high the walls or how brave the defenders, hunger was inescapable. Finally, because the people began to complain, the authorities feared a fifth column and some people were executed as traitors.

Eventually, the gates were opened. The emperor managed to slink away, and the remaining forces knew there was no point in prolonging the inevitable. On this occasion, while the Mongols did plunder the city, there was no wholesale slaughter. By now the Song had created a treaty with the Mongols so favourable that Song Chinese forces were marching with the Mongols to finish off the Jin.

In 1234, the last great city of the Jin, Caizhou, was under siege. The emperor, knowing his fate was sealed but not wanting to be remembered as the last emperor of the Jin, forced his title on to a loyal but unwilling general. Then the old emperor committed suicide and the new one let in the Mongol/Song forces, bringing to an end the Jin dynasty, which had lasted for more than a century. Ögedei could now claim new conquests that his father hadn't been able to achieve. The campaign had started poorly, but once the initial setbacks had been absorbed, the Mongols quickly and ruthlessly got on with the job. The Song dynasty remained, making it the last powerbase in China that was not Mongol.

Because of Subitai's Great Raid, the Mongols were aware of Georgia, which had faced the wrath of the Mongols once before but had not yet been conquered. It was a sign of Ögedei's resources and tenacity that even while the conquest of the Jin was being conducted in 1232, another army was sent to Georgia and Armenia and modern western Russia to make them vassal states. The fighting was over by 1235, although there would be rebellions later in the 1230s. The problem was that these countries were so far away and so relatively poor compared to the closer and vastly wealthier China (or even the Middle East) that it wasn't worth having Mongol forces remain in the area. The following history of Mongol activity in these two countries was cyclical. Each time the Mongols arrived, they defeated the locals and conducted various acts of punitive revenge, which stoked resentment, which led to rebellion, which led to the eventual return of the Mongol forces and punishment.

Somewhere in all this fighting, a tiny village centred around a religious community was burned to the ground. Its name was Moscow. It was rebuilt and used the Mongol trade network to turn itself into a trading hub, always making sure to pay tribute to the Mongol overlords. This worked well for a few generations until the now thriving community was once again burnt to ashes by the Mongols in 1293. The third foundation of Moscow was the first to have rudimentary earth and wood walls, for obvious reasons.

By now there was a third wave of attacks going on simultaneously with Jin China and Georgia/Armenia. Ögedei was aware that under his father's rule the Koreans had killed a Mongol envoy, and he was planning revenge. So, in 1231 (the same time as the Caucasus campaign and the China campaign were being conducted), Mongol forces invaded Korea from the north.

But before we get to Korea, let's pause to consider the number of dead Mongol ambassadors. Because communication is vital in dire circumstances, it was the custom to allow emissaries to go about their business unmolested. Even if harsh words were exchanged, ambassadors were only rarely the victims of violence. An exception to this were the Spartans who killed the Persian ambassador simply to antagonise the Persians, and Vlad III (the Impaler) who nailed their turbans to the heads of Ottoman messengers in order to provoke Mehmed II. The Mongols were reviled, which led to a much higher than average mortality rate among their emissaries, but at the same time, to provoke a culture with such a violent reputation was foolish and usually a sign of arrogance. Think of Muhammed II of the Khwarazmian Empire who believed in his own infallibility and assumed the irksome Mongol troublemakers wouldn't dare attack. These leaders were always proved wrong and always regretted their actions.

The Mongol General Saritai crossed the Yalu River, the northern border of the Kingdom of Korea, in the summer of 1231. The Mongols were joined by the Korean General Hong Bok-won, who could spot a winner. The Koreans mobilised a massive infantry army, which was exactly the wrong army to field against the Mongols, and every time they met on the battlefield they were surrounded and annihilated. But there was one thing infantry can do that the Mongols always had difficulty with, they could garrison a fortified city. So, the Mongols laid siege to the city of Kuju but were forced to break it off when the Korean king, having learned nothing from previous battles, raised a colossal infantry army of slaves (a reminder that slavery was not just a European creation). These slaves were forced to fight to the death, no retreat, no surrender. But they were less well equipped and organised than the huge infantry armies the Mongols had already defeated.

With the Korean king running out of men and the fall of the capital inevitable, he sued for peace and Korea became a vassal state. The Mongols exacted a heavy price for the Korean insolence that had included killing the Mongol ambassadors. Ögedei demanded a payment of 10,000 otter skins, 20,000 horses, 10,000 bolts of silk and clothing for 1,000,000 soldiers – oh, and all children and craftsmen would become Mongol slaves. Business was concluded by the end of 1231 when Saritai left 72 Mongol administrators stationed in various cities to ensure that the Korean king kept to the terms. Like those in the Caucasus, there were a number of revolts against Mongol rule. These were met with the kind of efficient brutality you would expect, and by the 1270s Korea had been brought to heel. As by this time the Mongols were also the Yuan Emperors of China, Korea would remain a Chinese vassal state for generations.

A few years later, Ögedei sent his eldest son to raid Song territory. The gains were considerable, and the death and destruction inflicted on the last remaining Chinese dynasty was terrible. But like the Jin, Song resources were so vast as to be able to absorb the initial shock. Having made their point, the Mongols left, but Ögedei had lost a son in battle in the process. Thanks to his harem there were others.

For the first time in this book (chronologically rather by chapters) we now have one of the steppe nomad tribes ordering the construction not of a military structure, but of a palace. By 1235 Karakorum was finished, but in comparison Westminster Abby or a palace in the Khwarazmian Empire, this building was on another scale. Starting at the outer edges was a mighty earthen wall surrounding many square miles of land. This contained a fort, lakes, hunting grounds and housing for the various peoples of his empire. The Mongols even constructed places of worship to cater for Confucian, Buddhist, Muslim, Taoist and Christian followers. It was said to be paradise on earth and is thought to be the inspiration for the legend of Xanadu. For the first time the Mongols were acting like emperors, not just warlords.

During this period of construction, the Mongols were also conducting raids into India; only the Delhi sultanate had even more resources than the Song emperor. So, once again, the Mongols proved a point with their raiding, but there were no lasting peace treaties or even any Mongol presence south of the Himalayas. That said, Ögedei had expanded the empire in every direction. There may have been doubts about his military prowess at the start of his reign, but he had proved to be a highly competent leader who had extended an already huge empire – and he had learned of more civilisations far to the west. In 1241, the Mongols invaded Europe.

There is a well-known and wonderful medieval legend about a ruler called Prester John. Christians in the West were vaguely aware of the fact that some early Christians (most notably St Thomas) went to the East to spread Christianity, and that there may have been some erratic communications between Nestorian Christians (an ancient sect of Christianity in Asia) and fellow Christians in Europe. These murky reports appeared to confirm that while the East was clearly full of magical beasts and men with the heads of dogs (a genuinely held medieval belief), in the midst of all that was fantastical and alien, the word of Christ was present, too.

The legend of Prester John began in the 12th century and became ever more embellished as time went on. He was a king and a priest; he was as wise and as wealthy as Solomon; his kingdom was vast. Of course, no legend is complete without fabulous magical objects, and Prester John reputedly had a mirror that allowed him to gaze on any part of his kingdom (an early version of CCTV) and, naturally, a fountain of youth, which would explain his remarkable longevity.

Prester John became the embodiment of wish fulfilment: everything wrong with Europe was fixed in the tale of this legendary ruler. It didn't help that a supposed letter from him circulated throughout Europe, adding hope that he would come to the aid of the Holy Land. Medieval maps were never that accurate at the best of times, but many that show Asia also show Prester John (as well as dragons). In the medieval mind, he was as real and as mysterious as India. In fact, it might well have been the Crusades that sparked these tales in the first place. Why didn't Prester John beat Saladin or save Jerusalem prior to the Third Crusade in the 1180s? There was always an explanation for his failure to appear, for instance an inconvenient flood was said to have stopped him from crossing a key river to the Holy Land, but everyone had it on reliable authority that he wanted to help and that he was coming.

The humiliating defeat and incarceration of the Fifth Crusade in Egypt added fuel to the fire. On his return from captivity, the Bishop of Acre came with good news: King David of India, the son or grandson of Prester John, (the exact relation to Prester John wasn't clear, but it was definitely a direct Christian relative and, therefore, a natural ally) was raising an army. The bishop was basing his information on persistent rumours about the massive defeats of huge and previously unknown Muslim kingdoms in the Far East. They weren't being attacked by any known European Christian force, so it had to be Prester John, or in this case, his grandson. Someone was killing Muslims, and surely, the enemy of my enemy is my friend.

Prester John revealed himself to Christian Europe not in the Middle East, but in Europe in the year 1241. The reports described above were the distorted echoes of Mongol conquests in Asia. As we have already seen, the Khwarazmian Empire, a major Muslim power, had been humbled not by Christians with a leader like Prester John, but by the shamanistic khans of the Temujin dynasty. Europe knew nothing about the Mongols, and even if it had, the continent was completely disunited, with its kings vying for power with each other, the Papacy and other petty powers. If mighty powers like the Jin Dynasty couldn't stop them in the 13th century, what chance did France have? Seen from the perspective of the Mongols, Europe was poorer than either Asia or the Middle East, but it had been ordained that the Mongols were to rule the world, so it was time to conquer Europe.

If Russia and Ukraine are considered parts of Europe (which they should be) then the Mongols had been in Europe for about twenty years, or a generation. But as this was very much on the fringes there was nothing for the scribes in western Europe to record. Therefore, the attacks in April 1241 came as one of the biggest surprises in history (it's comparable with the conquistadors arriving in Mexico) when the Mongols once again proved their martial organisation by conducting two surprise attacks in a pincer movement, with each strike at the opposite end of a 500-mile front – and they did this within days of each other.

The first major clash was the Battle of Liegnitz (Legnica) in modern southwestern Poland on 9 April 1241. The Europeans should have known something was coming. As the Mongols expanded westward, they had displaced the Cumans, a nomadic and ethnically Turkic race, in a manner that would have been familiar to the Huns or Avars. But as those conquests had happened centuries earlier, there was no contemporary understanding that the Cumans were being displaced by a more aggressive power from the East. The reason the Cumans had arrived in Hungary was the same as that for earlier steppe nomads: they were fleeing stronger, more aggressive tribes. Their arrival in Hungary marked the end of their journey across thousands of miles of steppe grassland and was the natural direction for them to take. It is also likely that when they arrived in the kingdom, they recognised similarities with their own culture. But the Mongol attack on Poland was a diversion from the main goal, which was the invasion of Hungary. The Mongols had thought to deter Hungary's neighbour in case it decided to come to Hungary's aid. This turned out to be unnecessary, as Europe was not well organised, nor was one country automatically going to come to the aid of another.

The Mongols started in Poland by burning the town of Sandomierz. After that there was the minor Battle of Tursko, where it seems the Poles did well with their heavy cavalry but got distracted looting the Mongol baggage train. The Poles fell out of formation and were wiped out by the Mongols who had likely conducted a feigned retreat to separate them from the rest of the army. This was followed a few days later by the Mongol annihilation of another small Polish army at Chmielnik. The Mongols were always heading west, and when they came to Kraków they burned it to the ground. To this day, every day at St Mary's church in Kraków, there is a ceremony in which a bugler plays a traditional call from a Polish trumpet but stops abruptly mid-tune. The story goes that in 1241 the bugler in the belfry of the church spied the advancing Mongols and tried to warn the population with his call, only to be cut short when a Mongol arrow tore out his throat and killed him. There is no evidence for this happening in 1241, but it is a poignant reminder of the death and destruction inflicted by this invading army remembered more than 750 years later.

When the Mongols next came to Wrocław (Breslau) they realised they would have to conduct a siege, which as we have seen was not a Mongol strong point. It also meant that as a besieging army they were vulnerable to attack from the rear. As their purpose was to seek out enemy forces in the field and neutralise them, they did not attack Wrocław, allowing the occupants to live another day. Besides, Mongol scouts had found the allied army of Henry II of Silesia, the main force in the area. If anything could stop the Mongols, it would be this coalition force of German princes, Polish nobility and the cream of chivalry, the Teutonic Knights. Like their brethren the Hospitallers and the Knights Templar, they were members of the military orders, pious knights who fought exclusively for God. They were the best trained, best equipped and most highly motivated heavy cavalry in the world.

When the two sides clashed on 19 April, it was a pivotal fight for both sides. The Mongols were at the end of impossibly long lines of communication back to Asia. Lose here and they would be retreating for a thousand miles over hostile territory. For the Poles, this was their last throw of the dice. If this army couldn't stop the rampaging Mongols who had already slaughtered armies and razed and burned three cities, there was nothing left to stop them.

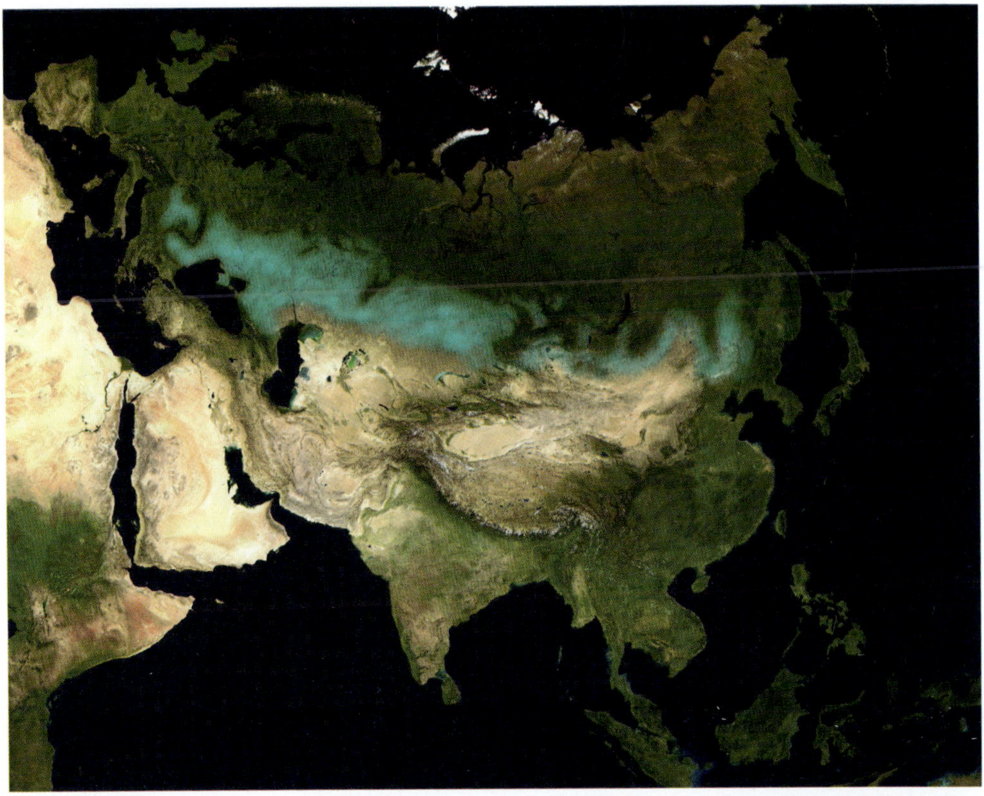

Above: The huge Eurasian Steppe belt, a largely featureless area punctuated by small ranges of low hills and rivers. (Public domain)

Right: The extent of Attila's empire *c.* 450. There is no capital, the 'centre' was wherever Attila's tent was. (Courtesy SJ, after Slovenski Volk)

Frisia
Old Saxony
Baltic Peoples
Germanic Peoples
Slavic Peoples
Turkic Khaganate
Metz
Avar Khaganate
Regensburg
Bavaria
Bulgars
Aquincum (Budapest)
Approximate extent of Avar settlements
Late Huns
Valcum (Fenékpuszta)
Slavic Peoples
Kutrigurs
Milan
Partiscum (Szeged)
Goths
Venice
Sirmium (Sremska Mitrovica)
Important Avar sites excavated
Ravenna
Lombard Italy
Singidunum (Belgrade)
Salona
Narona
Justiniana Prima
Philippopolis
Rome
Constantinople
Naples
Thessaloniki
Eastern Roman Empire

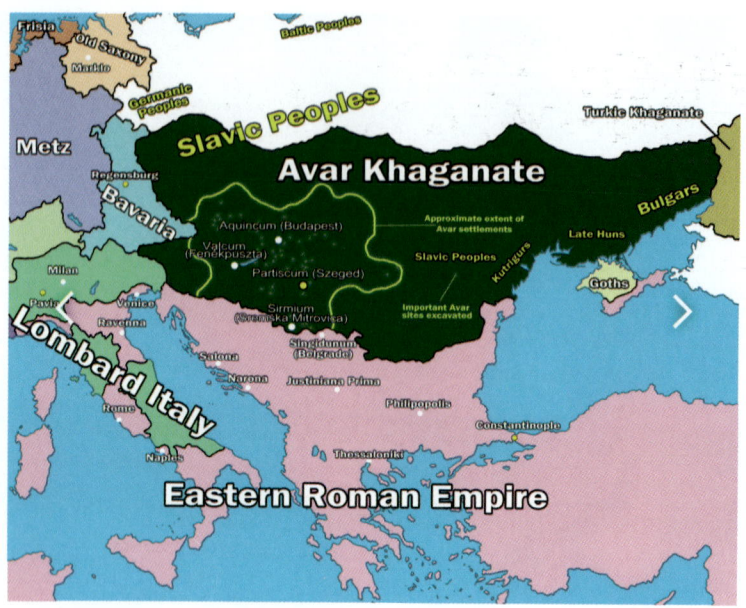

Above: 'Go West, young man.' The Avars did so to escape the hegemony of the Göktürks. The Khaganate *c.* 602. (Courtesy Wario2 under creative commons)

Below: Map courtesy SJ, after Arienne King.

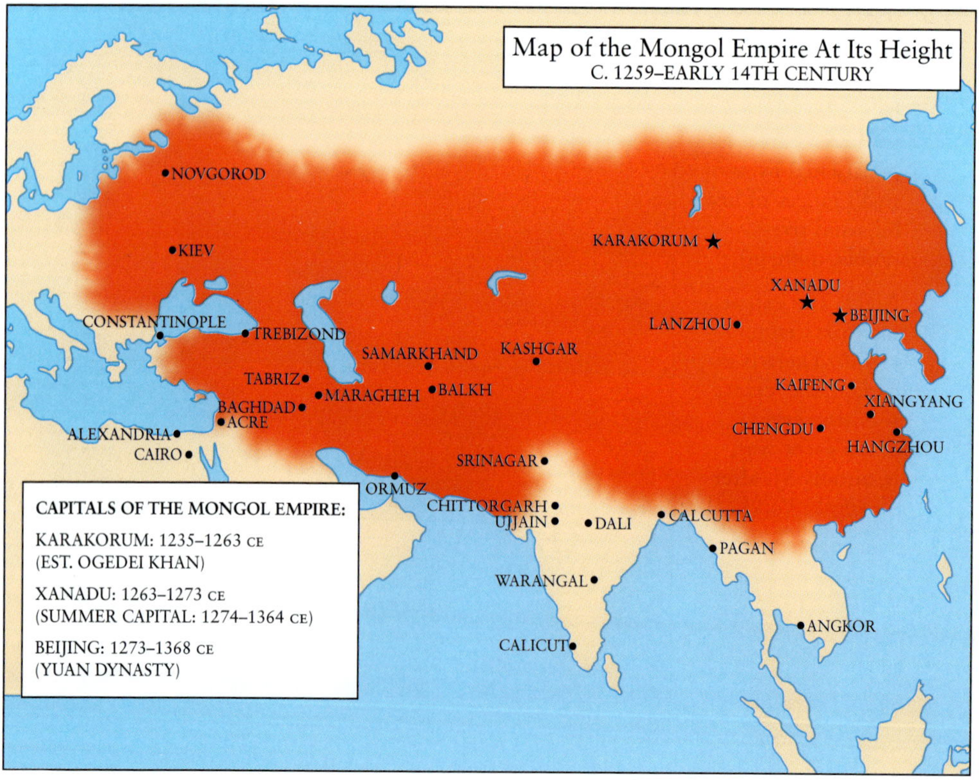
Map of the Mongol Empire At Its Height
C. 1259–EARLY 14TH CENTURY
NOVGOROD
KIEV
KARAKORUM
XANADU
CONSTANTINOPLE
TREBIZOND
LANZHOU
BEIJING
SAMARKHAND
KASHGAR
TABRIZ
MARAGHEH
BALKH
KAIFENG
BAGHDAD
ACRE
XIANGYANG
ALEXANDRIA
CHENGDU
HANGZHOU
CAIRO
SRINAGAR
ORMUZ
CHITTORGARH
UJJAIN
DALI
CALCUTTA
PAGAN
WARANGAL
ANGKOR
CALICUT
CAPITALS OF THE MONGOL EMPIRE:
KARAKORUM: 1235–1263 CE
(EST. OGEDEI KHAN)
XANADU: 1263–1273 CE
(SUMMER CAPITAL: 1274–1364 CE)
BEIJING: 1273–1368 CE
(YUAN DYNASTY)

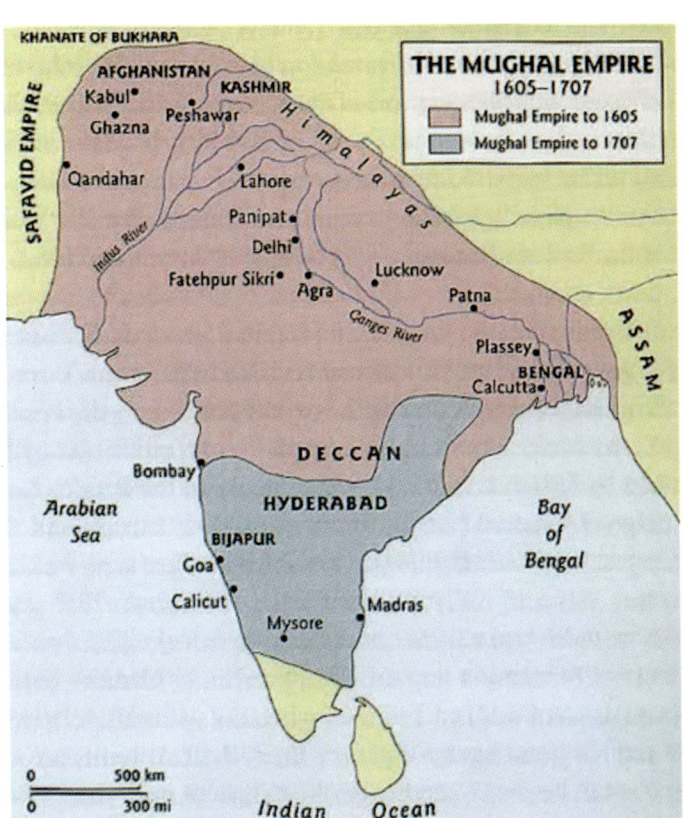

The gradual decline of the Mughal Empire was immensely useful to the British.

Genghis Khan's empire at his death. (Courtesy Postmann Michael, public domain)

Above: Attila the Hun is a name that has echoed down through the ages, appearing in diverse sources such as this 14th-century manuscript, the *Chronicon Pictum*, a chronicle of the history of Hungary – the nation he founded – written by Mark of Kalt. (Public domain)

Left: A horseman and his captive on the ewer from the Romanian Nagyszentmiklós Treasure of the 7th-8th centuries. The vessels were produced by Avar goldsmiths, the gold being tribute payments the Avar Khaganate received from the Byzantine emperors. (Wikimedia commons)

Below left: The meeting between Attila and Pope Leo depicted by Raphael during the Renaissance, a millennium after the event. (Public domain)

Right: Reconstruction of a typical Eurasian Steppe nomad helmet, considered to be Avar. Note the horsehair plume. (Courtesy James Steakley under Creative Commons 3.0)

Below: The Magyars' arrival in Europe as shown centuries later by their descendants in Hungary, from the *Chonicon Pictum*. (Public domain)

Left: Relief of a Seljuk Turk now in Armenia, with composite recurved bow. (Public domain)

Below: Soldiers of a royal court of the nomads as imagined by a sedentary, and therefore alien culture. From the mid-13th-century *Book of Anditodes of Pseudo-Gallen*, probably from Northern Iraq. (Public domain)

Above: Seljuk Turks were not originally Muslim but converted when they began conquering territory in the Middle East. From *Varka and Golshah*, battle scene 4, mid-13th century, Anatolia. (Public domain)

Below: A 19th-century image of Osman I, founder of the Ottoman Empire, by Konstantin Kapıdağlı. There are no contemporary images of Osman. (Public domain)

Mehmed II leads Ottoman forces in the conquest of Constantinople in 1453. The first time in history that gunpowder played a key role in victory. (Public domain)

The Battle of Mohàcs in 1526 was one of the Ottoman Empire's greatest victories and opened up Hungary for conquest; artist Bertalan Székely (1866), National Hungarian Museum. (Courtesy Székely Bertalan, public domain)

Above: The Süleymaniye Mosque in Istanbul is one of the pinnacles of Ottoman architecture. (Courtesy Hunanuk, under creative commons 1.0)

Right: Temujin, known to the world as Genghis Khan; from a 14th-century album of Yuan emperor portraits, National Palace Museum, Taipei. (Public domain)

Temujin after unifying the Mongol tribes is declared 'Universal Ruler', which in Uighur is 'Genghis Khan'. From Rashid al-Din Hamadani's early 14th-century history, *Jāmi' al-Tawārīkh*, written in part to justify Mongol hegemony over Iran. (Courtesy Bibliothèque nationale de France, public domain)

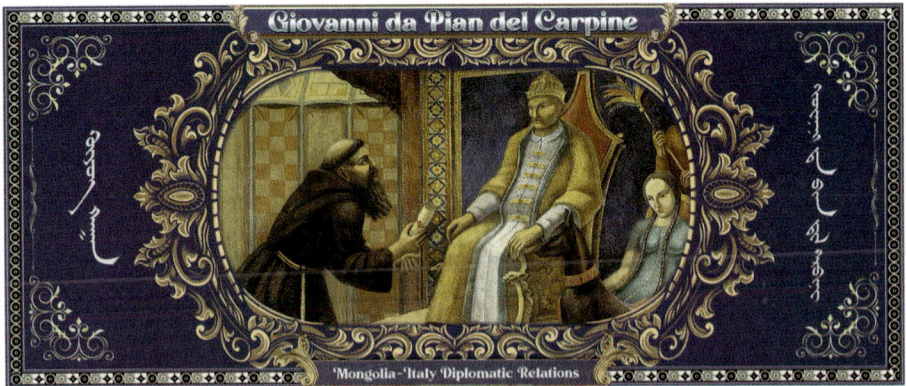

Giovanni da Pian del Carpine

'Mongolia–'Italy 'Diplomatic 'Relations

Above: A commemoration of Giovanni Carpine's trip from Europe to meet the Mongol Great Khan. To mark Pope Francis's visit to Mongolia in autumn 2023, the Italian Embassy released this special commemorative silver banknote. (Courtesy Embassy of Italy in Ulaanbaatar)

Right: A Chinese (Ming dynasty) depiction of a Mongolian warrior; hundreds of thousands, if not millions, of Chinese people would die as a result of the Mongolian conquest of China. (Courtesy Victoria and Albert Museum, London, public domain)

Below right: A medieval European depiction of the Mongol invasion of Europe, part of the Altar of St Hedwig of Silesia, mother of Henry II of Silesia who died in the Battle of Legnica, or Battle of Liegnitz, Poland, 1241. The souls of the killed Christians are shown carried to heaven by angels, while those of Tatars are swallowed by hell. (Public domain)

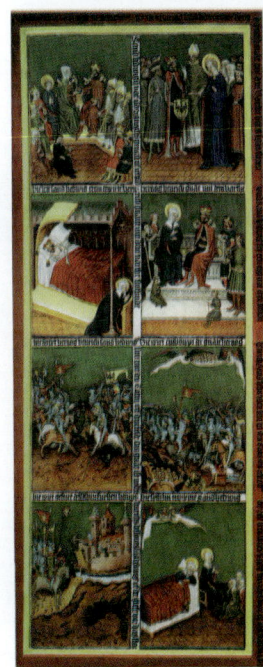
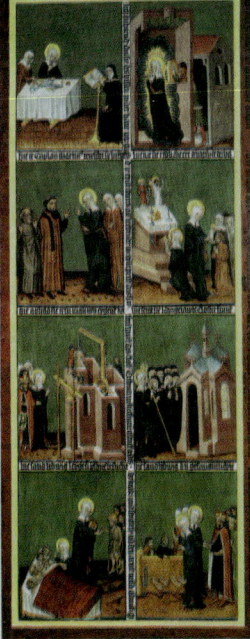

Left: A record of Toktamysh the great Mongol warlord's time in Moscow in the Facial Chronicle b.10, p.66. At the time, the people of Rus were a vassal state to the Mongols. (Public domain)

Below: Emir Timur is seen as a hero in some central Asian countries, and a bloodthirsty conqueror in others. A monument to Timur at Ak-Saray Palace in the city of Shahrisabz, Uzbekistan. (Courtesy Ljuba Brank under creative commons)

Right: The Battle of Ankara between Emir Timur and the Ottoman Sultan Bayezid was a titanic clash that would nearly destroy the Ottoman Empire. Held at Golestan Palace, Tehran, Iran. (Wikimedia commons)

Below: The mausoleum of Emir Timur at night; a curse would become associated with the great warlord's tomb that seemed to come to pass under the rule of Stalin. (Courtesy Bgag under creative commons 1.0)

Above left: Babur, the last of the great central Asian warlords who would found his own empire and dynasty. (Courtesy David Mauro under creative commons 4.0)

Above right: Babur invades northern India/Pakistan from his base in Afghanistan. (Courtesy Los Angeles County Museum of Art, gift of the Walter Foundation, public domain)

Left: The Battle of Panipat, victory for Babur and the defeat of the last of the Lodi sultans. From the *Bāburnāma*, the memoirs of Babur. (Public domain)

The Battle of the Pyramids by Jean-Antoine Watteau, where Napoleon faced the same kind of mounted horse archers that the Romans had with Attila. (Courtesy Musée des beaux-arts de Valenciennes, public domain)

Ottoman soldiers in the First World War with a heavy machine gun; the age of the horse archer is long gone, but the empire was to survive for a few more years. (Courtesy National Library of Israel, public domain)

Above: The Mongolian plains are like much of the Eurasian Steppe, their plentiful supply of grass and lack of major geographic obstacles allowed these groups to travel across the known world for centuries. (From *Across Mongolian Plains* by Roy Chapman Andrews, 1921)

Right: On the Tibetan plateau the old skills of firing a bow from the back of a galloping horse are still practised today. (Courtesy Antoine Taveneaux under creative commons)

Below: The Taj Mahal, arguably the most famous building constructed by one of the once nomadic empires. (Courtesy Jean-Marc Astesana under creative commons 2.0)

The Mongols display the head of Henry II, from Freytag's Hedwig manuscript, 1451, held at Wroclaw University Library. (Public domain)

Frustratingly, the sources for the battle are scattered and contradictory, so piecing together the most likely narrative, it seems the conflict unfolded in stages. The Europeans initiated contact with a charge by the Silesian heavy cavalry against the vanguard of the Mongol army. It appeared ineffectual and the Silesian cavalry was forced to pull back. But the allies decided that if at first you don't succeed, try, try again, and now it was the turn of other allied heavy cavalry units to attack. This time the Mongol vanguard retreated under some kind of smoke screen, but exactly what this was is unknown. The smoke seems to have been accompanied by flames, along with strange and terrifying noises, which implies some kind of gunpowder. If this was the case, it would have been the first ever example of gunpowder being used in Europe. The smoke enveloped the second heavy cavalry assault, which obscured the flanking movement of the Mongol horse archers and separated the European cavalry from the rest of the army. In a hail of arrows, the Europeans were wiped out.

The Mongols' final attack now fell on an allied army lacking the mobility of its cavalry, so the infantry was at the mercy of the mobile and highly effective Mongol horse archers. Henry II broke and ran. He was intercepted by Mongol light cavalry, promptly beheaded, and his head displayed on the end of a spear. At this, the rest of the European army disintegrated. Nobody knows the exact numbers of dead, but the casualties on the European side were devastating. Even the contingent of Teutonic Knights seems to have been all but wiped out. Meanwhile, Mongol casualties can only be guessed at, but as their forces never seemed to be in much danger, they had to have been very light. It was said (later) that to assess the scale of their victory, the Mongols cut the right ear off each fallen European in order to count the dead. The ears supposedly filled nine sacks.

So little was known about the Mongols and their agility on the battlefield, not to mention their brutal efficiency, that the term 'hordes' was applied to them. We have seen that the term was used by the Mongols themselves, but this was internally. The European use of the word is as a generic descriptor that indicates there were lots of them. The Europeans frequently overestimated the size of Mongol armies, and Western sources imply that the reason why their brave knights were beaten was because they faced countless numbers of the enemy who came at them like a swarm of ants. A horde is an incalculable number, but the reality was the total forces attacking Europe were likely to have been 5-7 tumens, and a tumen from the Mongol decimal system was 10,000 men, far fewer in number than the forces that rampaged across China. So if the Europeans thought 50,000–70,000 men was a large Mongol army (and compared to anything else in the West, it was), they clearly had no idea of the true numbers the Mongols could deploy. In truth, such low numbers probably meant they were more likely a reconnaissance force compared to the numbers fielded when their main goals were the conquests far to the east.

Just as the Poles were fleeing from the nightmarish death and destruction wreaked by the invasion, Hungary was also invaded from the East. The arrival of the Cumans had caused tensions in the kingdom, which, it should be remembered, had connections and customs in common with the Eurasian Steppe nomads. They even had their own version of the horse archers, but unlike the Hungarians, the Cumans had resisted conversion to Christianity. In March 1241, the arrival of this new threat led to revenge attacks on the Cumans and their leader was murdered.

The Hungarian king was Béla IV, who had come from a dynasty that could trace its beginnings back through many generations. Under normal circumstances he would have been a standard medieval monarch, but he was now facing an immigration crisis from the East, followed by an attack by the most efficient military machine in the world at that time. By that spring the Mongols, led by Subutai and Batu Khan had arrived at the capital Pest (Buda and Pest at this time were two separate towns divided by the River Danube). Batu was the son of Jochi and founder of the Golden Horde. The fact that a grandson of Genghis Khan and one of his most trusted generals were leading this campaign shows how important it was and how the Mongols were determined to leave nothing to chance. Béla IV forbade any attempts to stop the Mongols because he realised he needed time to gather his strength if he was to stand any chance of success against this onslaught. He wisely allowed the Mongols to raid with impunity as he carefully marshalled his forces. He was also hoping for some help to the west, but the other Mongol invasion force had tied up all his erstwhile allies.

Despite his wise caution, he faced internal power struggles with Frederick II Duke of Austria and Styria (known to history as Frederick the Quarrelsome). Frederick, against Béla's orders, engaged a small Mongol raiding party and overwhelmed them. This raised Frederick's profile and he boldly branded Béla a coward. The temperature in Hungary was rising and Béla was becoming increasingly unpopular. The Cumans were not welcome and their similarity to the Mongols made them appear to be natural allies of this new enemy, but they were the only force that had any experience of fighting the Mongols, one of the reasons Béla wanted them on his side. However, with their leader dead and increasing attacks against them by the local population, the Cumans moved out of Hungary, pillaging all the way, their betrayal becoming a self-fulfilling prophecy. Now that Béla's allies had left Hungary, despite their obligation to do so many of the local powers decided not to come to the king's aid, so Béla was weaker now than he could have been, and he had yet to engage the Mongol forces. All of this can be chalked up to bad luck. His strategy and diplomacy made sense, just not to the scared and insular people of his kingdom.

In short, Hungary was in a mess even before the Mongols started setting fire to settlements. Feeling he had done enough to raise his profile and lower Béla's, Frederick left the kingdom and went home. Some nobles who did send forces to the king were ambushed by the Mongols and never arrived. Just as the Mongol invasion of Poland had engendered complete chaos, so too had their arrival in Hungary. Béla, with what forces he had, sought to meet the invaders in battle, but the Mongols melted away, leading to yet more criticism of Béla as an overly cautious king – clearly these unknown people from the East had fled at the first sign of Hungarian men at arms. In reality, it seems the Mongols were hoping to lure the Hungarian forces into breaking formation and crossing the Sajó River where they would attack to maximise their impact. Béla was too smart for that, even if he did look like a coward to some of his nobles. Instead, he built a fortified encampment surrounded by the heavy wagons of his supply lines. It was almost like an instant fort and perfect protection from horse archers.

There was even better news when a slave escaped from the Mongols and warned Béla that the Mongols were planning a nighttime raid to capture a nearby bridge. A small force was led by the king's brother, the local master of the Knights Templar (like the Teutonic Knights in Poland, there are examples here of the elite of European chivalry facing the Mongol threat) and Archbishop Ugrin Csák. Even for the medieval era it was unusual for an archbishop to join in the fighting, but Csák was clearly more of an Old Testament kind of theologian than a New Testament one, where the message was to turn the other cheek.

This vanguard arrived just in time. The slave had been correct in everything he had reported, and the Mongols were thrown back with heavy losses. Many of them either drowned in the river or fell victim to the crossbow, a weapon of enormous penetrating power unfamiliar to the Mongols. Such moments are important. With all the Mongol successes, particularly Subutai's, it can sometimes feel like their tactics were infallible and their successes pre-ordained, but like every army in history, they had setbacks. The difference here though was they quickly learned from them and were able to adapt their tactics accordingly.

Having put in place a defensive force on the bridge, the Christians returned to camp and were able to celebrate a tactical victory. Unfortunately, as dawn broke, the Mongols revealed they really had left nothing to chance and had brought siege engines, including catapults, which they used to hurl stones at the guards on the bridge. The remaining Hungarians fled, stirring the three leaders of the night raid to sally forth from the waggon fort with their troops to deal with the next Mongol raiding party. But as the horse cavalry continued to pour into view, it was obvious to all that this was no raid, but the main Mongol force. The Hungarians had to retreat or be overwhelmed and returned to the fort hoping to rally the whole force. There were delays and confusion, which, critically, gave Batu the time he needed to get all the Mongol forces onto the other side of the Sajó River.

By the time the Hungarians had formed into lines and ventured forth from the safety of the fort, they were dangerously close to the Mongols. While Batu had managed to get his troops over the river, however, he now had a river to his rear; he was boxed in and without the means to carry out the manoeuvres and feigned retreats that would be standard in such situations. The Hungarians, with their heavy cavalry, were peppered with arrows, but they were able to get into the Mongol ranks and cut a swath through the invaders. The Mongols reported that dozens of Batu's personal bodyguard were killed in this part of the battle. At this point there had to be more Hungarians on the field of battle than Mongols, but the European sources for the Battle of Mohi are ludicrous, with some quoting a number as high as half a million for the Mongol army. Once again, we see a subconscious bias where the unknown numbers of the Asian force could only be described as innumerable, impersonal and inhuman. The reality was a far more modest tens of thousands.

Just when things were going Béla's way, Subutai arrived. He had been delayed when he forded the stream with his forces, and he arrived in the Hungarian rear with tens of thousands of fresh troops. After the battle Batu would admonish Subutai for taking too long, leading to unnecessary casualties, but in fact, they had carried out one the greatest pincer movements in military history.

Initially, the fort had been a good idea; the waggons were virtually arrow-proof. But unfortunately for the Hungarians, Batu brought up his catapults, and while they had been designed to shatter stone walls, they worked even better on wood. Some Mongols switched to fire arrows (Hollywood is obsessed with flaming arrows, which were incredibly rare on the battlefield, but this was one of those rare times when they were deployed), but these were as nothing compared to what came next, when the Europeans faced something they had no prior knowledge of, gunpowder.

What was described as naphtha bombs and flaming arrows could have been simple grenades or rockets packed with metal. There is no hard evidence for gunpowder weapons, but some of the accounts seem to imply their use (their use was also implied in the Polish accounts). Whatever the cause, the waggons were being blown to shreds and fire threatened to engulf the camp. Archbishop Ugrin Csák (along with another archbishop and three bishops who were also in the camp) died during the bombardment.

Béla and his brother managed to escape with a handful of men. When the day started, the Hungarians had around 80,000 men and had successfully repelled a Mongol night raid, but just a few hours later, the King of Hungary was running away from the burning battlefield, fleeing Mongol raiders, fearing for his life, his army in ruins.

King Béla IV managed to escape the clutches of the Mongols and ruled for nearly another 30 years, but this was cold comfort because the capital of Pest had been captured and burned to the ground. Any resistance from any town was, as usual, met with a massacre of the entire population, and any town that instantly capitulated could expect to see its men hauled away to join the peasant ranks of the Mongol infantry. It is estimated that over the next few months, half of Hungary's settlements were laid waste by the Mongols and that around a quarter of the country's population was either killed or marched over the horizon to Asia to become slaves.

The effects on Poland and Hungary were devastating, but the shockwaves were felt across Europe. When Pope Gregory IX died in August 1241, the story went that on hearing of the Mongol assault from the East, he fell ill and died of grief for all the dead Christians. True or not, the point was that this account was given serious credence; it was a distillation of the profound terror Europe had of the Mongols. It was in this summer that records began to talk about innumerable hordes of the devil's horsemen who were said to be the children of Gog and Magog, obscure references to evil from the Old Testament and the Book of Ezekiel. Technically, Gog was a person, and he came from the land of Magog, but such subtleties were irrelevant. According to the story, Gog and Magog could only be defeated by the Messiah and their arrival heralded the end of days; the

Mongols were the heralds of Armageddon, and nobody in Poland or Hungary would have disagreed with that assessment at the time.

Some of the largest, best equipped and most competently led armies in Europe had been swept aside in a matter of days. Europe rarely rallied together and even if it did, it clearly didn't have the resources or tactics to match the almost supernatural assault on central Europe. But then, just as quickly as they had arrived, the Mongols vanished. Reports filtered west that the armies had simply broken camp, packed up their tents and begun to ride east, past the borders of Europe and the known world. The Mongols rode into legend, to a land on the map's very edges, there be dragons. You would think Europe would be euphoric, but this inexplicable disappearance was almost as terrifying as their presence. Why did they leave? And more importantly, when were they coming back?

I have spoken to Poles who know why the Mongols left. Apparently, resistance by the brave Polish fighters had been so fierce and the Mongol casualties so high that they didn't dare return to Poland. If that story is what makes patriotic Polish hearts beat faster, they should feel free to believe it and skip the rest of the paragraph, but the simple fact is that there are no chronicles from contemporary sources that bear witness to heavy Mongol casualties. The Poles were annihilated, just like the Hungarians and the Jin and the Khwarazmian Empire. There is no shame in losing to the global military power of the age, but the reality was even more prosaic: Ögedei died. This meant that the Mongol armies in Europe had to travel six months to get back to Karakorum to induct a new khan. Added to that, the pickings in Europe were meagre compared to those in Asia or the Middle East. The reason why the Mongols didn't conquer Europe is the same reason why the Roman Empire didn't conquer Scotland. They could have done so, it just wasn't worth it.

The death of the second great khan heralded a lengthy period of debate about the succession. Each of the khans had multiple sons, but it is interesting to realise how much the women were involved. We know that Genghis Khan valued the input of both his mother and first wife in the affairs of state. Now, with the passing of his son, something similar took place. Ögedei's first wife was Töregene and she assumed the role of regent. While all the political jockeying for a successor was going on, she was in charge, refereeing the arguments and administering the affairs of the empire. But this time the selection process took years, and while Töregene got her way and her own son became the next great khan, Güyük only lasted two years before he died. Some say he died in a fight with a family member, but most records indicate natural causes. Either way, once again it took years to select a new ruler and this time it was Möngke Khan. He was not formally enthroned until 1251, about ten years after the death of Ögedei. It is therefore a testament to the capabilities of the generals and the ruling elite of the Mongol Empire that this was neither a period of disintegration nor one of civil war.

Despite all the war and bloodshed, the era of Ögedei and the decade after did have one positive effect: for the very first time the Silk Road, from its origins in China, all the way to the Middle East (roughly 85% of the journey) was now under one authority, that of the Mongols. This meant trade between East and West boomed. The Mongols excelled at imposing their will on an area either through force or the threat of it, and as such, greatly reduced crime along this most important trade route. While banditry could never be completely eradicated, this was a time of relative stability, and with just one border to cross, once traders were inside the Mongol Empire it was a long but straightforward and relatively risk-free journey to China.

In such a vast empire, communication was always a problem and was not helped by the limitations of technology. The distance from Kraków to Beijing is 4,436 miles (7,139 km), a considerable distance even now. But the Mongols had an answer and it was the Yam, in essence, the pony express – about 600 years before the American version. Dispatch riders would be sent out, and every 10-15 miles there would be a stable with fresh horses waiting for the riders who would switch mounts and keep riding hard. It was an ingenious way to expedite the flow of information. Riders, too, could be switched, so the message continued to make its way 24/7. A horse can gallop for limited periods at up to 30 miles an hour; by comparison an adult human can average 4 miles an hour, but he would need to stop and rest. This meant that the great khans were able to be more reactive to changing situations than any other emperors up to that point.

It is from this era we get the most unusual of eyewitness accounts, from an Italian monk called Giovanni Carpine. Both he and, a few years later, after branching off from the Seventh Crusade in Egypt, William of Rubruck, were European priests sent across the whole of Asia to engage with the great khans. These journeys were on an unimaginable scale to the medieval European mind. They were, in their own way, as big an achievement as landing on the moon. Europe had been shaken by the events of 1241, so emissaries needed to be sent and Asia needed to be explored. Rather optimistically, William had a secondary mission to convert the Mongol Khan to Christianity, so he would then be obliged to take orders from the Pope. I think you can work out how well that went. But the Europeans were surprised to find that there already were Nestorian Christians in the court, as well as Buddhists, Muslims and many more. In Europe, where there was only one acceptable religion, the idea of having a society with multiple faiths and treating them all as equal was shocking. Indeed, at the time in Europe, even deviations from the preached doctrine could elicit a visit from the inquisition, and a family could lose everything. Both of these literate European writers were able to record their experiences; obviously biased with an eye to exoticism, they were still vital documents in trying to piece together the story of the Mongols. Unlike the later Marco Polo, Rubruck did not fall for any folk tales, and his accounts are biased but believable. These are invaluable documents from nearly 800 years ago.

As for how well William's mission went, there follows his reply to Pope Innocent IV:

> You must say with a sincere heart: 'We will be your subjects; we will give you our strength.' You must in person come with your kings, all together, without exception, to render us service and pay us homage. Only then will we acknowledge your submission. And if you do not follow the order of God, and go against our orders, we will know you as our enemy.

So that's a no, then.

In 1251, with Möngke enthroned as the new great khan, the war with the Song was renewed and lasted for the whole of Möngke's life. In the period between Ögedei and Möngke, the old guard passed into history, and the supremely successful Subutai died. But a new generation had come to the fore with the same level of zeal for conquest and competence in leadership. In this case, Möngke's younger brother Kublai was one of the generals who carried out the conquests not just of most of the Chinese Song dynasty, but also of those in Tibet and Vietnam.

The Mongols, under Ögedei, conquered Tibet in 1240-1. It was the first time the kingdom had been successfully invaded by outsiders, and it was this invasion that encouraged future Chinese powers to invade, right up to the 20th century when

Mao invaded in the 1950s. To this day, China considers Tibet to be part of its territory, another example of how the Eurasian Steppe nomads have shaped the modern world.

Tibet was then an extremely influential force in the area. Ruled over the years by various dynasties, it was a religious epicentre that brought Buddhists from all over Asia to hear the decrees of its religious leaders (the first Dalai Lama was born about a generation after Yuan rule and there will be more on the Yuan Mongol emperor of China later), so it was a significant and valuable addition to the Mongol Empire.

Doorda Tarkhan was the Mongol general who brought Ögedei this conquest, but it was not an easy one. Tibetan terrain is about as alien as it gets compared to the gently undulating grasslands of the Eurasian Steppe. Now the Mongols faced jagged mountains higher than the treeline, apparently piercing the heavens themselves. Naturally, in such an environment, the Mongols could not use their usual tactics, and it was at this time they entered a new phase. When armies were led by Mongols, the strategy and tactics were devised by Mongols, but increasingly the Mongols employed the forces from subjugated nations. Later we will see great naval fleets created by the 'Mongols', who of course had no history of naval technology; these ships were built and manned by the Chinese. So, too, in Tibet, where the terrain dictated that any fighting had to be done largely by infantry because horses are notoriously poor at climbing mountains. That's a little flippant and some trails could take pack animals, but the overall lack of manoeuvrability meant that ways to outflank the enemy simply did not exist in Tibet. This campaign was one of pure brute force driving a massive army into sieges and overwhelming the sparsely populated country. By the reign of Möngke, Tibet had refused to pay tribute, so not only did Kublai have to fight the last Chinese dynasty, he also had to go into the foothills of the Himalayas to bring the Tibetans to heel; which he did.

When the fight to conquer the Song got bogged down in heavy fighting, with little ground being captured, the Mongols looked for an alternative direction of attack, and the result was their decision to invade Vietnam. The first invasion began in 1258 under General Uriyangkhadai. Once again, we see an army that was more ethnically Han Chinese than Mongol. Just like Tibet, Vietnam did not have the terrain for a traditional Mongol campaign. Dense jungle on sometimes steep terrain, regularly interspersed with rivers meant that infantry was the tool for the job. Uriyangkhadai was successful in capturing the Vietnamese capital Thang Long (modern-day Hanoi), which brought the Vietnamese rulers under Mongol control, and once again a sovereign nation became a vassal state. The subjugation of Vietnam achieved all the Mongol goals and allowed them to turn north and open up a new front against the Song a year later. The local chronicles mistook Mongol movement for a victory. In Vietnam it was thought that the Mongols could not withstand the oppressive heat and humidity, which had forced the invaders away. In reality, Vietnam was just an access point to the bigger target of the Song; the Mongols never intended to stay. Vietnam would rebel multiple times, so Mongol forces were dispatched regularly to deal with the uprisings. This usually led to more tribute but not always, and the fighting was slow and hard. The story is eerily similar to 1960s Vietnam when the Americans, rather than the Mongols, had far greater military power, but every time the Vietnamese faced defeat, they simply slipped into the jungle, away from the enemy. The Vietnamese have been resisting outside powers for a very long time.

Despite the successes in Tibet and Vietnam, the Song were the main target. The modern provinces of Sichuan and Yunnan in the south and southwest of modern China (bordering Tibet and Vietnam) were the first places conquered. General Uriyangkhadai led approximately a third of the Mongol army (which had already subjugated Vietnam) and the other two-thirds were led by Möngke. The next few years are a flurry of names and locations. At one point Kublai was besieging a city; at another, the Mongols were burning and destroying or beating a Song army in the field. Even though the Mongols had yet to vanquish their foes, the constant war, death and destruction led to revolts against Song rule. After all, if the emperors couldn't protect them, what was the point of them, or their taxes and officials? It was a period of total chaos in southern China.

The Song used everything in their power to try and stop the advancing Mongol menace, including the first true guns, called Tu Huo Qiang. Imagine a cannon with the barrel made of bamboo. The principle of a cannon remained the same: an explosive charge would send a projectile down the tube at the enemy, but in the case of bamboo, the barrels split so these 'guns' were a strictly one-shot weapon. The reality was that while they made a lot of smoke, fire and noise, they weren't effective weapons and were used more as a scare tactic to spook the Mongol cavalry.

In the summer of 1259, the Song finally caught a break when Möngke died. How he died is still a matter of debate. Most records say he died during a siege, and although there is some question as to whether it was from a rock thrown by a siege engine or a crossbow bolt, Persian sources say it was from disease. Both are equally likely, as sieges did invariably create unsanitary conditions, but either way, the fourth great khan was dead, and it was once again time for the Mongols to return to their home territory to find a new leader. The Song could breathe a sigh of relief, but for how long?

While all of this was going on in Asia, during Möngke's rule other forces were sent west into the Middle East. There has never been an Islamic equivalent of the Pope. Different sects have leaders, but even they tend to be more spiritual leaders than temporal rulers. In the 13th century, the closest position in Islam to a unifying religious leader was the caliph. The Abbasid Caliphs, based in Baghdad, could trace their lineage back to the early days of Islamic empire-building in the 8th century AD. While their power waned as that of other ethnic groups emerged (particularly the Turks as described in previous chapters, rather than the Arab rulers in the Middle East), the caliph was the unifying force in Islam in the 1250s.

Baghdad was an ancient city with imposing walls and a well-deserved reputation for being nearly impregnable. The caliph then was Al-Musta'sim, and as the Mongol General Hulagu (grandson of Genghis Khan and therefore a brother of Möngke and Kublai) approached Baghdad, the caliph received an ultimatum from the Mongols. Al-Musta'sim rejected the ultimatum, sat behind his thick walls and waited for the inevitable. He had made no plans for war, sent no messages to other leaders for military assistance or prepared a defence, extremely foolhardy failures, all the more surprising because he had to be aware of the consequences for his deliberate snub of the Mongol ultimatum. If they were victorious, he could expect no mercy.

Hulagu arrived in January 1258 and the city was rapidly enveloped by over 100,000 troops (not just Mongols but those from other regions of the empire, too). Hulagu demonstrated that the Mongols were not only master horsemen, but masters now of the art of siege warfare as well. The Mongol army dug a ditch and built a palisade (a wooden wall) around the city. This not only prevented any chance of escape, but also limited the options of a relief force. Then they set up siege engines to pound the walls. The people of Baghdad could not escape andt had to sit and take it. After a few weeks of barrage, it became clear that Baghdad was going to fall. Al-Musta'sim called for talks on surrender; Hulagu declined them. The Mongol rule was simple: immediate capitulation and unconditional surrender would save lives; resistance was met with annihilation. The caliph had chosen resistance but had failed to make any preparations for it, making him one of the worst military leaders ever recorded.

The fall of Baghdad in 1258 isn't widely remembered in the West, but it was a tremendously important event with massive implications. Al-Musta'sim was found and brought to Hulagu for judgement. The Mongols had a sacred rule that the blood of a king or emperor should never be spilled on the ground, so the Mongols rolled the caliph in a rug and rode their cavalry over him. The honour of this execution was probably lost on Al-Musta'sim. He was kicked to death by hundreds of hooves, his muffled screams the last sounds a caliph would ever make.

The death of Al-Musta'sim marked the end of the Abbasid Caliphate, which had lasted five hundred years and was never replaced (the Ottoman sultans would take the title from the 16th century onwards, but while they had supreme authority in their realm, their caliph 'credentials' weren't recognised by other Muslim rulers). Throughout the era of the Crusades, Islamic scholars were well ahead of their western counterparts; and while the caliph's death didn't cause the decline of Baghdad, it is seen as the end of the golden age of Islamic learning. Historians debate exactly when this era of learning began, most settling around the year 800 AD. Islamic centres such as Baghdad, Damascus and Alexandria poured out treatises on everything from complex mathematics to astronomy, medicine and the arts, and produced some of the most beautiful architecture ever created. The start date is debated, the end is not. Everyone agrees that 1258 and the Mongol destruction of Baghdad marks the end of this significant golden age.

For centuries Baghdad had been the repository of thousands of texts and manuscripts and was one of the key centres of Islamic learning, indeed of scholarship per se, but the Mongols deliberately destroyed everything. One eye-witness recounted seeing the Tigris run black with ink, so many documents had been thrown in the river. As a result, countless primary sources were forever lost to future historians. Although the intellectual loss was great, the human loss of life was far worse. Arab sources estimated the death toll at 200,000. It's tempting to see this as an exaggeration, perhaps meant to underline the enormity of the devastation – until you read that the Mongols claimed 800,000 deaths. The streets were greasy with human fat for weeks afterwards, the horses slipping on it wherever they went in the city. The level of death and destruction was so great that even the Mongols couldn't stand it, and for the only time in Mongol history, they moved out of a city they had only just ravaged, away from the site of their orgy of murder and the overwhelming stench of decay. This was one of the worst massacres in human history.

Unbelievably, it got worse. The Mongols were so determined to leave a permanent scar on Mesopotamia and Persia that they deliberately destroyed the ancient canal systems feeding hundreds of thousands of acres of soil from great rivers like the Euphrates and the Tigris. Today we think of central Iran and Iraq as barren, but they weren't always like that. It was the Mongols' destruction of the irrigation systems, along with the legacy of hugely reduced populations, that allowed farmland to shrivel up, blow away and become desert. It was one of the greatest pre-industrial ecological disasters ever, the consequences of which remain today, over seven hundred years later. There is now a name for the deliberate destruction of nature in war, ecocide. This is arguably the first example of it.

The Islamic world had had its cultural and spiritual heart torn out by the Mongols. Could nothing stop these monsters? Some historians believe that Islam was teetering on the brink, but I don't agree. The Mongols had no interest in imposing their shamanistic religion on anyone or in stopping any of the religious practices of their subjects. The beliefs of Islam weren't threatened, but the Muslim dynasties of the Near East were facing an existential threat like no other.

It was during this devastating invasion of the Middle East that the Mongols inadvertently did both crusaders and Muslims a favour. The previous century had witnessed the rise of the Hashashin, led by Hasan-i-Sabbah (as mentioned previously in chapter 5). They were despised not only because of their assassinations but also because as Ismailis, they were a separate sect of Islam, outside the Sunnis and Shi'as, so were often seen as the Islamic version of heretics. Consequently, they were reviled by the Sunni majority power bases of Islam as well as by the Christians.

The Assassins were equal opportunity murderers. Princes, warlords and generals of both cultures were targets for the Assassins, who often struck very publicly. As the assassins showed no fear of death, they almost always succeeded. This meant for such a tiny force they had a disproportionate impact on the politics of the near east for more than a century. No wonder movies and even video games have been made about them, they have an almost mythical aura around them.

The Hashashin embedded themselves in a string of castles in remote desert regions (mainly in modern-day Syria and western Iraq). These were essentially impregnable as no army could besiege such an arid region. Anyone can march into a desert, but then to besiege a location with no source of water meant that the army would be dead before the defenders were suffering from thirst. This allowed the group to spread terror from safe bases. Hasan-i-Sabbah became known as 'The Old Man of the Mountains', and future rulers picked up the same title.

But the Hashashin weren't the only ones in the assassination business in the Middle East. Both the crusaders and the Muslim princes were responsible for their own fair share of murders, so the Hashashin's exact number of successful hits will probably never be known. In any case, because the sect was so secretive and because almost all our sources come from their enemies, it is hard to separate fact from fiction.

This reputation of mystery and terror that surrounded the group was exactly what they wanted; and while the Hashashin never deployed large armies or conquered vast territories, they were important players in the region. Myths sprung about them, again some of the more fanciful ones are in chapter 5 about the Turks. No person in power from Acre to Astrakhan was safe, including the Mongols. While the Assassins kept a low profile within rising Asian power, they feared their independence could be threatened as the Mongols expanded westward. This led to several assassins being sent to the court of Möngke Khan as emissaries, but Möngke's bodyguard smelled a rat and the assassination attempt was thwarted. Clearly such a naked act of defiance could not go unpunished.

Hulugu was heading westward with his forces when he received the news and made sure to pay a visit to the assassin strongholds. The Mongols had already marched an army across the Gobi Desert, so they had proved their ability to prepare for such arid conditions. It turned out that the Hashashin's strategy of these remote desert strongholds worked against every known threat, except the Mongols. Now this isolation worked against them because with nowhere to go and with no chance of a relief force arriving, the strongholds surrendered, one after another. The Mongols then simply marched the occupants into the desert allowing thirst and dehydration to do their work for them. It was a death march where presumably women and children were part of the doomed Nizari Ismailis. Later, in the 1200s, there was a famous incident when Prince Edward of England (later King Edward I), on crusade in the Middle East, was attacked in his private chambers by a poison-knife-wielding assassin whom he beat to death with a wooden stool, but not before he had been cut by the poison blade. This incident shows that the Hashashin hadn't completely disappeared, but as a major threat to all powers in the Middle East they were effectively neutralised by the Mongols in the 1250s.

The great cities of Aleppo and Damascus were the Mongols' next targets, and they fell easily. The news of Baghdad preceded Hulagu, and as the Mongols had calculated, one massacre can lead to many cities throwing open their gates and suing for peace. The capitulation of these cities effectively ended the Abbasid Caliphate in the north (the caliphate in the south already had been destroyed by the Mamelukes).

This rapid surrender was the chief reason for the Mongols' success. Although they had several large and highly trained armies, they were a small population compared to many areas they were conquering, so if every Mongol target fought to the bitter end or required constant surveillance, Mongol gains would fade away as their troop levels were stretched across vast areas or declined due to attrition. But was it worth sacrificing your city and your life (and that of your family) to help the next city along the road? It was a clever, vicious piece of psychology.

Now there were crusader soldiers marching into cities which had, for a century and half, eluded them. Bohemund I had been the Norman mercenary on the First Crusade who set up the Principality of Antioch; 150 years later we have Bohemund VI brokering a Franco-Mongol treaty where the Crusaders were now acting in alliance with the Mongols against the old enemy, Muslim Egypt (under the new ownership of the Mamelukes). Bohemund VI was a minor player in events and was never going to be rewarded with large prizes, but Antioch was given a number of key forts and towns as a sign of gratitude. Bohemund VI's plan was working, and the key cities that had always threatened Christian lands in the north of Syria were now held by allies – terrifying and bellicose allies, but allies nonetheless.

Hulagu knew that the only viable remaining opposition was the new Mameluke regime in Egypt. He sent ambassadors to Cairo to demand capitulation or face the consequences. The new Sultan Qutuz had the envoys killed. As far as the Mamelukes were concerned, surrender was not an option.

By now Hulagu had conquered huge swathes of Persia, Mesopotamia and Syria. His forces needed consolidation, so he kept the bulk of his force in the north while he despatched General Kitbuqa (a Nestorian Christian) with two tumens (that's 20,000) of Mongol cavalry south to probe the Mameluke forces.

The Mamelukes are often confused with Turks. Indeed, the last great battle involving the Mameluke cavalry was the Battle of the Pyramids in 1798 against Napoleon, when the troops were resplendent in their silks and scimitars, the epitome of Muslim Arab imagery. However, the original Mamelukes (at this time) were a warrior slave cast, and all these very Arabic and Turkic sounding leaders were actually Christian boys who had been sold into slavery, converted to Islam and became the elite forces of the Muslim Egyptian powers. Where had all these Christian boys come from? A large number had to have come from the Caucasus and southern Russia as the Mongols pushed into the region in the 1230s-40s. While it's impossible to know the minds of long dead men, some had to have had firsthand experience of the Mongols as boys, after which their lives had been irrevocably changed, and as such, there had to be a few who saw the Mongols as a personal nemesis. From the Seventh Crusade in Egypt there are firsthand Christian accounts of the violent overthrow of the old regime by the new Mameluke regime. These were battle-hardened men, newly arrived on the scene, and every bit as hungry, expansionist and bellicose as the Mongols. If there was one force in the world that could genuinely match the Mongols, it was the Mamelukes.

In the meantime, Sultan Qutuz and his General Baibars, the two main leaders of the coup against their old masters, were determined to stay in power and rallied the largest army they could muster. The Mamelukes knew that they faced an enemy which had never been beaten in open battle, one that would show no mercy. Here it's important to remember that the Mamelukes had been raised as warriors, and their horse archers were comparable in skill and tactics to the Mongols. It is also likely that Qutuz and Baibars had been sold into slavery as the result of earlier Mongol raids, so there may have been certain personal dimensions to this conflict as well. The stage was set for a titanic clash.

While all this was going on, the once promising co-operation between the Mongols and the Christians soured. The Count of Sidon foolishly attacked the town of Damas, which was garrisoned by a small number of Mongols. It was a minor skirmish but one of Kitbuqa's grandsons was killed. The Mongols could not let something like this go unpunished and the city of Sidon was sacked.

This was an indication (if one were needed) that the Mongols were never going to be reliable allies. Their goal was global conquest, and it's impossible to ally with any group that has such a goal. Pope Alexander IV certainly saw it as an unholy alliance and forbade any further deals with the Mongols. So, when the Mamelukes sent envoys to Acre to ask for the safe passage of their forces through crusader territory (on their way to meet the Mongols), the crusaders (after some dissent and discussion) agreed because the Mongols, despite being erstwhile allies, were seen as the greater danger. The events at Leignitz and Hungary were still fresh in the minds of the Europeans. They would also have been aware of what had happened in Baghdad and while that was an atrocity against Muslims, the Mongols clearly had no qualms about who they annihilated. The Muslim dynasties of the Middle East, by contrast, had rules and could be reasoned with. Saladin hadn't massacred the Christian population of Jerusalem; Frederick II had been able to negotiate Jerusalem's return; and more recently, Louis IX had been well treated in captivity. Would the Mongols have done any of that? It was doubtful. The Christians decided it was a case of 'better the devil you know'.

So, the Mamelukes were granted free access through Christian lands to go to war with the Mongols. Meanwhile, Sultan Qutuz had managed to rally an army of roughly 20,000, approximately equal in size to that of the Mongols. It must have been a chastening sight to the crusaders as they watched their Muslim neighbours ride past their strongholds with an army they could never hope to match.

On 3 September 1260, the Mongols met the Mamelukes at Ayn Jalut. The name is roughly translated as 'the well of Goliath', as the mighty giant from Biblical times was supposed to have rested by a spring in the area. It was an aptly heroic name because the Battle of Ayn Jalut was one of the most important battles in history. It would also have implications for the Crusader States, even though no crusading army was present on the battlefield.

General Baibars was in the lowland region with a small part of the Mameluke force. Both the Mongols and the Mamelukes tried the classic strategy of charging within arrow range, loosing volleys from their re-curved bows and then feigning retreat to try and lure the enemy. It must have been like looking at mirror images. Similar-sized armies, similar tactics and both sides highly mobile. Eventually Baibars succeeded in luring the

Mongols into the highlands where Qutuz was waiting with the bulk of the Mameluke forces.

The Mamelukes tried enveloping the Mongol army, but the Mongols fought so fiercely that the left wing of the Mamelukes began to crumble under the sheer energy of the Mongol attacks. When Qutuz saw this, he joined this wing with the reserves, flinging off his own helmet so his troops could see their sultan leading the charge. During this intense fighting the Mamelukes revealed their secret weapon: a midfa, which seems to have been a very early arquebus or rudimentary musket. It is doubtful that they killed many people, but the loud explosions and flashes of light would have confused and frightened both Mongol soldiers and their horses. This wasn't a decisive ploy, but the fighting was so bitter and the forces were so evenly matched that every little helped.

The Mamelukes did just enough to push back the Mongols, and in the savage melee, Kitbuqa was killed. The loss of their general dealt the Mongols a psychological blow. By the end of a bloody day, the Mongol force was all but destroyed or fleeing. The Mamelukes had earned their hard-won victory. Casualty numbers are unknown, but they were obviously heavy, and for the very first time, the Mongols had lost a decisive battle. They had lost before, most notably in China, but this was in a campaign that continued and ultimately succeeded. Ayn Jalut turned out to be the high-water mark of Mongol expansion and influence in the Middle East. Even though, from a Mongol point of view, this had involved little more than a scouting army and the victory had been narrow, it was a blow to their reputation as invincible.

For the Mamelukes, this victory sealed their reputation as the premier military power in the Middle East. It also gave them the incentive and the momentum to keep pushing north and reclaim some of the Muslim land that had been held by Hulagu. The crusaders may have rid themselves of the devil's horsemen, but they were now in danger of being encircled by a unified Muslim empire run by some of the most formidable warriors in the world.

The universal approval Sultan Qutuz enjoyed after his victory over the Mongols was short-lived. On his return to Cairo he was killed by his own generals. Although Baibars was not at the scene, he was plainly the man behind the plot. Quite why this extremely effective partnership came to such a bloody end will always remain a point of speculation, but we can assume that Qutuz had inadvertently insulted Baibars in some unforgiveable way. So, the leadership of the Mamelukes, which had been taken in bloodshed, was transferred to another Mameluke under similar circumstances.

But let's pause to consider what would have happened had the Mongols won the battle of Ayn Jalut. The destruction of the Mamelukes would have seen the demise of a dynasty that in fact lasted into the 16th century. It would have meant that the whole of the Middle East was now Mongol territory, and we know there would have been at least another generation of Mongol expansion. Under the circumstances, it's hard to see the Crusader States lasting anything more than another couple of years. Further, the Ottomans were able to rise to dominance because of the power vacuums occurring in the Middle East (more on that in chapter 6 on the Ottoman Empire). With Mongol hegemony, that wouldn't have happened, and Osman and his followers would have been just another bunch of mercenaries for hire. So, no Mameluke Sultanate, no Ottoman Empire – and it is not wild speculation to say that had the Mongols wanted to head west, there would have been nothing to stop them.

Without getting too carried away, had the Mongols won at Ayn Jalut, they would probably have wanted the biggest and richest city in Europe, Constantinople. They had conquered larger cities in Asia, and there would have been nothing to stop them heading in this direction. So rather than falling to the Ottomans in 1453, Constantinople would probably have been captured by the Mongols by 1270, quite possibly accompanied by a Baghdad scale of destruction. Looking at events in this way, it is impossible to overestimate the significance of the Battle of Ayn Jalut.

But events after the death of Möngke need to be put into the wider context of, for the first time, the instability that followed in determining who would be the next great khan. Hulagu, warlord of the Ilkhanate, was fully occupied with the Middle East, which took him out of the conversation. It didn't help that another brother, Berke Khan, the warlord of the Golden Horde, was a recent convert to Islam and was incensed by Hulagu's devastation of Baghdad, so much so that the two briefly went to war. With that conflict going on in modern-day Iran, the Mongol leadership came down to two other brothers, Kublai and Ariq Böke. The latter had been made the military commander of Karakorum (the capital of the empire), which suggests that he was the preferred successor; however, no other favours or honours were given to him, and when Möngke died Kublai was in the field with one of the biggest Mongol armies.

Even though we are now in the mid-13th century, the records are reminiscent of the time of the Huns and Avars. We know clashes happened but have no relevant details, and while an exact date can be put on the Battle of Ayn Jalut, this was not the case with any of the battles among the four brothers. These titanic clashes, composed of hundreds of thousands of troops, were far bigger than any other campaigns being conducted on planet earth at this time, but the accounts are as vague and piecemeal as hints about the forced migration of the Huns 800 years earlier. We can only conclude that while Ariq Böke probably had the better claim, Kublai was in a better position, with more soldiers and more resources. While civil war raged until 1264, Kublai always seemed to have the upper hand and eventually vanquished his brother. Ariq Böke died just a few years later, still in captivity. The fact that he died so conveniently, with no real explanation, has led most historians to conclude that he was poisoned and quietly forgotten.

So Kublai became the next great khan and went on to further increase the empire's wealth, resources and fearsome reputation, but the civil war that preceded his victory showed the era of the Mongols was coming to an end. At the time of Genghis Khan's death, the Mongols had witnessed only the rise of their power, and they believed in his call for universal conquest. But we are now several generations removed, and the massive size of the different hordes shows that by the 1260s, while local warlords paid service to the great khan, they were concerned more with matters in their own gigantic domains than with the welfare of the Mongol Empire as a whole. Berke Khan's conversion to Islam indicated that the Mongols, without a strong cultural history of their own, were starting to 'go native'. By the time Kublai Khan's grandson Temür Khan succeeded him to become the next great khan, he was, in reality, a Chinese emperor of the Yuan Dynasty first and a Mongol khan second.

Another indicator of Mongol decline was that while there had always been delays between khans, this time there had been civil war and that would have denuded the number of fighting men. Further, and this cannot be definitively proven, there were likely to have been unsettled grudges between the various Mongol factions even after peace had been declared. In short, the Mongols' enemies were starting to get wise to their tactics and were able to present a stronger opposition just at the point where the Mongol military wasn't quite as effective as it had been. To quote Winston Churchill, 'Now this is not the end. It is not even the beginning of the end. But it is, perhaps, the end of the beginning.'

Kublai's reign started energetically when he stopped the civil war between Berke Khan and Hulagu. When Korea decided to stop sending tribute, a Chinese/Mongol force was sent back to the peninsula where it installed a Mongol puppet king. Vietnam was similarly brought to heel. In 1266, emissaries were sent to Japan for the first time demanding the nation becomes a vassal of the Mongol Empire. They were ignored, and Kublai would remember that. Meanwhile, Kublai reached out to the Song emperor and offered him a form of autonomy if his territories became a vassal state. Too much blood had been spilled for the Song court to accept this and they declined, knowing the full force of the Mongols would inevitably descend on them, which is what happened in 1267.

Between 1267 and 1273, the Mongols returned to Xiangyang, which had been reinforced by the Song as the de facto front line between the Chinese and the Mongols. Kublai put the full power of his giant empire into the area, but it is a testament to the leadership, effective defence and the Song's own formidable resources that this campaign took six years. At this point the Song had a boy emperor, a situation that also illustrated the resilience of the Song administration, because even with a child at its head, the empire could conduct constant warfare to frustrate the Mongols. But in the end, the Mongols broke through and seized control of both the Han and the Yangtze rivers, tearing the heart out of the Song Empire. Nevertheless, it would remain defiant until 1279 and the Battle of Yamen.

The Battle of Yamen demands consideration because up until now, this book has been almost exclusively about horse archers. But the Battle of Yamen was the Mongols' first large-scale naval battle. Because the likes of Kublai or Hulagu had no experience of naval combat, they would have been useless as admirals, so the 'Mongol' leader was the very Chinese Zhang

Hongfan. This Mongol victory had no actual Mongols present. It was also a testament to the Songs' continuing power even this late in their fight with Kublai Khan that they were able to muster (allegedly) 1,000 ships. Zhang Hongfan had a little over 50, but what he lacked in numbers he more than made up for in cunning when he chained his ships together to stop any enemy ships slipping between them. Then he tried to cluster the Song fleet together, hoping to finish them off in one blow with the introduction of fire ships (old ships packed with flammable materials which were set alight and sailed towards the enemy fleet). However, the Song admiral had anticipated this tactic and covered his ships in mud, which meant the fire ships did not set the Song fleet ablaze. Then Zhang Hongfan used the number of the enemy ships against them by keeping them boxed in. Unable to go anywhere, the ships, carrying tens of thousands of men, quickly ran out of food and potable water. Meanwhile, Zhang Hongfan had the enemy admiral's nephew kidnapped and threatened with harm to force a surrender, but to no avail.

Zhang Hongfan tried every trick in the book as the enemy weakened through hunger and thirst. Next, he separated his force into four groups, each group going to a point on the compass to 'surround' the much larger fleet. When they were ordered to play music, the Song forces believed some kind of ceremony or festival was taking place and let their guard down. When Zhang Hongfan ordered an attack, seven Song ships were sunk, and the Mongol forces (with their marines) boarded the confused, weakened and unprepared Song vessels. They cut through the outer vessels and were aiming for the centre where the enemy admiral, the Song Prime Minister and the child emperor were located. When the Prime Minister saw Kublai's forces breaking through, he took the boy emperor in his arms and jumped overboard, a defiant act of self-destruction. Rather

A park created in commemoration of the battle of Yamen in Xinhui, Jiangmen, Guangdong. (Courtesy Windless Long Night, under Creative Commons 3.0)

than fall into the hands of the destested enemy, many of the court officials, concubines and others did the same.

With the emperor and court all dead and the mighty Song fleet either destroyed or captured, the Song dynasty came to an end. It had lasted for over 300 years until it met the might of the Mongols. China was once again unified under one ruler, but that ruler was not Chinese, he was the Mongolian Kublai Khan who created the new Yuan Dynasty. Yuan is still used today as the name of the Chinese currency. Translated it means central, eternal, universal, the perfect name for a dynasty whose authority would spread into eastern Europe. It was Kublai Khan who would make Beijing the capital city of his empire.

This was the moment the Mongol Empire reached its zenith. Korea, Vietnam, the whole of central Asia, the Caucasus, Iran,

Iraq and parts of eastern Europe were all under the authority of Kublai Khan, who presided over the largest contiguous empire the world has ever seen (the British Empire was the larger, but it was not contiguous as it had territories spread all over the globe).

In 1274, Kublai Khan sent a fleet into the Sea of Japan to invade the country. Six times emissaries had been sent to the Japanese imperial court, and on every occasion they were ignored. The Mongols had never been masters of diplomacy, and they stuck to their always-successful strategy: after the threats came the knockout blow of invasion. The same blueprint would be used on the island archipelago.

Quite sensibly, the Mongol forces started with the closest Japanese island to the Chinese coast, Tsushima. When they landed, they totally overwhelmed the local garrison (although one record states that a solitary samurai killed 25 enemy before succumbing to his wounds). The Mongols, who had fought western knights in steel armour and assassins in the deserts of Syria were now fighting samurai on the beaches of Tsushima. (The samurai had begun around the year 1,000 AD and remained a viable military force into the 1800s). Then it was the turn of another small Japanese home island, Iki. The local castle was surrounded and again the small garrison quickly fell to the Mongols. The Japanese recorded that some of the women on the island were executed, stripped naked and tied to the bows of the invading ships when they arrived at the much larger island of Kyūshū.

The arrival of the Mongols heralded a rapid response from the local forces of samurai, and on the second day a sizeable Japanese force met the Mongols at the First Battle of Hakata Bay, where the invaders displayed a mixture of Chinese and Mongol tactics. The invaders had not brought horses but they had brought plenty of archers, and the samurai had to contend with a blizzard of arrows. Added to that were the phalanx-like formations of infantry which could beat off frontal assaults, and gunpowder rockets; the samurai had never before fought anything like this enemy. Indeed, at the time, Japanese warfare was heavily ritualised. Often a samurai would come to the front of the formed ranks to lay down a challenge to a specific enemy samurai. During this campaign, a few samurai tried this, but the Mongols, not knowing or not caring, simply had the archers kill the challenging lone warrior. That tradition finished with the Mongol invasion of Japan, so the Mongols changed Japanese culture just as they had changed the cultures of other conquered lands.

The Japanese were roundly defeated, and while larger armies lay on other Japanese islands, the emphatic outcome of every clash showed that the Mongols had nothing to fear from this new enemy. The night after the First Battle of Hakata Bay, a huge tropical storm blew up. When the surviving Japanese arrived to spy on the enemy encampment the following day, they discovered that the Mongols had all gone. The typhoon had forced their armada to retreat, and in the high seas most of the ships had foundered or been scattered. The Japanese had been saved by mother nature. It had been a very close-run thing.

Kublai Khan had not forgotten how he had nearly brought another nation under his authority, so shortly after the Song had been vanquished, plans for a second invasion of Japan were drawn up. More than a thousand ships were amassed, and more than a hundred thousand troops were assembled. Because there were no longer any enemies in the vicinity, Kublai could focus all his resources on this one challenge, and this time he had more than enough men and ships to carry out a two-pronged attack, using an Eastern and a Southern Route force. Once again, the islands of Tsushima and Iki fell with ease, but the Japanese authorities weren't dumb. The reputation of the

Mongols preceded them and the Japanese knew they would be back, so preparations had been made, including bonfire sites on the coast which could be lit as an early warning signal.

The Eastern Route was supposed to wait for the Southern Route at the island of Iki, but things were going so well that they proceeded ahead of schedule. The Eastern Route fleet split their forces in half and simultaneously attacked Hakata Bay and Nagato Province. A total of three hundred ships attacked Nagato but were driven off and forced to return to Iki. The remaining force was large but only about a quarter of the soldiers that had been planned were there when the Mongol forces attacked Hakata Bay, now heavily fortified with a defensive wall and positions for archers to shower the landing area with arrows. The Mongols were forced back and dropped anchor at the two tiny islands of Shika and Noko. That night Japanese defenders sailed small fishing boats to the Mongol fleet and carried out a daring night raid. One samurai returned with 21 heads heaped up in his boat. The brief landing at the bay and the subsequent raid became known as the Second Battle of Hakata Bay, but once again, the anchored fleet was annihilated by a powerful typhoon, and once again, an invasion had been thwarted not by tactics or bravery, but by storms.

These were the most daring attempts to invade the Japanese home islands until the Second World War. The idea that Japan was blessed by the gods, that divine powers would not allow the Japanese to be invaded, were spun into legend. The typhoons were no longer regarded as natural weather events and were given a new name: kamikaze, divine wind. The name gained global notoriety during the closing stages of the war when Japan defended its islands with a new divine wind manifested in the suicide pilots who smashed their aircraft into allied shipping. This was an echo of Mongol history in the 20th century.

It was at this point, at the height of the Mongol Empire, that a Venetian trader called Marco Polo headed east to meet with the great khan to try and arrange favourable trading terms. He travelled with his father and uncle, but it was Marco who seems to have caught the attention of Kublai's court, and later it was Marco who would write of his experiences in *The Travels of Marco Polo*.

The book was not without its controversies. At the time of publication, it was seen as a fantasy, a new version of the Arabian Nights, as the sheer wealth and complexities of the Chinese civilisation was thought to be exaggeration, tall tales told by a master storyteller. Later still, there were criticisms about place names and what some historians thought were glaring omissions. However, by the end of the 20th century, textual analysis revealed that while there are omissions and exaggerations, the place names doubts had been resolved and the sheer level of detail about everything from salt production to the accurate description of currency (the Mongols had introduced the first unified paper currency, something completely unknown in Europe) meant that this was a unique outsider's view of the Mongol Empire. It appears that Marco Polo served as a foreign diplomat throughout the eastern part of the empire and beyond, into Southeast Asia, including Vietnam (which still had periods of revolt) as well as the non-vassal states which had all tasted potential invasion by Mongol forces, including India, Sri Lanka, Myanmar and Indonesia.

Marco Polo sometimes focussed on specific events and people, such as the Assassins, but he also knew how to tell a tall tale, one of which was thought to be the story of Khutulun. She was a real woman (and her existence is verified in another source) whose very existence countered the arguments that the Mongol court in China was going soft, something that was not the case in other areas of the empire. Khutulun was a member of the royal family, so she was a princess, only she did not go in for tiaras and ballgowns.

Living in central Asia, in the heart of the Eurasian Steppe, Khutulun was every inch the epitome of the Mongol ideal. The story goes that she wanted to marry well and that she would select as her husband the man who could beat her in a wrestling match. Mongolian wrestling is still incredibly popular in the country today, so while it was even then unusual for a woman to do it, it was not unheard of. The man who could beat her would gain her hand in marriage, but when any potential candidates lost, they had to give her 100 horses. Apparently, she gave up looking for suitors after winning 10,000 horses, a reminder that since the era of the Huns steppe nomads measured personal wealth in the number of horses they possessed. When there were rumours that Khutulun was having an incestuous relationship with her father, she finally picked a failed marital candidate (one she liked) to be her husband and quashed the rumours. Is any of this impossible? No, but the tale of Khutulun is a good one to tell around the campfire. Khutulun was fierce, proud and totally uncompromising. Personally, I hope it's a true story, but we will never know.

At a time when there were no other written records, Marco Polo's writings preserve the rich elements of a mighty empire that did not exist seventy years earlier and will have vanished in another seventy years. In 1281, Kublai's favourite wife Chabi died and he began to withdraw from public life. His last few years saw military failures when the Mongols attempted invasions of neighbouring territories; the closest he came to outright victory in the late 1280s was the attempted invasion of the kingdom of modern Myanmar, which became a vassal state. Vietnam was always a hotbed of resentment. Tibet also revolted and was successfully suppressed at the cost of the death of thousands of Tibetan civilians.

Closer to home, members of Kublai's extended family were constantly vying for political power, which at times led to outright civil war (that Kublai won), and not just in China but in the broader empire. Then there was his relationship with his son and chosen successor Zhenjin. This is not a Mongolian name but a Chinese one. Zhenjin was a Confucian and learned how to administer under the tutelage of his father, but when allowed to do this on his own, he used the Chinese administrative model, which was effective but also a sign that the young man saw himself more as a Chinese Yuan emperor rather than a Mongol warlord. As Kublai grew older and became more insular it was suggested that he abdicate in favour of Zhenjin. This incensed Kublai. He refused to speak to his son, who lapsed into alcoholism and died in 1286. Kublai was distraught. When he realised that his health was irrevocably failing, he named Zhenjin's son Temür as his heir. When Kublai died in 1294, he was not buried in his Yuan capital of Beijing; his body was returned to his ancestral home in Mongolia. And so Temür became the sixth great khan of the Mongol Empire and the second emperor of the Yuan Dynasty in China. Unlike his father, Temür had a Mongolian name and had ridden by the side of Kublai Khan during the civil war in the 1280s. But he ruled using Confucian ideas, and in an early edict he ordered that Confucius should be revered, showing that this was really a Chinese emperor playing at being a Mongol.

Temür lacked the global vision of the other great khans. Sensibly, he stopped preparations for a third invasion of Japan and shored up relations, either through diplomacy or force, with the usual nations in southeast Asia. But a close look at his forces reveals they are all Chinese, with Yuan imperial fleets and tens of thousands of Yuan infantry. Temür never ventured further west than the borders of China, and while other areas of Mongol administration paid lip service to him being the great khan, this was not like the era of Ögedei, where total authority emanated from the great khan's court, and nobody even thought to object. And as for the tactics and culture of the Eurasian Steppe nomads, like the Ottomans, these Mongols remembered their roots as a type of legend, while their day-to-day lives, influences and culture were a world away from living in a yurt with only your horse, your bow and your falcon. As we will see, Mongol power and influence over the Eurasian Steppe would continue for generations to come, but the age of empire was over.

9

EMIR TIMUR

On each occasion, when a new Eurasian Steppe nomadic group arrived on the scene, a substantial amount of time had passed since the previous group's arrival. Often it was centuries, but the gap between the death of Temür, grandson of Kublai Khan, and the birth of baby Timur from an inauspicious family in central Asia, was less than 30 years. Their names are similar, but they couldn't have more different backgrounds, careers and legacies.

Before we come to the life of Timur, we must consider what was going on with the Mongol khans to the west of Yuan China. In 1299, while Temür was carrying out diplomatic missions with his far eastern neighbours, Hulagu's territory of the Ilkhanate was now run by Ghazan. He was a direct descendant of Hulagu, but he was raised as a Buddhist who then converted to Islam. However, in 1299, he decided to pick up where his ancestor had left off and went to war with the Mamelukes; over a year he conducted a lightning-fast campaign that would capture the whole of the levant. Huge cities like Aleppo and Damascus fell, but there were no massacres. The Mamelukes were met in the field at the Battle of Wadi al-Khaznadar and were swept aside by the Mongols. The fighting included the classic horse archers, feints and cavalry manoeuvres, although there was heavy melees at times. This is what the Mongols were remembered for rather than the fleets and infantry forces of Yuan China. The victory was reversed in 1303 at the Battle of Marj al-Saffar, which was fought in an identical way, only this time the Mongols lost. The battles between the Mamelukes and the Mongols show that they were martial powers of equal efficacy.

In 1300, the Mongols captured Jerusalem. This sent shockwaves around Europe. Now was the chance to reclaim the Holy City once and for all from the Muslim infidel. This was completely wishful thinking as Ghazan was Muslim and would never have relinquished Al Quds (the Arabic for Jerusalem, which means 'the Holy') either as a new convert to Islam or as a Mongol warlord. The fighting went on until 1313. Ghazan had died by then, and he was succeeded by his equally vigorous brother Öljaitü (although his other name was Mohammad-e Khodabande, which shows that he had also become a convert to Islam). His invasion culminated in an unsuccessful siege of Rahbat in Syria. This marked the end of the attempts to expand into Syria and the Holy Land, but the Mongols remained a significant power east of the Euphrates River. Indeed, the Ilkhanate was never conquered; the Mongol ruling elite simply interbred itself into the local population.

By the 1330s, the Yuan dynasty was in the grip of civil war and would eventually be replaced by the Han Chinese Ming dynasty; which brings us to Jani Beg, khan of the Golden Horde that stretched across the north of the Eurasian Steppe as far as the Black Sea coast to the west. Kaffa was a Genoese trading outpost on the northeastern coast of the Black Sea. It was one of the terminus points of the Silk Road, and from there, the Genoese were able to take goods on either to Constantinople or to the Dardanelles and into the Mediterranean, where they could be plugged into their extensive trade network.

Jani Beg was very much from the old school of Mongol principles. To become the ruler he had to order the execution of two of his brothers, and he spent a large amount of his reign bullying the vassal princes of Muscovy. He, also, was a convert to Islam, but like a lot of the Mongol converts (and as we shall see with Timur) that didn't stop them doing some very un-Islamic things, like drinking himself into a stupor. In 1343, he tried to besiege Kaffa but was unsuccessful as the Genoese had full access to the sea and a relief force arrived to break the siege. (These events were happening after the birth of Timur who, far to the east as a boy, was oblivious to them.) As we have seen before, the Mongols throughout their primacy were never masters of siege warfare, but they were masters of sheer bloody-mindedness. In 1345, Jani Beg was back, and this time he was better prepared for a longer siege, even bringing rock-throwing siege engines with him. However, he could do nothing about the threat that all besieging forces faced, disease. Humans are more susceptible to illnesses caused by bad water than anything else. Cholera and dysentery can be lethal. Malaria is a consequence of mosquitoes breeding in stagnant water, and despite all the descriptions of bloodshed in this book, malaria has killed more humans than anything else, ever.

But the illness that developed in this siege was different. It involved an unusually high fever and weakness so extreme it was hard to tell who was alive and who was dead. Then there were the buboes, black swellings on the groin and in the armpits, sometimes with bleeding. The result was a scene of nightmares, and it was spreading. Jani Beg was furious. He had carefully planned his return and his revenge on Kaffa, but disease was robbing him of his prize. He ordered the dead to be loaded onto his trebuchets and fired into Kaffa. Imagine what this was like for the occupants, surrounded by the feared Mongols, not knowing when relief would arrive. Then, something comes arcing through the air: not a rock, but a man who silently smashes onto the dirt street where his body bursts, spreading blood, viscera and infection everywhere. Today we understand germ theory (the idea that micro-organisms such as bacteria and viruses cause disease, became only widely accepted in the late 1800s), but at that time, even though the causes of disease were unknown, nobody was going near that mess.

Bodies rained down on the terrified Genoese, and the sickness soon began to spread behind the walls of Kaffa. The Genoese had no option but to leave. They were a trading nation, so they had ships ready to go, and they fled to their three hubs in Genoa, Messina and Constantinople, carrying the disease with them. Exactly how the Black Death arrived in Europe in the 1340s is still debated, but in the author's opinion this is the most plausible explanation. Everyone agrees that the plague had its origins in Asia and was bound to have spread along the Silk Road where vast stretches were still under Mongol control. So, if Jani Beg's assault on Kaffa was the cause of this pandemic, his catapults were the most lethal weapons in history. Records are patchy but historians who research disease estimate 50% of Europe's population was wiped out by this pestilence. Half of Europe was dead by 1349.

Despite the fading away of the Mongol Empire, Timur's early life took place during a period of relative calm. The Ilkhanate, Golden Horde and Chagatai Khanate (south of the Golden Horde but north of India, right in the centre of Asia) were still vast territories. There were intermittent clashes among them, but it was not a period of instability and constant warfare. Timur himself was born in the Chagatai Khanate, and there has been much debate around his heritage. Because he was to rise so high, later annals like to link him to Genghis Khan's extended family. I think this is unlikely as he went out of his way to marry Saray Mulk Khanum, his first wife (and therefore the most senior of the wives), who was herself a direct descendent of Genghis Khan.

Then there was the question of exactly how wealthy Timur's father was. Again, some later records downplay his estate, which makes Timur's rise even more remarkable. This could be true, or again, the writer could have had an eye on what makes a good story. Even his birth year is contested. Most historians agree on the late 1320s, but many records specifically put the date as 1336. This date is important as it implies a link to the Ilkhanate in the year it disintegrates. So, splitting the difference, he is likely to have been born of a Mongol family which might have had a distant connection with the royal lineage of the great khans, but as the family holdings were modest, either the family had suffered a substantial fall from grace or were very much on the fringes of the main event.

Either Timur's parents failed to teach their son about boundaries, or the family had fallen on such hard times that banditry was required to supplement their income, but by his late teens Timur had gathered a group of close friends who carried out raids on traders and local shepherds. Even though we are talking about the 1360s, this rough-and-ready lifestyle would have been an upbringing Genghis Khan or even Attila the Hun would have recognised and is a reminder that while separated by centuries, these peoples shared common threads of culture, tradition and martial prowess.

In his early twenties, in the process of stealing some sheep from a local shepherd, the young Timur failed to make good his escape and was struck by two arrows; one tore off two fingers on his right hand and the other struck him in the leg, after which he was paralysed down one side of his body. Timur is arguably the greatest general in history, and he became so with all the limitations of his paralysis. These limitations meant he had to be helped into the saddle, an incredibly ignominious requirement for someone of Mongol stock, but as we shall see, he didn't let his disability get in the way of his goals. (If he were to enter the modern Paralympics, he would be classified T42).

His paralysis led to his nickname, Timur the Lame, which was condensed into English as either Tamerlane, or in the case of Christopher Marlowe's play, Tamburlaine the Great. So, in the West we remember a man by a name he never used, wouldn't have recognised and would have considered a huge insult (after translation) had he been aware of it. The reason for the title of this chapter is that as he rose in power he used the title Emir Timur, and if that's what he wanted people to call him, I will happily carry out his wishes because he was so feared his reputation has echoed down the centuries.

It must have taken months for Timur to stabilise from his serious injuries, but his small band of horsemen was gaining a reputation, and Timur became a warband leader under the Chagatai khan, unhelpfully called Tughlugh Timur Khan. As Timur gradually proved his ability to lead, his influence grew. When Tughlugh Timur died, his son managed to provoke Timur into rebellion with a local warlord chieftain called Amir Husayn. This led to a campaign in which one side tried to outmanoeuvre the other, and eventually Timur fought against this previous ally. This period of fighting culminated in the siege of Balkh, a large town in the western part of modern-day Afghanistan. It had once been much bigger, until Genghis Khan at the head of a Mongol army had razed it in 1220. A century and half later it had only recently been rebuilt. The siege lasted only a few days. Amir Husayn's forces were the same as the horsemen that Timur had and, as such, he did not want to sit it out. So, on the first day they rode out and attacked Timur, forcing him to retreat, but he was back the next day, and when Amir Husayn's forces tried the same tactic, Timur was ready for them. As the enemy forces came through the bottleneck of the town's gates, he attacked and pushed his way into the town.

While Timur's forces began sacking the town, Amir Husayn retreated to the central fort, and from this citadel he negotiated with Timur. He offered to leave the area and go on pilgrimage to Mecca, never to return, if Timur spared his life. Even after this was agreed, Amir Husayn tried to hide, but he was captured and handed over. Timur kept his promise and, without harming him, let him go; however, Amir Husayn was immediately killed by a chief who had had a previous feud with him.

By now Timur was the premier military power in the Chagatai Khanate, but he had a dilemma and started issuing missives about how he was a descendant of Jochi, Genghis Khan's first but illegitimate (by now this had probably been forgotten) son. His rise to power echoed that of his role model Genghis Khan, but if he truly was from the family of the great khans, why would he depose another family member? Also, while he was a Muslim, he couldn't claim to be a caliph as he didn't have the Arab or Islamic heritage to back it up. So, when he became far more powerful than the khans of the various Mongol territories who became his puppets, he took the title 'emir', which simply means general (in Arabic, again revealing his connection with Islam). Emir Timur would gain many epithets from both allies and enemies, but perhaps the most apt was 'sword of Islam'. And what was to come was 35 years of conquests. Alexander the Great earned his name because of his 8-year unbeaten campaign across the known world. Timur was unbeaten for 35 years, and he not only did it paralysed down one side of his body, he also left a far more positive legacy for his heirs. Because of this he should be better remembered in military history.

As Timur's power grew, a young Mongol princeling called Tokhtamysh failed to take over the Golden Horde and was forced to flee. He sought refuge in Timur's court where Timur was only too glad to have a Mongol prince of Genghis Khan's bloodline on hand. Timur gave him support and resources so he could try again. Tokhtamysh not only lost the next battle, he was wounded as well and only survived by swimming across a river, putting him out of the reach of his enemies. After attempt number two, he was back in Timur's court where he was once again warmly welcomed. However, hot on his heels were emissaries from the khan of the Golden Horde, demanding that Tokhtamysh be handed over. Timur was loyal to the would-be warlord and declared Tokhtamysh the new khan of the Golden Horde. This compelled the current khan to send an army towards Timur's nascent empire, only for there to be a standoff over the winter of 1376-77; after this, the khan was forced to retreat and Timur installed Tokhtamysh in the town of Otrar.

Once he was installed in his own power base, Tokhtamysh never looked back. He began expanding westwards, steadily winning territory from the khan of the Golden Horde. All of this was happening as Timur began his expansion into modern-day Iran and Afghanistan. His first target was the oasis city of Herat, a vital stopping point on the Silk Road. The occupants made the mistake of resisting without having an effective army to resist with, and consequently, we see the very Mongol tradition of showing what happened to cities that did not immediately capitulate. This massacre was on the scale of the atrocities carried out by the Mongol Empire, but Timur went further and reduced the city to rubble, torching everything and pulling down the remains. It was ten years after Timur's death that the first attempts to rebuild this important waypoint began.

But it wasn't all death and destruction. Early on in his rise to power, Timur had fewer troops than his lofty goals required. There's a famous story that he arrived at one walled city and exaggerated his forces while demanding an immediate surrender.

His troops were deliberately spread out over the neighbouring hills to make the force look larger than it was. Indeed, had it been attacked at that point, with his men so thinly spread, it would certainly have resulted in a crushing defeat. Timur was counting on the active imaginations of the local population rather than looking at the hard facts of the situation. After he gave the locals a night to think about it, he ordered each of his men to set a campfire that usually signalled a hub of soldiers. Anywhere up to a dozen men might congregate around one, so what was the point of wasting all that fuel for one man? The answer again was image. From the perspective of the anxious inhabitants, it seemed the surrounding hillsides were covered in the fires of the enemy force. It was a simple and effective way to exaggerate the size of the force by at least a factor of ten. When Timur went back the next day to seek an answer from the local ruler, the gates were flung open. Nobody had died and a victory was secured by intelligent subterfuge rather than brute force.

Similarly, a little later in his reign, when Timur came to another walled city, his emissaries demanded capitulation. This time the local chief said that he would accede if he could conduct a one-to-one duel with Timur. The messengers returned to Timur to ask what he wanted to do, and to everyone's surprise Timur accepted (his paralysis and that he was missing two fingers from his right hand meant he was likely to lose). Timur arrived the next morning at the gates of the city, resplendent in his robes, with a scimitar in its sheath. He was ready to fight. It must have been at this point that the local leader realised his folly: if he lost, he would be killed, and if he killed Timur, his men would surely want revenge. And so, the gates were opened and Timur rode in with no opposition or violence; it was only the suggestion of violence that was needed in this case.

In an eerie foreshadowing of the 20th century, Timur also had to deal with rebels in Afghanistan who hid from the invading forces in cave networks in the mountains. In more recent times both the Soviet Union and NATO have had problems fighting entrenched forces on this terrain, and they had guided missiles and attack helicopters. Timur had no such advantages, but he ordered his men to climb the mountains, and from the heights lower themselves down in baskets to the mouths of the caves where the occupants were threatened with archers or by simply stacking hay up at the front and igniting a fire to smoke them out.

After Afghanistan, Timur pushed into Persia and captured Khorasan. The citizens knew what was coming and surrendered immediately. But a year later, presumably thinking that Timur would be too busy conquering other territories, they rebelled. Timur was just as thorough as the Mongols and returned to slaughter the occupants, singling out some to be cemented alive into the new walls. As we have seen confirmed on multiple occasions, the Mongols could be cold and calculating mass murderers, but Timur added a new layer of cruelty to it.

This was demonstrated in Isfahan when this major city capitulated immediately and was shown clemency. But then, for reasons known only to the local population, the city's inhabitants killed Timur's tax collectors and the garrison. The response was as predictable as it was brutal. Timur arrived with an army and slaughtered everyone. But that was only phase one. Timur knew that there were always survivors of these massacres; there was always a basement missed or a warrior bribed to spare a rich family. So, he waited a week and came back and killed all the survivors. That was phase two. In all of Mongol history this had never been done before. But there was a phase three. With no surviving witnesses to these horrific acts, Timur needed to provide proof of his iron will as a warning to others. A contemporary record states there were over 28 pyramidal towers constructed of about 1,500 heads each, laid out around the edges of this scene of destruction. The pyramids confirmed the deaths of 42,000, although the actual death toll is thought to have been about three times that.

Timur was conquering what a generation earlier had been the Ilkhanate, so it was a sign of how far the martial powers of this area had fallen to have been overwhelmed so quickly by a new force from the East. Some have argued that too much emphasis has been put on the bloodshed, pointing out that the intellectual elites and artisans were spared, and it has been shown that the highpoint of Persian miniature painting occurred during this era. While all of this is true, I find it disingenuous to say consider all the great art and forget about the death and destruction.

By around 1390, Timur was attacking Georgia, which was then suffering from its third wave of Eurasian Steppe nomads (the Turks, the Mongols and now Timur). Unlike Subutai more than a century and a half earlier, Timur's forces were not a reconnaissance force but a main army. Georgia simply did not have anywhere close to the resources required to match Timur and quickly became a vassal state. Over his lifetime, Georgia would always wait for Timur to be a long way away before rebelling, which they did multiple times, only to face the inevitable vicious onslaught of a Timurid army returning to wreak its retribution in blood and fire.

After his initial conquest of Georgia, Timur turned south and captured Baghdad without much of a fight and from there moved into Syria. The only thing stopping him from advancing on Egypt was an unexpected new enemy. The previously mentioned Tokhtamysh, a descendant of Genghis Khan, was now an important khan within the Golden Horde, thanks in no small part to Timur who, in the early days of his rise to power, had given him refuge and had helped and protected him. After that, Tokhtamysh had been consolidating his position and pushing further westwards, where he confronted Novgorod, a rising new nation that covered a vast area of eastern Europe in what is now modern-day Belorussia, Ukraine and western Russia; Novgorod is seen as the progenitor of these countries. In 1382, Tokhtamysh decided that as a vassal territory of the Golden Horde, this new nation wasn't submissive enough and attacked. First, he arrested all Novgorodian traders in his territory of the Golden Horde, then he confiscated their boats, which allowed him to get his army across the formidable natural barrier of the Volga. When he arrived in Novgorodian lands, the grand prince immediately capitulated. According to the rules of steppe warfare, the lands were left unmolested. Moscow, however, had other ideas, and Grand Prince Dmitrij of Moscow did not immediately give tribute. Instead, he came up with the very practical solution of leaving a large garrison in Moscow while he went to friendly neighbours to see if he could gather more forces. But before the prince could return, Tokhtamysh arrived at Moscow in the summer of 1382, and again, cunning rather than brutality won the day. By using another Novgorodian prince, they tricked the garrison into opening the gates after only three days of siege. Tokhtamysh's army flooded into the town, killing the occupants, sacking the city of all its goods and razing it ... again. The early history of Moscow really is little more than its periodic destruction at the hands of Eurasian Steppe nomads. Tokhtamysh was now the dominant force in the northern steppe territories, which ran from eastern Europe to Siberia. There was nowhere left to expand that didn't involve heading into Timur's rich lands to the south.

Tokhtamysh had finally conquered the Golden Horde by 1385, and things came to a head during Timur's campaign in Persia, when Tokhtamysh repaid all the help he had received from Timur by invading eastern Persia. Timur was justifiably furious and what followed was ten years of cat-and-mouse manoeuvring, raiding and shadow boxing between these two most powerful Eurasian warlords over thousands of miles of steppe. Their fight consumed a decade of each of their lives.

Once again, we see the same issues we saw in the first few chapters with the Huns, Avars and Magyars. The internal power struggles of these groups were never far away, and even came to the fore in what became the civil war that preceded Kublai Khan's confirmation as the great khan. Unfortunately, we have only fragmentary evidence for the war between Timur and Tokhtamysh in what was, for its time, the most important and probably the largest conflict on earth. Disappointingly, this war has fewer records than those for the Ottoman expansion into the Balkans or the Hundred Years' War in Europe (both events are contemporary to this), conflicts that are seared into the consciousness of the nations involved. All we can say with any certainty is that they were sideshows compared to the gigantic but mysterious clashes going on in central Asia. We know that both sides used their highly mobile horse archers as the main body of their forces, just as they had done in the preceding millennium. So much had changed in the world over those thousand years (the fall of the Western Roman Empire, the rise of Islam and the invention of gunpowder to name just three), but this effective form of warfare was still lethal and fit for purpose centuries later.

Tabriz in eastern Azerbaijan was the first place Tokhtamysh attacked. He had no intention of taking it but plundered it to humiliate Timur. When Tokhtamysh retreated to friendly territory Timur was forced to follow him into the great grass ocean of the Eurasian Steppe. A few locations can be confirmed in this clash of two warlords, where the prize was a gigantic territory that dwarfed western Europe. The first phase involved chasing Tokhtamysh out of Timur's lands, and the two armies would occasionally skirmish as they moved over a thousand miles northwest until they met in 1391 at the Battle of the Kondurcha River. The location is a few hundred miles north of the Caspian Sea in modern-day southwestern Russia: the middle of nowhere.

This was a classic cavalry engagement. It is thought that both forces were of similar size, but actual numbers are unknowable. Tokhtamysh's tried to get around the flanks of Timur's army to block it off from retreat and annihilate it. However, Timur's force stopped the manoeuvre which was followed by flanking attacks that Timur was able to withstand. Due to his attempts to encircle the enemy, Tokhtamysh's army was now spread thin, and this allowed Timur to attack the enemy centre, which lost its cohesion, and Tokhtamysh was forced to retreat. It had been a clear victory for Timur, but Tokhtamysh was still in the field with most of his army intact. This kind of fighting would have been familiar to Attila the Hun, and yet it was happening nearly 1,000 years later, emphasising the connective tissue between these nomadic steppe groups.

Tokhtamysh withdrew beyond the horizon and escaped Timur's forces. There followed several years of searching for Tokhtamysh and his men, but he remained out of sight until he revealed himself in 1395 when he again attacked Timur's empire. Of course, Timur responded, and they cautiously shadowed each other along the Terek River in the Caucasus. They were on opposite sides and neither wanted to commit to crossing the natural obstacle as this would break their formations and slow them down as the horses struggled through the water; the perfect opportunity for an ambush. Timur showed his guile by carefully splitting his forces in such a way that Tokhtamysh didn't notice, and further along, out of sight, part of Timur's force forged the river and sprung a surprise attack on Tokhtamysh's right flank. At this point (and presumably after the exchange of secret messages) some of the leaders of Tokhtamysh's left flank declared for Timur and began attacking their own army. This allowed Timur to cross with the rest of his force, and Tokhtamysh's Golden Horde was shattered. When Timur descended on the homelands of the Golden Horde, he sacked several cities and claimed the Golden Horde's lands as part of his empire, nearly doubling it in size. As usual, he did not become the official khan; he gave that title to one of his family members, but everyone knew who the great overlord was. Now that this foe was out of the way, Timur could focus on more important targets.

Tokhtamysh escaped Timur's personal retribution by always staying one step ahead, but he had lost almost everything and was no longer a threat. After this final blow he arrived with a small force in Novgorod and fought as little more than a mercenary warband chief. This conflict did not go well for him, and he was forced to leave. He spent the early 1400s trying to rally support and had modest success in some areas of Siberia, an area that had once been under his control. Timur had been a costly distraction and Tokhtamysh was killed in battle by an enemy warlord in 1406.

Timur had proved himself against the forces that fought in the traditional horse archer way. He had experience in sieges and had fought against a western nation like Georgia, but those had been easy victories and nothing, apart from Tokhtamysh, could have been considered a serious threat. It was time to test his mettle against stronger foes.

But first there was a rather strange diversion. In the early 1390s, Timur attacked several key Ismaili towns. The Nizari Ismailis were what the Assassins had evolved into (this sect of Islam exists today and has completely turned its back on its violent medieval past), but Nizari Ismailis are not Sunni Muslims, and it seems Sunni Timur felt it was his duty as a *ghazi* (a holy warrior) to eradicate the heretics. They were no real threat, but the fighting in Anjudan showed yet again that Timur could think his way out of a problem. There was no field of battle, no massed ranks; instead, the locals fought in tunnels that connected many of the buildings in the town. This one tactic neutralised both Timur's numbers and his main mode of fighting, as horses are not natural burrowers. Timur's solution was ingenious and brutally pragmatic. He used the manpower of his forces to redirect a local river down into the tunnels, drowning all the locals.

What separates Timur from the pure shamanistic Eurasian Steppe nomads are his links to Samarkand and Islam. The modern capital of Uzbekistan is Tashkent, but Timur's capital was Samarkand. Because his base was in a city and not a tented itinerate community, Samarkand was lavished with the wealth of his conquests. Palaces and, in particular, mosques were erected using the finest artisans captured in his conquests. Narrowed domes, almost cupola-like, were the preferred style. The outer walls were covered in brightly glazed tiles. Due to the restrictions of iconography in Islam, the images were not of people or animals but complex geometric patterns and intricate calligraphy of Quranic texts. Timurid architecture is distinct and recognised as separate to other Islamic architectural traditions by art historians today. For the first time, the steppe nomads are connected to a unique architectural style.

Timur's time was contemporary with the Ottoman Empire (as we shall see), and as such, it was not surprising that people who originated as steppe nomads had taken the Islamic faith. As both Timur and the Ottomans became more sedentary, they decided to build for Allah, which also provided a means of displaying their own wealth and power. However, before we give too much weight to Timur's faith, it is worth pointing out that like many other Eurasian nomads, he liked a drink (alcohol is forbidden in Islam). His feasts, while pork-free, were heavy on the booze, and there are many accounts of Timur and his closest friends drinking themselves into unconsciousness. A Spanish traveller recorded this account given by a man named Clavijo, who described how Timur's eight wives entered and sat on a dais (Islam forbids the intermingling of the sexes outside of family), each one positioned slightly lower than the last to show a clear hierarchy of the wives (with his first wife, Saray Mulk Khanum, in charge). Clavijo also described their ornate clothing and the way the wives covered their faces in white lead makeup. From this we can conclude that Timur was pragmatic in his faith rather than devout. He followed the teachings of the Quran right up to the point where he didn't want to, and then he did his own thing.

Timur's next opponent had the very Muslim name of Nasir-ud-Din Mahmud Shah Tughluq of the Tughluq Dynasty. You might assume that he was a Syrian chieftain, but no. Nasir-ud-Din Mahmud Shah Tughluq (who will now be called Nasiruddin for simplicity's sake) was the Sultan of Delhi. In the next chapter we will look at how some proud Muslim leaders in India have been made more Hindu friendly, but a sizeable part of northern India was under Muslim rule during Timur's time (although many subjects were Hindus or Sikhs).

The Mongols had tried to invade the Delhi sultanate on several occasions a century earlier, but they were limited to raiding and plundering rather than taking on the sultans in pitched battle. Timur was out to conquer this Islamic empire, and consequently, both sides drew up outside Delhi in 1398. Timur brought his huge army of mainly cavalry across the Indus River in late September and attacked Tulamba, a city now in Pakistan, but at the time part of Nasiruddin's lands. The city fell easily and Timur sacked it for good measure, but there was no wholesale slaughter of the occupants. Opposition melted away as, by now, Timur's reputation had preceded him, and while Nasiruddin's military capabilities had been proven in a short civil war before becoming sultan, this had only ended a year earlier.

Despite this early defeat Nasiruddin was not deterred. He was proud of his army; it had won him the throne, and it was enormous (exact numbers extrapolated from medieval sources is a cottage industry, but let's say 100,000). The two sides squared up for the Battle of Delhi, with Timur fielding an army of a similar size but which, unsurprisingly, consisted mainly of horse archers. And it was at this point that Timur faced a problem that looked insurmountable. Nasiruddin not only had his own ranks of infantry and thousands of cavalry, both heavy and light, but he also had dozens of war elephants. These mighty beasts were draped in chain mail, had blades like scythes attached along the tusks and small wooden structures on their backs from which archers could loose their arrows on the enemy in relative safety. If the elephants were a terrifying sight for the men in Timur's army, it was even worse for the horses. A horse is a herbivore, a prey animal, and prey animals are naturally skittish; it's what keeps them alive in the wild. If in doubt, run away and live to eat another day. Horses don't like things that are bigger than they are because that could be a predator. Given all of this, it comes as no surprise that horses will not charge elephants, and this was a huge problem as maybe 90% of Timur's forces were cavalry. The way he won battles was with his horse archers, but if the horses wouldn't go near the elephants (and even the men might think twice before trying to go up against the medieval equivalent of a battle tank), how could the action take place?

As we have seen before, Timur used his brain rather than brute force. He ordered his men to dig trenches around the flanks of his force to protect the horses from the elephants. This was highly unusual. Ditches and trenches had been dug in battles before, but always to protect infantry from cavalry, not cavalry from something else. The tactic calmed the horses and made the men feel safer, too.

Next, Timur ordered the camels from the baggage train to be brought to the front where their loads were packed with wood and hay. The camels were not part of the usual fighting force, nor are camels interested in charging at anything, let alone an armoured-plated elephant. However, Timur knew that there was one thing that had the same effect on all creatures, whether camels, horses, elephants or humans – fire. He ordered that the camels' loads be set alight. The camels, smelling the smoke and feeling the heat of the flames, panicked and began galloping away from what they thought was the source of the fire towards Nasiruddin's awaiting army. As this wall of flames came ever closer, accompanied by cries of pain from the camels, the mighty war elephants panicked and stampeded. This had happened previously in history when the Romans, faced with the war elephants of the Carthaginians, circumvented the problem by using very long spears as well as covering the backs of pigs with flammable substances and sending them in the direction of the elephants. The sight of the pigs sent the elephants into frenzies so that they ran amok, and in the process trampled the units around them. Presumably, this also meant that after winning the battle the Romans had a hog roast ready meal to celebrate.

When the flaming camels arrived at the front lines of Nasiruddin's army, chaos ensued. The elephants went wild, attacking, trampling and goring anything near them. The trumpeting elephants charged the Delhi cavalry, whose horses panicked and bolted in all directions, while the men on the front lines would have turned and fled from the oncoming camel inferno. Timur added to the mayhem by ordering his siege catapults to attack the enemy ranks with any flammable ammunition and the horse archers showered the front ranks of Nasiruddin's army with fire arrows. What could have been a decisive defeat or a hard-won battle was one of the easiest victories of Timur's career.

Nasiruddin could only watch in horror as he was outsmarted by his opponent and lost before the two armies had even (technically speaking) met. Nothing now stood in the way of Timur, who plundered this fabulously wealthy city and enslaved the population on the grounds that Delhi had resisted. When the local population revolted, he switched from taking slaves to killing everyone, men, women and children alike. It is estimated that at least 100,000 were killed.

As usual for Timur's conquests, if the local leader swore an oath of loyalty, he could continue to govern, provided he paid a regular tribute. As such, Nasiruddin remained the Sultan of Delhi but with a dramatically diminished level of authority. Timur's invasion marked the beginning of the end for the dynasty as multiple territories claimed independence and broke away. Timur could now boast that he had captured a city of immense wealth and prestige that no other steppe nomad, not even the mighty Genghis Khan, had conquered. This, along with all his other victories, makes him one of the mightiest military leaders in all of history. But he wasn't done yet.

At this time, far to the west was the Ottoman Sultan Bayezid I, nicknamed Yildirim (the lightning bolt). He was a teenager when he saw his father murdered during the infamously bloody Battle of Kosovo, and he had terrorised crusades and kings in eastern Europe for years. In 1402, as Timur was beginning to focus on this small but expansionist empire, Bayezid had turned his attention to the one great prize that had so far eluded him, Constantinople. Since all his battles and conquests had been land-based, he had had no need for a navy, and he lacked the siege craft and equipment to capture the city. Even if he could hastily construct a navy, he would have been unable to match the quality of ships produced by the established Italian fleets ... so Bayezid stuck to what he was good at. He waited it out at the walls of Constantinople and kept pressure on the city. The major relief force the Byzantines had been desperately awaiting had been destroyed at Nicopolis. It was only a matter of time until Constantinople surrendered and, as Bursa and Nicaea had demonstrated, the Ottomans were more than willing to wait years for a major walled city to capitulate. But then, in a completely unexpected twist of fate, Constantinople was saved not by some Christian relief force, but by an apparent force of nature. As fearsome and as proficient a warlord as Bayezid was, he wasn't the only one.

Bayezid was still besieging Constantinople when he heard the news that Timur was moving into Anatolia (after sweeping through Syria with little to no resistance; again his reputation paved the way for his successes) with an entire army. Bayezid reluctantly left the Byzantine capital, allowing it to catch its breath until he returned. By the time Bayezid heard that the local Turkish chieftains in central Anatolia were switching their allegiances to Timur, he could almost hear the hooves of Timur's troops. Bayezid did not underestimate the force he was up against. It was reported by multiple sources that he gathered the largest army the West had ever seen, and while it may not have been as big as the entire might of Rome's legions, it is still estimated to have been around 85,000-strong. Compare that to the Battle of Agincourt in 1415, when the French and the English between them could muster only around a quarter of that number. The size of Timur's army is unknown but was even bigger, not unrealistically, probably twice the size of Bayezid's.

The Ottoman sultan marched his army across Anatolia in the searing summer heat until the two sides met in the field of Çubuk, just outside the small town of Ankara, in an epic clash between this generation's greatest military leaders (I have a soft spot for Henry V, but he wouldn't have stood a chance against these men and their resources). Neither Timur nor Bayezid had ever before lost a battle, but one of these men was about to taste defeat for the first time.

I think the Battle of Ankara was a pivotal historic clash, because the impact of the events of 20 July 1402 would be felt for many years to come by those in many different lands. It was far more important than the Battle of Agincourt. Shakespeare never wrote a play about Bayezid (although Marlowe wrote one about Timur); this pivotal conflict remains obscure in the West because nobody from the West fought in it. Actually, that's not strictly true. Bayezid would have brought together forces from all over his empire, so Greeks, Serbs and Bulgarians would have been fighting on that day, but they were Ottoman subjects who never got to tell their story to the chroniclers in Italy or France. The chronicles report that Bayezid's Serbian wife, Olivera Despina, sometimes rode out with him, and she was with him on this campaign.

The days leading up to the battle were a deadly game of cat and mouse. Bayezid knew Timur's force was almost entirely cavalry and, as such, was fast and mobile. He spent days scouring the area trying to find Timur and his vast army. Timur, however, was always one step ahead of Bayezid, at one point resting his troops in one of Bayezid's abandoned encampments after he had moved on with his Ottoman army. Both men were the master of manoeuvre warfare and both generals were now facing their most capable enemy. When more than 200,000 soldiers faced each other in central Anatolia, it was Timur who had chosen the site of the battle, and even though Bayezid had the home advantage, his troops were tired from constant marching. Timur brought not only cavalry but also war elephants from his victories in India. Some say he had managed to equip the elephants with rudimentary flame throwers. After Timur had seen what happened when elephants mixed with fire, this seems implausible. Another theory is that the description of a flame thrower is actually that of a rudimentary cannon, though again, the skittish nature of elephants makes this unlikely. He probably opted for the traditional arrangement of a small platform with protective wooden walls and a couple of archers on the backs of the elephants. Either way, not only did Timur have the advantage of numbers, he also had armour-plated war elephants, something that Bayezid had probably never seen. Consequently, his cavalry was all but 'hobbled' because, as we now know, horses won't charge elephants.

Accounts of the battle are fairly sketchy and often contradictory regarding events when the two armies finally collided. What is clear is that a pivotal point in the battle took place when some of Bayezid's Anatolian vassals switched sides or melted away, meaning that he was at an even greater numerical disadvantage. However, the core of the Ottoman forces (including the Serbs and the Janissaries, two groups which might not have been expected to fight hard in such an historic confrontation) fought bravely. The resulting carnage was both widespread and brutal. By the end of the day, it was said that around 50,000 Ottoman troops lay dead; the same was said of Timur's force. If these numbers are correct (and there's no way of knowing), it was one of the bloodiest battles in world history prior to the 20th century. Bayezid might have been up against a man who was his equal in leadership, but Timur had more of everything – and some armoured pachyderms. Bayezid had thrown all of his empire's resources into the battle, but he couldn't overcome the fact that Timur's empire was bigger. By the end of that violent and sweltering July day, Bayezid's army was in tatters, and he and his wife Olivera Despina had been captured, showing that Bayezid had personally fought to the bitter end. Timur was now the undisputed leader of the Muslim world.

The Ottomans had two unlucky rulers in quick succession: Murad was the first and only sultan to die in battle, and his son Bayezid was the only sultan ever to be captured in battle. There was a story that Bayezid was taken east in a golden cage, but Timur always respected a formidable foe, and it was likely that even as a captive Bayezid would have continued to enjoy all the luxuries befitting a sultan, except, of course, his freedom. Bayezid was escorted across the vast interior of Asia, through Persia and on towards Timur's capital of Samarkand in modern-day Uzbekistan. But Bayezid never reached the capital. He fell ill and died on the journey east, and his body was returned to the Ottomans. Along with other Ottoman rulers, he is buried in the family mausoleum in Bursa. His wife Olivera Despina returned with her husband's body and moved back to Serbia, where she split her time between the courts of her brother and her sister. She died peacefully in 1444. As for Timur, his conquests proved to be ephemeral, much like those of Alexander the Great, and his deeds are not well remembered anywhere other than in Uzbekistan.

The Battle of Ankara threw the political landscape of the Ottoman Empire into turmoil. Bayezid had four sons old enough to take power (a fifth joined in later) and, rather than talk things through (or strangle each other), they fought a civil war that was to last for more than a decade. A century earlier, the Ottoman Empire had barely existed; now it threatened to shatter and become a distant memory. When reading about Constantinople and the fact that Bayezid had already started besieging the city, readers might be thinking it really should have fallen by now, but most people remember that this only happened with the final siege of 1453. How could it possibly have hung on for another fifty years? The answer is the Battle of Ankara. It left a power vacuum in the Ottoman state and made the Byzantine emperors sigh with relief as the Ottoman princes fought for the throne. So, another impact of the battle was a reprieve for Constantinople.

As stated in chapter 6, there was now an Ottoman interregnum for a decade, as the princes of the empire feuded. With hindsight we can see that the empire would recover and go on to even bigger conquests, but at the start of the 15th century that was far from certain, and yet again we see that there was no love lost between the different groups that once inhabited the Eurasian Steppe. The Ottomans and the Timurids had a similar form of warfare in common, religion and languages were also similar, but when the chips were down, might made right and Timur was mightier than Bayezid.

As a side note, I once planned to make a documentary about the incarceration of Bayezid. I wanted to ride a horse from Ankara to Samarkand to retell the story of the Eurasian Steppe nomads. As well as a kind of re-creation of a historical event, it would also be a travelog. It nearly got to development stage, but with all the instability in the region, such a journey became too dangerous. But here's the interesting fact: after poring over maps and researching average horse speeds, that journey would have taken a little over three months, and that was only if everything had gone according to plan. It was that research which brought home to me how hard the riding and how vast the distances for all these warriors. 'They thundered across the steppe conquering all before them' is a great line, but things just didn't happen that way. The fact that Timur had been able to see Samarkand, Delhi, Georgia and central Anatolia made him one of the most travelled men in history up to that point.

Timur had conquered everything Genghis Khan had conquered and more, except for China. The Yuan Mongol Dynasty had been deposed by the Ming Dynasty in 1368, so for nearly 40 years Timur could have fought against an old enemy of the Eurasian Steppe people. Instead, he had headed west rather than east.

After his victory over the Ottomans, he began to plan a campaign against Ming China. However, by 1404, Timur was roughly 70. He ordered the incarceration of some Ming envoys as his way of declaring war on China, but as the situation was evolving Timur was increasingly in failing health. He was no longer able to ride and was being moved on a litter. The best doctors from his empire attended to him as he sweated and writhed in pain. He summoned his family and whispered to them that he knew his soul was about to leave his body and to start praying and reciting Quranic texts so that he would reach heaven. He gathered his generals and made them swear an oath of loyalty to his heir Khalil Sultan, his grandson, and they wept as the great leader neared death. To Timur's credit and despite great pain, he was concerned that a smooth transition of power would be conducted to create a positive legacy for his new empire.

Timur died of presumed stomach cancer in Farab (a small town on the Silk Road in Kazakhstan) in February 1405. After all his successes against a wide variety of enemies, it's hard to see the Ming doing anything but falling to his sword. But what actually happened was that Khalil Sultan released the Ming emissaries and order was restored. Timur's death saved China from another invasion of Eurasian Steppe nomads.

The story of Timur's family and descendants will be the focus of the last chapter, here we will finish with examples of how Timur's fearsome reputation lasted for centuries after his death.

Timur was buried in the purpose-built Guri Amir, a mausoleum in Samarkand. The style is distinctively Timurid and is notable for its fluted dome covered in azure ceramic tiles inscribed with Islamic calligraphy. It is a testament to the artisans of Timur's empire that this was arguably the greatest structure on the Eurasian Steppe at the time. It is a beautiful site that has been heavily renovated since Uzbekistan's independence from the Soviet Union.

But Timur was not done with this world; there is believed to be a curse which says that great leaders must not disturb his tomb lest their kingdoms fall to a mighty army, the embodiment of Timur's wrath. It is worth remembering that Christopher Marlowe's play *Tamburlaine the Great* was written in the 1580s, nearly 200 years after his death, and while almost every fact in the play is wrong, what Marlowe emphasises is how brutal 'Tamburlaine' was. Tudor England was about as far away as you could get from the real man and his deeds, which shows that his reputation for violence had spread across the world. But this is a history book, and none of this would be worth mentioning until we come to the most bizarre set of coincidences.

In 1740, Nader Shah Afshar of the newly energised Persian empire conquered parts of central Asia including Samarkand. He knew all about Timur, so after capturing his capital, he tried to remove Timur's sarcophagus, but in the process it was broken, and a jade tablet was taken. Almost as soon as it was removed, Afshar's apparently unstoppable campaign became bogged down in one piece of bad luck after another. Even worse, his son became seriously ill, and it was then that Nader Shah Afshar was told about the curse, and the jade tablet was immediately returned. Afshar went on to rule for another seven years, and his son eventually recovered to full health. An interesting story, but just a coincidence? There's more.

In June 1941, Stalin ordered archaeologists to exhume the body to see if it really was the great man. When the team arrived, they were handed a piece of paper warning them of the curse and the dangers they would surely unleash. The Soviet archaeologists were atheists and men of science, so they were not going to be deterred by superstition and proceeded with their work, but when they opened the tomb, a terrible stench was unleashed (this is similar to the account of the excavation of Tutankhamun's tomb about 20 years earlier, so we can probably put it down to some local embellishment), and the electric lights and other equipment consistently malfunctioned. That was nothing compared to what happened just days later when Hitler's war machine amassed millions of troops and thousands of tanks, aircraft and artillery pieces and invaded the Soviet Union in the opening stages of Operation *Barbarossa*. This was the biggest invasion in history, leading to the loss of thousands of miles of Soviet territory and millions of soldiers of the Red Army, and the virtual destruction of the Soviet air force. It was about as crushing a defeat as invaders could ever hope for.

Stalin had bigger issues to deal with and he did not return to the issue of Timur's remains until November 1942. He ordered his body to be reinterred in his mausoleum and five weeks later, Stalin could claim victory at Stalingrad, the largest battle in history and the beginning of the end for Germany in the Second World War. Now, as a historian I can only talk about facts, rather than myths or legends, but these are the facts, and they make for a great story.

10

BABUR AND THE MUGHAL EMPIRE

Owing to their peripatetic lives most of the Eurasian Steppe nomadic groups rarely forged a unique identity in the world. The Huns, Avars and Magyars may have created the nation and language of Hungary, but they couldn't compete with castles, Christianity and chivalry, and their origins just melted away. The Mongols did establish a capital in Mongolia and certainly had an impact on Chinese history, but the Yuan dynasty was just another Chinese imperial dynasty in a long list. An image of Kublai Khan could be that of a Ming dynasty emperor.

It was only Osman of the Seljuk Turks who forged a distinctive Ottoman culture, one differentiated from its neighbours. Timur, like the Mongols, had the opportunity to create his own unique empire but chose not to. Although it is true that there was a distinctive architecture under his rule, Timurid mosques and madrassas were not being built in Damascus or Delhi. Timur had chosen deliberately not to take the title of Khan or Shanenshah, but Emir. He was confident enough in his own abilities not to need the vapid trappings of titles and crowns, but that led to a problem with his legacy. After the death of the great warlord, places like Georgia or the Golden Horde owed his successor no loyalty. If might was right, the mighty had passed away; time to return to business as usual. These territories had not been transformed into a different society. Indeed, the only thing that had glued the empire together was violence, cruelty and fear. As a result, Khalil Sultan inherited an empire that was straining to break apart. The only way to keep it together was to continue in his grandfather's footsteps as a conqueror, and Khalil Sultan was not the only grandson with a claim to the empire. It was a tall order for anyone to duplicate the military successes of one of the greatest generals.

As this is the last chapter in the book you can probably guess what happened next. While Khalil Sultan consolidated some power, other family members either broke away or challenged him in civil war. It wasn't that Khalil was a bad general or ruler, but his grandfather was a unique talent and had surrounded himself with loyal allies who owed their livelihoods to him. Khalil Sultan was, in essence, the first among equals.

What happened next seems to hang on Khalil Sultan's first wife Shad Mulk and results in the kind of plot found in a historical romance. Shad Mulk was unpopular in Samarkand, exactly why is unclear, but women usually become unpopular in history when the overreach their position in society. However, Khalil Khan stood by his wife, which reflected poorly on him in the eyes of his generals and the governing officials. She was, allegedly, trying to replace the landowners with low-born people, which annoyed those in power but makes her look a force for good to the modern reader. All of this was exacerbated by a famine, the first time such an event was a problem for a Eurasian Steppe culture and a reminder that these people were no longer nomadic but had become sedentary, much like their neighbours in Ming China and the Sultanate of Delhi. They were no longer living off the land and following their flocks across the great grass ocean of the steppe, and a bad harvest could undo royal authority just as quickly in this empire as in any other.

Meanwhile, the youngest son of Timur, Shah Rukh Mirza (an uncle to Khalil Sultan), was based in the rebuilt and repopulated Herat. In 1409, he marched on Samarkand, and in the ensuing violence managed to capture Shad Mulk while Khalil Sultan was away from his capital, busy fighting yet another challenger to the throne. Khalil Sultan surrendered to Shah Rukh Mirza to get his wife back. The two were reunited and Khalil Shah was demoted to the position of Governor of Ray. He died in 1411 and Shad Mulk, not wanting to live without him, committed suicide. (If Hollywood would like me to write the screenplay, please get in touch.)

Under Shah Rukh Mirza the empire had been greatly diminished in size. The Golden Horde broke away, as did Georgia and the Sultanate of Delhi. Western and central Iran were once again invaded by steppe nomads, this time by a group called the Ak Koyunlu (they were small scale compared to the other groups, but this shows the dynamism of this culture a millennium after Attila the Hun). Shah Rukh Mirza moved the capital from Samarkand to his base of Herat but was left mainly with Kazakhstan, modern eastern Iran, Uzbekistan and Afghanistan, a large area to be sure, but a rump of the former empire of Emir Timur. However, this large stretch of territory encompassed the main Silk Road routes out of China and across eastern central Asia, and this trading lifeline between east and west continued to be a highly lucrative source of revenues for the Shah.

After the initial bout of violence in the civil war that brought him to power, Shah Rukh Mirza became the model of diplomacy. He started nation building in a way completely alien to his father but reflective of the similarly evolving Ottoman civilisation. He improved the administration, he codified the laws, and he continued to build in the architectural styles his father had introduced, but he was a far more pious Muslim than Timur ever was. His reign was a long and relatively peaceful one, and Shah Rukh Mirza died in 1447. Ulugh Beg was the next ruler but he only lasted for a couple of years. The most notable point about him was that he was a renowned astronomer and mathematician. This is the first time any such scholarly expertise has been mentioned in connection to any of the leaders discussed and underlines that, like the Ottomans, the move away from the warlord chieftain of the past had been huge over just two generations. Over the next two decades there was a flurry of short-lived rulers until we get to Umar Shaikh Mirza II, who began his rule in 1469. Like Shah Rukh Mirza, he was a devout Muslim and an effective administrator, but it seems the fire had gone out of the belly of the lineage at this point. However, in 1494, in a freak accident, Umar Shaikh Mirza II was crushed under a collapsing building, which made his 11-year-old son the new ruler. His name was Babur.

Because Babur was so important to Indian history, we tend to think of him today as Indian. This is not helped by the fact that in his court in India, he is depicted in typically Indian style, just like Kublai Khan's paintings show him to be Chinese. The comparison between these two men separated by about 200 years is useful. It is true that later in their successful careers they would wear and be depicted in the styles of the vanquished nation they ruled, but they were both born far from the borders of the places they are mainly associated with and adapted themselves to completely alien cultures. Indeed, through various elements of the family, Babur was related to Kublai Khan and was also a great-great-great grandson of Timur. In truth, Babur had more of an affinity with the Eurasian Steppe than with Delhi. He was also a Muslim and the son of a devout Muslim ruler.

Babur ruled from Fergana (a wide valley in modern Uzbekistan), and just two years after assuming power, aged 13 or 14, he led an army to recapture Samarkand. He succeeded but, in the process, lost Fergana to other enemies. Still, how many in their early teens have been recorded as successfully conquering a city?

Babur would go on to capture and lose Samarkand three times. This convinced the young ruler that he needed assistance and he reached out to the two most powerful Muslim powers to the west, the Ottomans and the new Safavid power in Iran. With his western borders now at peace, and from the Safavid perspective the central Asian horsemen looking elsewhere for trouble, Babur could now focus on a new prize, a territory not threatened by the Timurid dynasty since the time of the founder, Timur himself. It took him nearly thirty years to refocus his power base and look at India, but as he had come to the throne at such a young age, he was still only in his early 40s in 1524.

Babur, like his Ottoman allies, had evolved. His use of diplomacy showed nuance that had not existed in the earlier times of Attila, Genghis Khan and Timur. Their challenge to neighbouring powers was capitulate or face our wrath. Babur could be diplomatic and magnanimous when he wanted to be, but he was also capable of unleashing the death and destruction that his forbears had inflicted on so many peoples. His use of these strategies allowed him to re-establish his claims over Kabul in Afghanistan, and after that, he reached the borders of India.

The term Hindu Kush seems to imply ownership by the Hindu powers of India, but that is not what it means. Hindu Kush is translated as 'Hindu Killer'. The first recorded version of this name was annotated by the great Muslim traveller Ibn Battuta in the first half of the 1300s. The name is thought to indicate that thousands of Indians were captured by the Mongols or other similar groups who conducted raids into the Indus Valley and then marched their captives through the mountains and onto the Eurasian Steppe, where they would never be seen again. The nomads wanted the Indians for slaves, and if a percentage died on the journey, so be it. There must have been times when the mountain passes were littered with the remains of these unfortunate souls. The name is a reminder that the mountains were not an impenetrable barrier keeping the people of the subcontinent safe but, instead, a crossroads of death and ruin, used for centuries to facilitate the grim trade of slavery.

When Babur crossed the Hindu Kush, he was imitating his ancestors. His opponent was Ibrahim Lodi, the ruler of the Delhi Sultanate, so there were two Muslim rulers clashing in a country we now associate with Hinduism. This is important because the narrative about Babur isn't that he was a Muslim ruler, exclusively fighting rulers of a different faith, an interloper in a Hindu world; huge swathes of India had already been ruled by Muslims, so the most that would change was the name of the ruler.

The Sultanate of Delhi had been crumbling for decades. It wasn't in its prime as it had been when facing Timur, and even then, the Battle of Delhi had been a crushing defeat. What seems to have enabled Babur to capture more than just the Punjab (as Timur had done) were all the defecting governors coming to Babur's court. Like rats leaving a sinking ship, these men recognised the rising power and hoped that if they switched sides early enough, they could secure their own powerbases. So, as Babur began to move south, resistance largely melted away.

When Babur arrived at Lahore (in modern-day Pakistan) the enemy army made the mistake of leaving the safety of the city's defences to meet him on the battlefield. They were poorly led and up against a battle-hardened leader; the army shattered and fled. Then Babur employed an all too familiar tactic and ordered Lahore to be burned to the ground. His forces regrouped and he moved on.

Babur's character is revealed in his remarkable autobiography called the *Baburnama* (not to be confused with Bananarama, which was an 80s all-girl British pop group). The work is in stark contrast to the illiterate society of the Huns or that of Genghis Khan. In it he recognises the Yassa, the collection of oral codes of law created by the Mongols, but he sees that it has been transcended by the Quran. Although he wrote in the traditional central Asian language and not Arabic or Sanskrit, like the Ottomans, his society was evolving and transforming into something new. He was moving with the times and showing an open mind as to how society should be structured. But he didn't slavishly follow Islamic codes either; he drank alcohol, remarking at one point, 'I am drunk, officer. Punish me when I am sober.' Babur later gave up alcohol for health reasons and made the rest of the court do the same. He did take opium in various edible forms but never to excess.

While a formidable general on the field of battle, he was remarkably shy in the bedroom. There are a number of stories about him being bashful not only with some of his early wives, but also with a young man in the court (although it's unlikely that relationship was consummated). We know this because he remarks on it in his autobiography; however, he had enough wives and concubines to ensure he did eventually have a male heir.

The next target for conquest was Diplapur, which also easily fell, but when Babur sent some of his generals with an army to attack Delhi itself, this time they were pushed back. Ibrahim Lodi, the Sultan of Delhi, was in the centre of his powerbase and his capital; it would not fall so easily. It was inevitable that the two leaders would meet in battle, and the confrontation took place in April 1526 at what is now called the first Battle of Panipat.

Ibrahim Lodi wanted to end this existential threat to his authority once and for all, and he brought every soldier he could muster to the battle. Numbers of 70,000 have been given for his forces; over half were cavalry. He was also accompanied by an estimated 100 elephants. As his ancestors had done before, Lodi had each elephant draped in a thick covering of armoured plate and chain mail. Scythe-like blades were attached to the tusks, and the animals' backs had small palanquins where archers could loose their arrows from their elevated positions. Babur had a much smaller force of around 20,000, but in a sign of the times, while Lodi had brought a vast army, Babur had taken onboard the innovations seen in the Ottoman army. He came with more than a dozen field guns, early cannons, which were even more inefficient and hard to manoeuvre than the gun carriages of the Napoleonic era. But any cannon would cause huge casualties to tightly packed mass formations, and all the smoke and noise would panic horses and elephants. Thousands of Babur's troops were not archers, but gun men, firing rudimentary matchlock muskets, a much cruder weapon compared to the beautiful composite bows of the Eurasian Steppe. The matchlocks were lucky to fire two rounds a minute and were impossible to use on horseback, but learning to fire a gun took only hours of training, not the years needed to hone archery and equestrian skills. The musket was less accurate, too, but the sound and flash of gunpowder was enough to make peasant conscripts panic and flee.

Babur had the conquering zeal of his ancestors but had evolved beyond the old tactics of the Eurasian Steppe nomads. For the first time in this narrative we see a leader whose military effectiveness did not lie with the rapid manoeuvrability of cavalry and carefully rehearsed feigned retreats. The strength of Babur's army lay in fixing positions and using cover to reign down fiery death on the enemy, virtually the antithesis of the old ways. As innovative as all this was, we know that Babur was not the first leader to do this. The rise of the gun was unstoppable; combatants either moved with the times or faced annihilation.

Ibrahim Lodi gave Babur enough time to set up his forces exactly the way he intended. Babur secured his flanks by having the right anchored against the city of Panipat. On the left there were no natural obstacles, so a trench was dug and covered with tree branches to create a defensive position with a good field of fire. In the centre, he placed roughly 700 waggons tied together but with a gap between each of the carts. These gaps were filled with wooden palisades where his matchlock men waited to engage from behind their defensive lines.

Babur still had cavalry and allowed it to work independently. When Lodi arrived on the field of battle he realised his army was so broadly spread out it wouldn't be able to get to Babur's forces, so he reorganised his army to fit into the bottleneck that Babur had prepared. As Lodi advanced, Babur's cannons and matchlocks fired, and the cavalry began an innovative double pincer movement to attack the flank of the Delhi forces (Babur's name for this new movement was the taulqama). The noise of the gunpowder panicked the horses, and the frightened elephants began ploughing into the surrounding infantry. Between the fire from the front, the attack on the flank and the utter chaos going on in Lodi's army, a force of 70,000 men rapidly turned into a maelstrom of terror, screams and crumpled bodies. In the ensuing rout thousands were cut down by either sword or shot. Ibrahim Lodi himself died in this carnage and was beheaded. It is thought that around 20,000 of the Delhi forces were killed on that morning. Babur's casualties are unknown, but seeing that Lodi's forces never engaged the front lines, they had to be light. In Babur's own words: 'By the grace of the Almighty God, this difficult task was made easy to me and that mighty army, in the space of a half a day was laid in dust.'

It is the sort of thing that you could imagine Genghis Khan or Attila the Hun saying. Babur had defeated and killed one of the most powerful rulers in India, and the way was open to march on Delhi and then Agra. But there were still rulers on the subcontinent who were not going to allow Babur's expansion unopposed. The other main power in northern India was the Rajput Confederation led by Rana Sanga. Like Babur, he had expanded his power by a mixture of diplomacy and highly effective military might. Babur described Hindu Rana Sanga as 'the greatest infidel king of India'.

The exact nature of the history between these two warlords is hotly contested and is further muddied by Indian nationalism, but what we can say with certainty is that diplomatic channels were open between the two leaders. Any point of agreement must have been achieved despite deep suspicions, as both recognised a predator when they saw one.

When Babur approached Agra, he was confronted with a number of forts creating a defensive ring around the city. They were Dholpur, Gwaliar, and Bayana, and it was in dealing with them that Babur once again showed his flexibility. He knew time was of the essence; he needed to have control over the forts before Rana Sanga arrived. So, he offered them generous terms to surrender, and they did. This move gave Babur the defensive advantage as one of the most formidable warriors in India began to advance on Babur's newly conquered territories.

The two sides met in March of 1527 at the Battle of Khanwa. In the year since the battle at Panipat, Babur had been able to bolster his numbers not just from his homeland, but with Indian forces, too. His army had swollen to around 50,000, more than double its previous size. By contrast, Rana Sanga had brought together an even larger force than Ibrahim Lodi had done, with at least 80,000 men and roughly 500 war elephants (naturally). The battle took place a little over 20 miles from Agra, so whoever won the battle would claim the city. Again, like Panipat, Babur focussed on anchoring his forces to defensive positions with a fortified encampment reinforced with portable walls. This time the carts were linked not with leather straps, but with iron chains. Babur knew that if his matchlock men were caught on open ground by the Rajput cavalry, they would be torn to pieces.

In this battle that we see the first innovation in artillery mentioned in this book. A cannon blasts out projectiles in a flat trajectory at oncoming targets, but Babur this time had mortars as well. Mortars fires in an arc and can fired from behind cover, so they are particularly useful in sieges. On this occasion they could fire out from Babur's fortified encampment and trenches, and the Rajput forces had no effective response to the threat.

Rana Sanga saw that Babur's troops had amassed in the centre, and consequently, if he could break that he could engulf all of Babur's forces and annihilate them. Attacking the strongest defences would mean heavy casualties, but the Rajput forces greatly outnumbered the enemy, so the losses would be acceptable if the plan worked. But, once again, the use of gunpowder showed its advantage over the old ways to wage war. As before, the matchlock and artillery fire panicked both horses and elephants, and as before, the elephants began to rampage, turning on their own forces and killing and wounding thousands. (War elephants can work as a shock tactic and, under some circumstances, can be a formidable opponent. Timur himself used them to good effect in the Battle of Ankara, but they have been seen as a complete liability in this book.) However, unlike the battle at Panipat, the heavy casualties did not turn into a murderous rout. Rana Sanga marshalled his forces back into a cohesive army and began to attack both of Babur's flanks with his remaining men. As the gunners had prepared for a frontal assault, this meant that the Rajput coalition were no longer under such heavy fire, even though the mortars could be repositioned.

The fighting was brutal and as Babur's numbers were fewest on the flanks, they faced being overwhelmed. So Babur ordered the taulqama, but on the two occasions his cavalry attempted this double pincer manoeuvre they were pushed back by Rana Sanga's men. At this point there is a controversial story about some of the Rajput forces switching sides. Some historians say this was a later addition to add spice to the account, while others say it actually happened. In any case, the battle hung in the balance and could have gone either way. But it was around this time that Rana Sanga was struck by a bullet and lost consciousness. His body was hidden from view by his bodyguards who moved it out of harm's way, and a Jhala general called Ajja took over the command. While Rana Sanga was a gifted military leader, Ajja wasn't. He did not have the innate authority to lead the Rajput coalition, nor were his tactics what were needed. As the fighting went on, he kept battering away at Babur's flanks, which, over hours, were steadily reinforced, meaning that Rajput's men were increasingly less likely to achieve a breakthrough.

With the main Rajput forces now at the flanks, it meant their centre was visibly weaker. This was the moment when Babur decided to go on the offensive, and he tore into the middle of the army. General Ajja realised his blunder and went into the melee with as many of the Rajput generals as he could rally, but it was too little too late. The death of so many key players meant the giant army was now effectively leaderless. The Rajput forces carried out one final charge into Babur's left flank, but this achieved nothing, and they were cut to pieces. With this, the giant army began to retreat from the battlefield. Babur held the battlefield by the end of the day, but the fighting had been fierce, and the casualties were high for both sides. Babur was unable to charge down the retreating enemy forces, but what he did next was a reminder to India and to history of his roots. He ordered the dead bodies to be decapitated and a tower of enemy heads to be built on the battlefield. This was a gruesome marker of victory, echoing what Timur had done nearly a century and a half earlier.

The Battle of Khanwa may not have been an unalloyed success for Babur, but it stopped any immediate threat to his Indian gains. The battle solidified his grip on modern-day Pakistan and northern India, but it was not the end. Rana Sanga recovered from his wounds and other powerful princes were still in the field. This led to the Battle of Chanderi in January of 1528.

Medini Rai was the lord of the city of Chanderi and an ally of Rana Sanga. Chanderi is situated in north central India and, as such, was a key location that could be used to muster troops to carry out an attack on Babur's lands. Babur approached the city, which had formidable fortifications, and gave Medini Rai reasonable terms for surrender. Medini Rai rejected them, and Babur set to work besieging the city, or so it seemed. In reality, he was hoping for a lightning-fast assault, and in the dead of night he captured the key outer fortifications. On a roll, Babur tried his luck and went for the central citadel, which fell within an hour. Even Babur was surprised at his rapid progress, and now, with his forces on the city walls, Medini Rai knew the game was up. Except for what happened next.

While this had precedent in Indian history, it is a shocking first inclusion here. Medini Rai ordered the women to commit ritual suicide by fire to save their honour from would-be attackers in a traditional Jowhar ceremony. The screams and the smell of burning flesh would have been pervasive within the city walls. The guards also carried out ritual suicide, not by fire, but with the blades of their weapons. In the space of two days Babur had gone from standing in front of the walls of a city to standing in the centre of a charnel house, and none of the civilian deaths were caused by his forces.

Rana Sanga had stopped wearing a turban and now wore a simple cloth, the sign of a penitent. He refused to return to his capital until he had vanquished Babur. Ten days after the fall of Chanderi, he died of poisoning. Some say it was Babur's assassins, but it seems, on balance, more likely that his court did not want any further fconflict with Babur and got rid of the last man standing in the way of a peaceful resolution.

In hindsight, the courtiers should have waited just a couple of years as Babur died, of natural causes, aged forty-seven in the winter of 1530/31. He had been campaigning since he was a young teen. Life in the saddle and on the battlefield is a hard one, so it seems that he was simply worn out. He was initially buried in the newly conquered Agra, but true to his ethnic roots, about ten years later he was reburied as he had wished in Kabul. His tomb in the Gardens of Babur is still there in the suburbs of the Afghan capital. As he was a great Muslim warrior who scored victories over 'the infidel', his tomb has been left unmolested by the Taliban and other Islamic powers in modern Afghanistan.

A mosque was built in his honour in the city of Ayodhya in northeastern India. This has become a battleground of ideologies in today's India. Now referred to as the Babri Masjid (literally Babur's Mosque), it is an important place of worship for Muslims, but it appears to have been built on the ruins of a Hindu temple. As such, various Hindu nationalist groups have wanted to tear it down, and it became the focal point of Muslim/Hindu tensions in the region. A new Hindu temple was consecrated on these grounds in January 2024 against a background of many international concerns over the eradication of Islamic heritage in India.

If Timur is incorrectly known as Tamerlane in the West and that is all that is known about the man, Babur is even more obscure. You will invariably find his story in books about Indian history but not Mongol history. The area of Babur's initial conquests is often referred to as Transoxiana, while the territories in India that he conquered were referred to by himself as Hindustan. Today, there are many nations whose names end in 'stan', for instance Uzbekistan or Kazakhstan. Stan in Arabic means 'the land of', so Kazakhstan is the land of the Kazakhs. It makes complete sense and is therefore a fairly accurate description of India as the land of the Hindus.

Mirza Nasir-ud-Din Muhammad was Babur's eldest son and his heir. On his accession to the throne he became known as Humayun. Humayun is not referred to as the ruler of Hindustan or Transoxiania but as the second Mughal emperor (Babur was the first). To the average westerner the Mughal Empire is as Indian as Chicken Tikka Masala, and they would be right because neither is authentically Indian. The name Mughal Empire is a corruption of the name Mongol Empire and was a term relating to Genghis Khan's vision of conquest; it was still a major power into the 19th century.

The Mughal Empire lasted for centuries, an amazing legacy created by Babur. Again, just like the Mongols in China, with a limited culture of their own, the Mongols in India were absorbed into the local culture and gene pool, but they always remained Muslim. It was the legacy of the Mughal that shaped the modern subcontinent: in negotiations with the British Empire the Hindu majority refused to be ruled once again by Muslims. They wanted separate countries for the Muslim population of imperial India, and so Pakistan and Bangladesh were created in 1948. The mass migration of peoples during this time (called Partition) was a tragedy, leading to an irrevocable change in cultures, disputed borders and deaths measured if not in millions, then in the hundreds of thousands. The blame has been laid at the feet of Britain, but it is worth noting that it wasn't British soldiers massacring local populations. A more nuanced reading of events is that the impact of the Mughals on the folk memory of the Hindu majority population led to what amounted to Islamophobia on a national scale.

It was the fifth Mughal Emperor Shah Jahan who built the Taj Mahal. It is the most famous structure in India and one of the most famous in the world. People assume it is a Hindu building, but it is no such thing. It is a tomb built for Shah Jahan's beloved wife Mumtaz Mahal. The name is a corruption of the term the Palace of Mahal. If you look at Ottoman architecture of this period and Timur's tomb in Samarkand, you can see the Islamic influence. The Taj Mahal is very much in the style of Shah Jahan's ancestors rather than copying the style of a contemporary Hindu temple. As is the case with any mosque's minarets, this building's four giant minarets were meant to be used for the call to prayer, a purely Islamic ritual, not a Hindu one. The main Islamic architectural influence is seen around the edge of the central arch, beautifully carved and inlaid with Quranic scripture. It was built for the love of a wife and the honour of Islam and is for some an uncomfortable reminder of India's multi-ethnic and multi-religious past in modern Hindu India.

The decline of the Mughal Empire began in 1712 after the death of Bahadur Shah I. The Martha powers began to tear away chunks of their territory, culminating in the sack of Delhi. The Mughal emperors reached out to the now independent rulers of Afghanistan for assistance, an attempt to reignite old alliances, but it was too late. By the early 1800s, not only were they competing with local warlords but with the British (in the guise of the East India Company) and other European powers with superior resources and technology. The war between the Mughals and the East India Company in 1857-8 led to Bahadur Shah Zafar, the last Mughal emperor, leaving his powerbase for exile.

The very last hurrah of the Eurasian Steppe nomads as a military force took place during the Russian Revolution when Mongolia tried to break away from the communists. Unfortunately for them, it was now the 20th century, and aircraft could easily spot large groups on the open steppe. Thanks to the inventions of the machine gun, the rife and hydraulic artillery, the famous Mongol cavalry were cut to pieces before they could even get into battle. Against the modern machines of war, the horse archer was obsolete.

Even though they were finished as a military force, the Mongol story continued in the political realm. I mentioned earlier on that the descendants of some of these people (known to history as Tatars) settled in the Crimea. By the mid-15th century, they had broken away from the Golden Horde, formed what became known as the Crimean Khanate and later allied with the Ottoman Empire. The two sides worked well together: the khanate supplied irregular scouting forces and the empire protected them. It is estimated that between 1500-1700, the khanate enslaved around two million Europeans, most of whom would have ended up in the slave markets of the Ottoman Empire. However, as Russia's power grew, this alliance waned until the khanate was abolished and absorbed into the Russian Empire. Then in the 20th century, the Russian Empire became the Soviet Union and Germany invaded. When the Red Army finally recaptured the Crimean Peninsula in 1944, Stalin accused the Tatars of collaboration and moved the entire remaining population from the Crimea to central Asia. Thousands died in the process.

After the fall of the Soviet Union, hundreds of thousands returned to their homeland of Crimea, now part of Ukraine. In 2014, the President of Russia, Vladimir Putin ordered a bloodless coup in Crimea, catching Ukraine and the rest of the world by surprise. In 2022, Putin tried to take the whole of Ukraine, but this time he did not have the element of surprise, and a full-scale war broke out in what is the largest conflict in Europe since the Second World War. Although the Crimea remained in their hands at the end of the first year, the Russians were pushed back. Fighting bogged down in the second year, not quite into a stalemate, but the Ukrainian advance was slow-going. In September 2023, Ukrainian President Volodymyr Zelensky replaced his defence minister Oleksii Reznikov with Rustem Umerov. How is this relevant? Umerov is a Crimean Tatar. His appointment was a clear signal to the Kremlin that Ukraine won't stop until it gets the Crimea back, so the Eurasian Steppe nomads are still making history in the 21st century.

CONCLUSION

When we talk about the great cultures and peoples of history, Ancient Greece, China and Alexander the Great are often mentioned. Renaissance artists like Leonardo Da Vinci may have created marvels of the art world, but did these exquisite pieces, seen by only a select few rich and powerful people, really change the world?

Ancient Greece is a myth. It was a series of warring states whose impact on the larger world was minuscule. It was only some of their writings and philosophical/political concepts that had any impact, and many of these only came to light centuries later. China was and is a powerhouse of ideas and culture, but throughout its long history, China never sought to export its culture globally. Alexander was a conqueror, a warlord who imposed his will by brute force, but Genghis Khan started with less and conquered more. Timur not only went to most of the places Alexander did, but he went further and did it all despite his serious physical limitations.

The Eurasian Steppe nomads are often dismissed when it comes to world cultures. True, they didn't develop philosophies like the Greeks or invent the technologies China did, but they mattered. If the Silk Road, which lasted for millennia, was the highway that connected Europe, the Middle East and Asia, it was these nomads who, for most of its existence, had the greatest impact on it, as they protected it or plundered it. China's ancient and impressive history was regularly punctuated by their fear of invasion by these people, and for a time this became a reality. In the annals of military history, Attila, Subutai, Genghis Khan, Timur and Babur are some of the giants who achieved far more than the national heroes revered in most countries.

Like the Vikings, these people killed, enslaved, plundered and destroyed. But they also traded, explored and changed the history of sedentary populations across the globe. Also like the Vikings, much of what we know about them has been written by their enemies, the vanquished foes who, understandably, remember the bloodshed but have little or nothing to say about their impact and influence on the wider world.

Without the tough living conditions forged on the merciless steppe and without the martial culture and close family bonds of the steppe nomads, there would be no Hungary or Republic of Türkiye; there would be no Taj Mahal or Great Wall of China. Iraq would be a more verdant country, and had the Islamic Golden Age not been brutally terminated in 1258, who knows where Islamic culture would be today? Without the nomads, the Black Death would never have come to Europe, and the continent's history and populations would have been completely different. Finally, Japan wouldn't have had the kamikaze to hark back to during the Second World War when defending itself from Allied invasion.

Looking at the list above, it's hard not to think of the Eurasian Steppe nomads as the single most impactful people in the history of the world. Their successes and excesses tower over those of most other cultures in global history. In other words, no other group has affected so many vastly different places for more than a millennium. Attila the Hun fought the Romans in the age of galleys and bows. The last Ottoman sultan fought against the British in the age of the aircraft and the radio. The Eurasian Steppe nomads deserve more understanding, more study and more respect.

BIBLIOGRAPHY

Attila The Hun: A Barbarian King and the Fall of Rome 2006, John Man

Deus Vult: A Concise History of the Crusades 2014, Jem Duducu

India in the Persianate Age: 1000-1765 2020, Richard M. Eaton

Storm from the East: From Genghis Khan to Khubilai Khan 1993, Robert Marshall

Tamerlane: Sword of Islam, Conqueror of the World 2012, Justin Marozzi

The Avars: A Steppe Empire in Central Europe, 567–822 2018, Walter Pohl and William Sayers

The Babur Nama (Everyman's Library Classics) 2020, Babur, William Dalrymple, et al.

The Hungarians: A Thousand Years of Victory in Defeat 2021, Paul Lendvai

The Huns (Peoples of the Ancient World) 2015, Hyun Jin Kim

The Mongol Empire: Genghis Khan, his heirs and the founding of modern China 2015, John Man

The Napoleonic Wars in 100 Facts 2015, Jem Duducu

The Romans in 100 Facts 2015, Jem Duducu

The Silk Roads: A New History of the World 2016, Professor Peter Frankopan

The Sultans: The Rise and Fall of the Ottoman Rulers and Their World: A 600-Year History 2019, Jem Duducu

INDEX

Afghanistan 168, 181, 236,
    238-240, 261, 263, 272, 274
Alexander the Great 16, 157,
    168-169, 181, 237, 254, 276
Alp Arslan 85-86, 88
Anatolia 82, 84, 86-87, 89, 91,
    93, 98-99, 103-105, 107,
    110-112, 124, 143-144,
    251-253, 255
Ankara, 1402 Battle of 252-253
Assyrian Empire 15-16
Attila the Hun 9, 10, 11, 19, 22,
    38-60, 64, 69, 75, 80, 90,
    92, 127, 138, 147-148, 156,
    177, 235, 244, 261, 263, 267,
    277-278
Augsburg, 910 Battle of 79
Avar Khaganate 64-65, 73, 130
Avars 61-79, 81, 113, 127, 157,
    191, 219, 243, 259
Ayn Jalut, 1260 Battle of 216-219

Babur 80, 259, 262-273, 275, 277
Baghdad 35, 83, 208-209, 213,
    216, 219, 241
Bayan I 65, 66, 68, 69, 72, 92,
    130
Bohemund 89, 90, 93, 95-97. 99,
    213
Bohemund IV 213
Bleda 41-42, 43, 44
Black Sea 8, 32, 130, 132, 142,
    145, 232
Börte 150, 153, 158, 159
Bulgaria (Bulgarians) 14, 32, 34,
    44, 70, 71, 75-76, 79, 119,
    124, 252
Byzantine Empire 66, 68-69,
    70-71, 83-86, 88-90, 94, 103,
    107, 110, 117, 118, 121,
    125-127, 154, 251, 254

Catalaunian Plains, 451 Battle of
    48-51

Caucasus 26, 32, 131, 142, 171-172, 186-187, 214, 223, 244

Charlemagne 71-76

China 8-9, 11-12, 20-22, 26-31,-33, 62, 68-69, 158-159, 162, 166-167, 175, 181, 183, 185-187, 195, 202, 205-207, 217, 223, 227, 229, 231-232, 255-256, 260-261, 273, 276-277

composite bow 24-25, 71, 90, 266

Confucius 188, 229

Constantinople 34, 36, 38, 43, 45, 46, 58-59, 69, 70, 83, 86, 108, 114, 117-125, 138, 218, 232, 234, 250- 251, 254- 255

Constantinople, 1453 siege of 117-125

Crimean Tatar 12, 21, 32, 81, 131, 133, 135, 138, 142, 172, 275

Cuman-Kipchaks 76, 83

Crusades, the 12, 88, 145, 189, 209, 250

Danube river 14, 17, 31, 35, 37-38, 42, 58, 69, 71, 76, 129, 132, 134, 145, 196

Delhi 188, 247-249, 250, 255, 259, 260-262, 264-265, 267, 274

Dengizichi 58-59

Egypt 14-15, 87, 97-98, 131, 139-141, 146, 190, 203, 213-214, 241

Emir Timur (see also Tamerlane) 9, 22, 231-258, 261

Eurasian Steppe 7, 8, 10, 11, 14-24, 28, 31, 32, 36, 60, 61-64, 70, 71, 74, 76, 81, 82, 102, 106, 113, 127, 130, 151, 152, 158, 160, 162, 166, 171, 172, 181, 195, 205, 228, 230, 231, 232, 241-243, 246, 255, 256, 259, 260, 262, 263, 266

Flavius Aetius 36-37, 41, 47-53, 57, 58

France 47-48, 72, 92, 128, 131, 138, 140, 142, 144, 146, 190, 252

Franks 33, 46-47, 71-74, 77, 88

Genghis Khan (see also Temujin) 9-12, 22, 40, 64, 107, 138, 157-171, 174-179, 180-182, 185, 187, 189, 191, 193, 196, 202, 208, 220, 234-238, 241, 250, 255, 263, 264, 267, 273, 276-277

Golden Horde 180, 196, 219, 232, 234, 237-238, 241- 242, 245, 259, 261, 275

Hashashin 100-101, 211-213

Holy Roman Empire 132, 133, 136

Honoria 46, 47, 51, 53, 54

Hulagu 208-209, 213-214, 217, 219, 221, 231

Huns/Hunnu 11, 26, 31, 32, 34, 35, 37-47, 49, 50-65, 68, 70, 72, 75, 77, 79, 81, 82, 103, 113, 138, 157, 191, 219, 228, 243, 259, 264, 274-276, 277, 278

Hungary 14, 22, 34, 60-63, 78, 81, 127-129, 132, 135, 137, 191, 195-197, 200-201, 215, 259, 277

Ibrahim Lodi 264-268

Ilkhanate 219, 231-232, 234-235, 241

India 12, 139, 188-190, 227, 234, 247, 252, 262-264, 267-268, 270-274

Islam (see also Muslim) 72, 83, 85, 87, 92, 98-100, 109, 111, 114-115, 119, 139, 146, 207, 208-211, 214, 219-220, 231-233, 237, 243, 245-247, 256, 265, 272-274, 277

Jamukha 152-155

Japan 12, 221, 224-226, 229, 277

Jerusalem 87, 98-100, 189, 216, 232

Jochi 153-154, 158, 167, 178, 196, 237

Justinian I 64-66, 119, 127

Kadesh, Battle of 15

Kamikaze 226, 277

Kilij Arslan 88-91, 99

Kondurcha River, 1391 Battle of the 244

Korea 186-187, 221, 223

Kublai Khan 10, 204-205, 207-208, 219-225, 227-228, 231, 243, 259, 262

Kyiv 12, 76, 172, 174

Leo I, Pope 19, 52-53

Lombards 51, 65-66, 72

Magyars 9, 22, 32, 60-61, 76-78, 81-82, 103, 113, 243, 259

Mamelukes 103-105, 140-141, 213-218, 231-232

Manzikert, 1071 Battle of 83, 85

Marco Polo 10, 100, 204, 227, 228

Maurice, Emperor 69

Mehmed II 113-114, 117-127, 146, 186

Mehmed IV 132, 138

Mehmed VI 145

Mohács, 1526 Battle of 128-29

Mohács, 1687 Battle of 137

Möngke Khan 202, 204-205, 207-208, 212, 219

Mongol (Mongolian) 7, 9, 10-12, 17-19, 21-22, 27, 30-31, 40, 62, 70, 100, 102-104, 113, 130-131, 143, 145, 148-149, 151, 153-188, 190-238, 240-241, 247, 255, 259, 263-264, 272-274

Moscow 12, 126, 144, 186, 242

Mughal Empire 259, 273, 274
Muslim (see also Islam) 19, 77,
    83, 85-87, 91-92, 95, 97-99,
    100-103, 113-116, 128, 140,
    155, 166-168, 178, 188, 190,
    203, 209, 211, 213-214,
    216-217, 232, 237, 245, 247,
    253, 261-264, 272-273

Naimans 156, 157
Napoleon 138-142, 214, 266

Ögedei Khan 154, 163, 178,
    180-182, 184-188, 201-202,
    204-205, 230
Osman 104-114, 126, 140,
    145-147, 218, 259
Ottoman 12, 82, 104-139,
    142-148, 186, 209, 218-219,
    230, 243, 246, 250-256, 259,
    261, 262-263, 265-266, 273,
    275, 278

Panipat, 1526 Battle of 265-266,
    268-269
Poland 12, 64, 191, 197, 200, 201

Rana Sanga 267-270, 271
Roman/Roman Empire 7, 8,
    10-11, 19, 26-27, 30-35,
    37-38, 40-59, 64-66, 72, 83,
    92, 103, 125, 126, 127, 139,
    201, 243, 249, 278
  Eastern Roman Empire 34, 40,
    44-46, 65-66, 72, 103

Western Roman Empire 34,
    45-46, 48, 51, 54, 64, 243
Romanos IV 84-86
Rouran Khaganate 31-32, 62, 63
Ruga 38, 40-41
Russia 23, 31, 62, 126, 139,
    142-144, 145, 158, 172, 183,
    185, 190, 214, 242, 244, 274,
    275
Samarkand 20, 246, 254-257,
    260-262, 273
Samurai 224-226
Scythians 8, 32, 34, 42, 56, 58,
    248, 265
Seljuks 83-88, 91-94, 98, 102,
    104, 107, 110, 148, 150, 154,
    168, 171, 259
Shamanistic practices 19, 20, 48,
    53, 167, 190, 210, 246
Silk Road 8, 21, 30, 68, 130-131,
    159, 167, 168, 202, 232, 234,
    238, 256, 261, 276
Song, the 183-185, 188, 204,
    206-207, 221-223, 225
Subutai 169-174, 182-184, 196,
    198-199, 204, 241, 277
Suleiman (Ottoman Sultan) 116,
    127-132, 134, 137

Taulqama 267, 269
Tamerlane (see also Emir Timur)
    10, 13, 21, 138, 236, 272
Tashkent 20, 246

Temujin (see also Genghis Khan) 148-159, 162, 167, 177, 178, 190

Temür 220, 229, 231

The Mongol Khan, play 11

Theodosius II 37-38, 40, 43, 52-53

Toghrul 153-154, 155, 156

Tokhtamysh 237-238, 241-245

Thrace 34, 37-38, 45, 58, 68-69

Türkiye 21, 82, 117, 146, 277

Turks 9, 12, 19, 32, 62, 65, 68, 82-83, 85, 87-92, 102-103, 106, 114, 118-119, 123, 135, 147, 171, 208, 212, 214, 241, 259

Uelun Ujin 150-153, 158-159

Ukraine 12, 31-32, 64-65, 142, 172, 190, 242, 275

Uldin 35-38, 45, 59

Valentinian III 46-47, 52-53, 57-58

Vandals 33, 36, 43, 46, 53

Vienna, 1683 Siege of 132-137

Vikings 22, 72, 75-76, 84, 277

Visigoths 36, 42, 46, 48-50

William of Rubruck 203-204

Xia (also Xinjiang) 159-161, 162, 174-176

Xiongnu (see also Huns) 11, 26-31, 32

Yamen, 1279 Battle of 221

Yuan Dynasty 187, 205, 220, 223, 229, 231-232, 235, 259

Zhenjin 229

Also available from Amberley Publishing

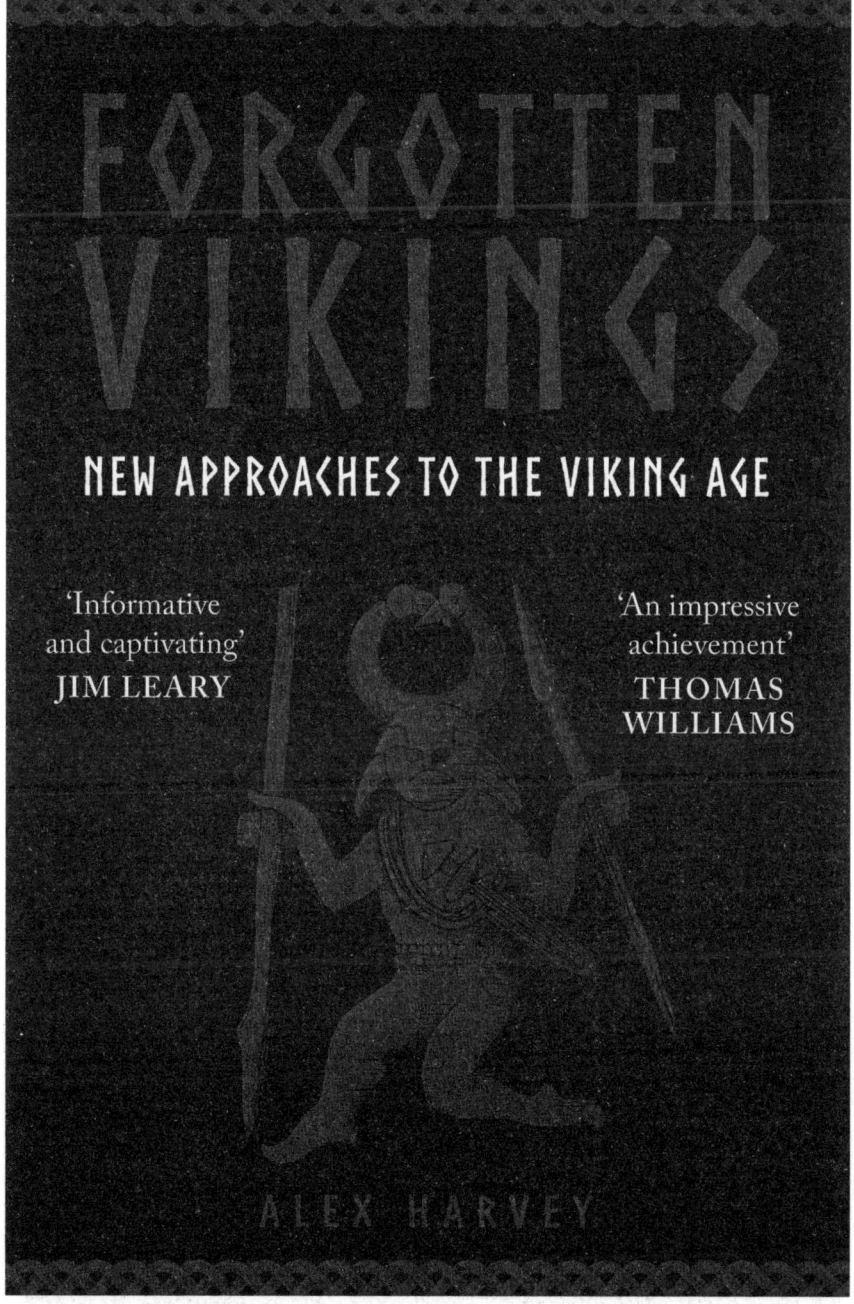

FORGOTTEN VIKINGS

NEW APPROACHES TO THE VIKING AGE

'Informative
and captivating'
JIM LEARY

'An impressive
achievement'
THOMAS
WILLIAMS

ALEX HARVEY